War and American Women

Also by William B. Breuer

An American Saga
Bloody Clash at Sadzot
Captain Cool
They Jumped at Midnight
Drop Zone Sicily
Agony at Anzio
Hitler's Fortress Cherbourg
Death of a Nazi Army
Operation Torch
Storming Hitler's Rhine
Retaking the Philippines
Devil Boats
Operation Dragoon
The Secret War with Germany
Sea Wolf
Hitler's Undercover War
Geronimo!
Hoodwinking Hitler
Race to the Moon
J. Edgar Hoover and His G-Men
The Great Raid on Cabanatuan
MacArthur's Undercover War
Feuding Allies
Shadow Warriors

WAR AND AMERICAN WOMEN

Heroism, Deeds, and Controversy

William B. Breuer

I.C.C. LIBRARY

PRAEGER

Westport, Connecticut
London

Library of Congress Cataloging-in-Publication Data

Breuer, William B.
    War and American women : heroism, deeds, and controversy / William
B. Breuer.
      p.   cm.
    Includes bibliographical references and index.
    ISBN 0–275–95717–9 (alk. paper)
    1. Women and the military—United States. 2. Women in war.
I. Title.
UB418.W65B74 1997
355′.0082—dc20   96–9013

British Library Cataloguing in Publication Data is available.

Library of Congress Catalog Card Number: 96–9013
ISBN: 0–275–95717–9

First published in 1997

Praeger Publishers, 88 Post Road West, Westport, CT 06881
An imprint of Greenwood Publishing Group, Inc.

Printed in the United States of America

The paper used in this book complies with the
Permanent Paper Standard issued by the National
Information Standards Organization (Z39.48–1984).

10 9 8 7 6 5 4 3 2 1

Dedicated to the memory
of my mother
MARY BENTLEY BREUER
an American patriot who devoted
a lifetime of service to her country and its armed forces.

U.S. Army nurse, post commander of the American Legion, board member of the USO, national president of the American War Mothers, benefactor of veterans.

Contents

Photo Section follows page 134

1 ❖ A Nightmare in Vietnam

Crump! Crump! Crump! The nearby explosions split the night air and abruptly awakened Major Lillian Lewis in her quarters in Saigon, South Vietnam. Then came the angry chatter of automatic weapons. Saigon had largely escaped damage during the war, as most of the fierce fighting had raged in the countryside amidst the rice paddies and the thick jungles. But now, Lewis knew, all hell had erupted in the city. It was the early hours of January 30, 1968.

"We women dashed to the rows of sandbags that had been placed around a men's barracks next door," Major Lewis recalled. "Smoke was all over the ground. We even had a number of snipers in the immediate area. One [sniper] shot out the side of one of our bedrooms and must have continued on down the hall."[1]

Lillian Lewis, an officer in the Women in the Air Force (WAF), was one of the several hundred American military females on duty in Saigon, which the Pentagon considered to be one of the safe places in the war-torn country. For the first time since World War II, American women in the services, other than nurses, found themselves caught in an enemy attack.

Communist forces had broken a truce agreed to by both sides so that the Vietnamese people could observe their Lunar New Year (Tet) and launched a powerful, coordinated assault. Within forty-eight hours, the Vietcong and the North Vietnamese People's Army struck at thirty-six South Vietnam provincial capitals; five autonomous cities; seventy-two district towns; and many airfields, military bases, and headquarters.

Few Western nations have a holiday nearly so important to their people as Tet is to the Vietnamese. It is not only a time of revelry—of fireworks and street festivals—but also of worship, at the family altar, of revered ancestors. For several days the entire countryside is on the move as folk visit their ancestral homes, and all business—even the business of war—comes to a halt. Consequently, hundreds of Vietcong (Communist guerrillas) had infiltrated Saigon in civilian clothes, their arrival concealed by the throngs of travelers moving about for the holiday.

The ease with which the Vietcong were able to infiltrate Saigon was reflected by an incident a short time earlier. As a newly arrived American

senior officer walked with an experienced adviser along a low bank sepa-
rating rice paddies, he saw a group of men wearing the Vietnamese peas-
ant's traditional black pajamas, which the Vietcong wore also. "How do you
know if they're the enemy?" the new arrival asked. "If they salute," the
adviser replied, "they're friendly. If they shoot, they're Vietcong."

North Vietnamese General Vo Nguyen Giap, a shrewd tactician and the
mastermind behind the Tet onslaught, had targeted Saigon for special
attention. A teeming metropolis of some 2 million people, Saigon was not
only the capital of South Vietnam, but the location of the imposing six-story
United States embassy which represented great symbolic significance—the
presence, prestige, and power of the United States.

One of the first targets to be hit was the embassy compound. If it could
be seized, the Communists would achieve a stunning propaganda bonanza,
making the United States look inept in the eyes of much of the world. Led
by a man the Americans called Satch, who had worked in the U.S. mission
for five years, fifteen Vietcong (VC) blasted a hole in the sturdy wall that
surrounded the compound. Two GI guards killed the first two VC to enter
through the hole, but they also died in the exchange of gunfire.

Two U.S. soldiers on jeep patrol responded to a call for help, and they
were gunned down as they drove up to the embassy, unaware of what was
taking place. A fifth American, a Marine corporal, who climbed atop a
building to fire into the compound, also was killed. At dawn, a platoon of
U.S. airborne troops landed by helicopter on the roof of the embassy and
wiped out the remaining intruders. One of the dead VC strewn around the
grounds was Satch.

None of the attacking force had entered the building. By noon, the U.S.
ambassador to South Vietnam, Ellsworth Bunker, and his staff were back at
their desks.

Elsewhere in Saigon, a group of VC, wearing South Vietnamese army
uniforms, attacked the Presidential Palace, but all were killed or driven off.
VC in battalion strength occupied a cemetery and a race track but eventually
were killed or chased away by South Vietnamese troops. On the outskirts
of Saigon, a VC force of up to three battalions assaulted Tan Son Nhut, a
major U.S. facility of prefabricated metal buildings, a large airfield, and
other installations, including the headquarters of MACV (Military Assistance Command, Vietnam).

There Lieutenant Colonel June Hilton, who had been the first member
of the WAF to arrive in Vietnam, was jolted from a sound sleep by the
exploding shells. "Within a minute or two, all of Tan Son Nhut looked
ablaze," she remembered. "There were over one hundred rounds of mortars
and rockets within a fifteen-minute period. The chapel was hit and burned
to the ground. Six airplanes were ablaze. The fire was terrifyingly close."[2]

As daylight peeked on Tan Son Nhut, planes, helicopter gunships, and
artillery pounded the VC, some of whom took refuge in buildings not far

from where Lieutenant Colonel Hilton and other military women were quartered. When the firing died down, 326 VC bodies were counted.

The Geneva Conventions held that military nurses were noncombatants, but that provision provided small consolation to the women when rocket rounds began exploding. "The Vietcong seemed to think that the red crosses on our tents were targets at which to aim," recalled an Army nurse.[3]

A primary target of General Giap was Danang, a coastal city in the far north of South Vietnam and location of a major U.S. air base that was essential to the air war against the North. An estimated battalion of VC hit the perimeter defenses, and fierce fighting raged.

Among the Americans in Danang was Major Eunice Splawn, who, along with seven other nurses, had arrived only two weeks earlier. They were assigned to the 22nd Casualty Staging Facility, whose mission was to stabilize wounded GIs and put them on aircraft that flew to hospitals at Cam Ranh Bay in South Vietnam, the Philippines, Japan, or Okinawa.

Until the arrival of the women, there had been only male nurses at the 22nd Casualty. They bore some resentment against the newcomers. If the Vietcong were to attack Danang, the men felt that they would not only have to take care of the patients but the women nurses as well.

During the first hours of Tet, Eunice Splawn counted about thirty rocket attacks, most of which were aimed at the nearby airport runway where planes were steadily lifting off with wounded GIs. Splawn recalled: "It turned out the male nurses did not have to 'take care' of us girls. We had one male nurse who was so scared he actually beat the patients to the bunker. He had to be sent out a few days later—he couldn't take it any more."

Splawn and the other women nurses worked thirty hours without sleep once the Tet casualties started pouring in. She remembered:

"There were fires everywhere, and rockets and mortars were dropping all around. That night the chaplain and I crawled around underneath beds with patients who were not able to go to the bunkers—you took as many as you could to the bunkers, and the ones who could not get to the bunkers, you put them on stretchers and got them underneath the beds. Some of them were mental patients, guys who had just broken under all the strain of combat."

Patients were kept only overnight before being shuttled on to some of the big hospitals for surgery or other major treatment. This situation proved quite frustrating to the 22nd Casualty nurses—they would never know if the GIs who had temporarily been in their care lived, died, or made it back to The World, as servicemen and -women in Vietnam called the United States.

Eunice Splawn recalled: "Casualties were heavy during Tet. In my ward, I had to take care of everything myself, with just a wardmaster and a technician. One day, we handled more than one hundred and sixty patients.

We had them in the hallways, we had them laying on stretchers everywhere, we even put them across the street in another small building."[4]

Meanwhile, at the 24th Evacuation Hospital at Long Binh, a sprawling American base and headquarters of the U.S. Army, Vietnam, fifteen miles northeast of Saigon, Lieutenant Kathleen Cordova, an Army nurse, often was working twenty-hour shifts during the Tet fighting. She and the other nurses wore fatigues both on- and off-duty. During brief lulls, they slept in bunk beds in stifling huts. Bathroom facilities were crude showers and outdoor toilets. Everything, including the perspiring nurses, was covered with dust. Wounded GIs were helicoptered in—many barely breathing—with arms and legs torn off, faces ripped apart, eyeballs missing, backs broken, gaping holes in chests, bloody intestines hanging out of stomachs.

During emergencies, Lieutenant Cordova, as with nurses in other evacuation hospitals, pitched in, performing surgeon-type duties like triage, tracheotomies, debriding wounds and closing them. Cordova, again as with most nurses, built an insulating shell around herself; otherwise she would have fallen to pieces and been unable to function.

Cordova was an athletic, adventurous young woman. A few months before being shipped out for Vietnam, she had joined a skydiving club at Fort Hood, Texas, and made many leaps from airplanes "just for the hell of it." Yet she was hardly prepared for what she encountered in Vietnam.

"The war was all around us during Tet," Cordova recalled. "There was automatic-weapons fire. Shells dropped very, very close. You never knew who the enemy was—the Vietcong looked just like the civilians. Anybody could walk into the [nurses'] compound and start shooting at you."[5]

One night Cordova was thrown out of bed when the Vietcong blew up an ammunition dump a short distance away. Half asleep, bruised, and mildly shocked, she stumbled down the hall to find someone who knew what had happened. As is often the case in war, no one knew anything, other than that there had been "one hell of a huge blast."

Cordova and a few other nurses dashed outside and saw a large mushroomlike cloud that looked to them like it had come from an atomic-bomb explosion. "I mean, we figured [President] Johnson had finally done it, the son of a bitch," Cordova remembered. "He had dropped the atom bomb—and near to our hospital."[6]

Fighting was on all sides of the 24th Evac. "There was always fear," Cordova recalled. "Fear that you were going to be shot, fear that the hospital was going to be shelled, that you were going to open the locker in your room someday and a mine [planted by a VC] would explode. You suppressed the fear and went on with your job."

On a steady basis, mutilated young American soldiers and Marines were brought to the 24th Evac. With the arrival of each new batch, Cordova had to steel herself to the ordeal.

"I put too many of those boys in black body bags," Cordova remembered. "Often there were only pieces of them—arms, legs, and other parts—shoved into the bags. The last sound I heard was the sound of the zipper. Each time I would go out in the back and cry my eyes out. Then I'd come back and do it all again."[7]

Cordova was consumed with bitterness. "I had never had any reason before to hate anybody or to develop anger for anything," she remembered. "Now I blamed the government for allowing this [killing] to happen. I blamed the military. We had the clout to do something to end the war and we didn't. Why did it go on? Why did they allow so many young men to die?"

Coping with the fear and nightmarish sights of blood and multiple amputations and dying American boys not long out of high school was a way of life for the Army, Navy, and Air Force nurses who served in Vietnam. Like the young fighting men, nurses could be killed—and eight did die during the war. One of them, Army Lieutenant Sharon Lane, was tending to a group of grievously wounded GIs at the 312th Evac at Chu Lai when a Vietcong rocket exploded, killing her instantly.

In the fertile flatlands of the Mekong Delta southwest of Saigon, troopers of the U.S. Special Forces (popularly called the Green Berets) also were under attack at their isolated base camp. One of their missions was to help organize and train South Vietnamese guerrillas who, hopefully, would ultimately grow enough in strength and skill to successfully tangle with the VC in the region. But mainly, the Green Berets relished raiding VC camps and ambushing VC soldiers.

A visitor in the base camp at the time of the Tet attack was Martha Raye, the Hollywood star, upon whom the Green Berets in Vietnam had bestowed the honorary rank of colonel. So she was called Colonel Maggie by thousands of admiring GIs in the country.

During the preceding two years, Raye had visited the troops in Vietnam numerous times. On one occasion, she begged Army authorities to let her extend her tour through the Christmas season, explaining that she had no family at home. "These gallant boys are my family," she said. Once when performing several shows in a steaming-hot hangar for thousands of GIs, she collapsed on stage and had to be hospitalized. Yet she refused to go home as doctors recommended, and continued her tour of American bases to entertain the troops.

The U.S. commander in Vietnam, General William C. Westmoreland, said of Colonel Maggie, "A great soldier!"

During the Tet attack, the Green Berets' camp in the Mekong Delta was pounded by VC mortar shells and rockets, and several men were wounded. There were no nurses at this remote outpost, so Colonel Maggie, wearing her green beret, combat boots, and a white surgical smock over her camouflage fatigues, helped tend to the wounded troopers. She also assisted the

Green Beret surgeon who operated on the casualties in a makeshift room—even as shells and rockets exploded periodically.[8]

Many Americans survived wounds from which they would have died in earlier wars because evacuation by helicopter to hospitals was so swift. No GI was ever more than a few minutes from medical treatment, although combat conditions on occasion might have caused a delay in his removal from the battlefield. Wherever humanly possible, skilled military nurses, surgeons, doctors, and wardmasters were always on hand to promptly go to work to prevent the wounded men from dying.

One of the most astonishing medical feats of this or any war was performed by Navy Captain Harry H. Dinsmore, who volunteered to remove a live sixty-millimeter mortar shell from the chest wall of a soldier. Assisting Dinsmore through much of the procedure were women nurses. Although the shell's impact fuse had been partially activated and the projectile could have exploded at any time, the Navy surgeon performed the delicate surgery calmly and skillfully, saving the soldier's life.[9]

Heavy fighting raged at many places in South Vietnam, but after a week to ten days, the Tet onslaught ran out of steam. In ancient Hue, South Vietnam's third largest city, it required twenty-five days for a South Vietnamese division, assisted by three U.S. Marine battalions, to clear out the die-hard VC.

After early successes gained by surprise, the Vietcong and the North Vietnam army regulars had suffered a frightful mauling. U.S. intelligence estimated enemy losses to be about 72,000, a figure that would gain credence when Truong Nhu Tang, the Vietcong minister of justice, admitted "We lost a lot of fighters in Tet. All of our divisions ended up with not even half of their forces."[10]

Even for the victors, war exacts a stiff price in blood and suffering. During the Tet fighting, about 1,000 Americans and 2,800 South Vietnamese soldiers were killed. Thousands of others were wounded.

From General Westmoreland down through the ranks to the GI grunt and leatherneck face-to-face with a clever and tenacious enemy, it was generally agreed that American women had conducted themselves most admirably under often dangerous and demanding conditions. These servicewomen and paramilitary females like Martha Raye had carried on a tradition for courage, dedication, and perseverance first established by Army, Navy, and Marine Corps women in World War I, more than a half-century earlier.

2 ❖ Female Trailblazers

Inside a nondescript bunker near London, a British wireless monitoring team intercepted and decoded a message from Berlin to Mexico on the morning of January 22, 1917. The communication indicated that the German government of Kaiser Wilhelm had approached Mexico for an alliance in case of war with the United States. As payment, Germany promised to help Mexico recover huge portions of land it had ceded to the United States after the Mexican War of 1846–1848. That territory included the regions of California, Nevada and Utah, most of Arizona and New Mexico, and parts of Colorado and Wyoming.

War in Europe had been raging since 1914, with Germany and her allies on one side and Great Britain, France, and their allies on the other side. The alarming message intercepted by the British, along with the sinkings of many U.S. merchant vessels by German U-boats (submarines), persuaded President Woodrow Wilson, on April 2, 1917, to tell Congress, "The world must be made safe for democracy." Four days later the United States declared war on Germany.

America was totally unprepared for the brutal conflict. But tens of thousands of young men rushed to volunteer, and large numbers were drafted and headed for training camps. Soldiers, sailors, and civilians sang George M. Cohan's "Over There" to let Kaiser Wilhelm and the entire world know that the Yanks were coming.

Not all the Yanks were men. For the first time in the history of the United States, thousands of women also would march off to war. They would be pioneers, traveling unknown paths, for the same reason men answered the call to the colors—duty, honor, and love of country.

Soon after war was declared by Congress, one of the pioneers, young Mary Louise Bentley of Mauston, Wisconsin, joined up as an Army nurse and left for Fort Riley, Kansas. It had been a wrenching decision: She had never been far from her home and parents.

Devout and dedicated, Mary Bentley had volunteered out of a sense of patriotism. But her motive had no impact on the gossips back in Mauston, where her father Michael was the chief of police. She was painted as a "camp follower" and a woman of loose morals. Otherwise why would she be chasing off to a place where there were thousands of soldiers?

In Mauston the tongue-waggers did not know that Nurse Bentley was toiling fourteen-hour shifts, seven days a week, or that she and other women were caring for hundreds of soldiers laid low by a deadly strain of influenza that killed scores of them at Fort Riley. She herself had contracted the disease and had been placed in the terminal ward before slowly recuperating.

Barely a month before America went to war, Secretary of the Navy Josephus Daniels had been convinced that the United States was headed for the conflagration in Europe—and soon. He was concerned that the Navy could not meet its clerical and secretarial needs because men would be called up to join the fleet. So he asked an aide, "Is there any law that says a yeoman must be a man?" "No," came the reply. "Good," Daniels said. "Get moving on it!"[1]

A week later, on March 19, 1917, the Navy authorized the enrollment of women in the Reserve. So when the nation entered the conflict, the wheels for recruiting females already had been greased. The new women recruits would be known as Yoemanettes.

Many young women rushed to sign up. One of them, eighteen-year-old Lillian Peterson, timidly strolled into a Navy recruiting office, heretofore an all-male domain. The male recruiter pointed to a small room and said, "Go in there and take off all your clothes." Even though it was for a medical examination, Peterson was mortified. In those days, women didn't even get into a bathtub without wearing a nightgown, but she took off her hat, skirt, blouse, shoes, wool stockings, corset cover, corset, three petticoats, and ruffled bloomers.

A weeping female recruit told her, "You act like you don't mind having no clothes on." Hoping to boost the other's spirits, Peterson quipped, "Oh, after the first few times you get used to this sort of thing." Not knowing she was joking, the other woman let loose with an even greater flood of tears.

Navy recruits, officially designated Yeoman (F), for females, were supposed to serve on ships, and many had volunteered with visions of travels to exotic ports of the world. Recruiting signs always said, "Join the Navy and see the world." However, Navy regulations prohibited women from going to sea. So this knotty problem was solved by assigning many of the Yeomanettes to tugs tied up or resting on shallow bottoms of the Potomac River near Washington, D.C.

During the war, 11,882 Yeoman (F) served stateside, and 57 of them died in the service, mainly from the deadly influenza epidemic that swept across the land in 1918.

Meanwhile, the Navy Nurse Corps expanded from 406 at the beginning of the war to 1,386 members. They served in the United States, the Philippines, Guam, Haiti, the Virgin Islands, Samoa, and in field hospitals in Europe, on loan to the Army.

Leading elements of the American Expeditionary Force (AEF), commanded by General John J. "Black Jack" Pershing, began landing in France on June 26, 1917, with bands playing the stirring "Over There." Hard on their heels were contingents of Army nurses who arrived in time to care for the first battle casualties.

Army nurses, for the first time, had to minister to soldiers badly wounded by new types of weapons for killing in large numbers—machine guns, tanks, and poison gas—as well as by conventional rifles, pistols, bayonets, and artillery. One especially horrible type of German shell released mustard gas, the cause of the most casualties.

Effects of mustard gas did not become apparent for up to twelve hours. Then it began to rot the body, inside and out. The skin blistered, the eyes became excruciatingly painful, and the victim was racked with nausea and vomiting. Worse, the gas attacked the bronchial tubes, stripping off the mucous membrane. The pain was almost beyond endurance, and nurses had to strap their patients to beds. Death took up to four or five weeks.

A U.S. Army nurse wrote home:

> I wish those people who write so glibly about this being a holy war and the orators who talk so much about going on no matter how many casualties it takes, could see a case—to say nothing about fifty cases—of mustard gas, could see the pitiful things burnt and blistered all over, with blind eyes . . . always fighting for breath, with voices a mere whisper, saying that their throats were closing and they know they will choke to death, slowly, horribly.[2]

Among the first sixty American nurses to go overseas was Helen Fairchild. At Casualty Clearing Station No. 4, she treated patients exposed to German mustard gas. Fairchild fell gravely ill and died three days later. Her death was listed as gastroenterostomy, but her family said records indicated that she had been heavily exposed to mustard gas while near the front.

Like the Doughboys (as the American soldiers were called), the Army nurses had two implacable enemies—mud and water—in every season except summer. Nurses, along with doctors, in tented field hospitals often had to work in ankle-deep mud. Sometimes the mud was so thick each small step became an effort.

As the American casualties continued to pile up at an alarming rate, it had become clear to General Pershing and his battle commanders that there was an urgent need for more military doctors. To meet this shortage, the surgeon general in Washington proposed giving commissions to women doctors. In rejecting the recommendation, the War Department told the

surgeon general that only persons "physically, mentally, and morally qualified" could be granted commissions as medical officers.

Efforts to recruit a large number of male doctors fell far short, however,
and the War Department changed its policy. Altogether, 350 American
women doctors served overseas, most of them in Europe. One female
graduate of the University of Minnesota Medical School was refused an
appointment to U.S. military hospitals—she happened to be black. Undaunted, she made her way to Europe and served with the color-blind
French army as an ophthalmologist at a hospital for soldiers who had been
gassed.

Earlier, the American Women's Hospitals asked the War Department to
accept their female doctors for overseas assignments. The request was
rejected. Undaunted, the AWH members decided that they would go to
Europe anyway. So in July 1918 the first AWH began functioning in Europe,
and its women served soldiers and civilians throughout the conflict.

During mobilization, the War Department had assigned the American
Red Cross to provide morale services, supplies, and funds where needed
to soldiers; 4,610 American women served in that capacity in France. The
Red Cross Nursing Service recruited and trained the bulk of Army and
Navy nurses, and more than 10,000 Red Cross nurses served overseas,
mostly in Europe.

Late in the war, Jane Delano, director of the American Red Cross Nursing
Service, was on an inspection tour of military hospitals in Europe when she
became ill. She wrote a friend: "I do not suppose that I should complain,
after the men put up with so much more." She died a few days later in
Savenay, France—in a Red Cross hospital.

High on the list of unsung heroines of The Great War were the women
known as "reconstruction aides." Years later, persons in their trade would
be known as rehabilitation specialists. It was their agonizing task to help
young, mutilated men—often those without arms or legs—to become
functional despite their enormous handicaps. More than 160 reconstruction
aides assisted in the recovery of thousands of badly wounded soldiers.

Also playing an important role in the American war effort in Europe were
233 young women recruited and trained for overseas duty by American
Telephone & Telegraph (AT&T). Dubbed the "Hello Girls"—a moniker of
which they were proud—these bilingual telephone operators served with
the U.S. Signal Corps, and their job was to improve communications
between various U.S. headquarters and the French army. The Hello Girls
served in nearly eighty French cities, but mostly in Paris.

Although 21,482 nurses had volunteered and were on duty at home and
abroad, the Army clung to its regulation prohibiting enlisted women from
joining up. Only after the U.S. forces had been suffering heavy casualties in
the bloody trench warfare in France did the War Department agree to let
Army units in the United States employ civilian women for clerical and

secretarial jobs to free men to fight. With the approval came a warning to unit commanders: "With careful supervision, women employees may be permitted inside camps without moral injury either to themselves or to the soldiers" if the women were "of mature age and high moral character."

In March 1918, powerful German armies struck savagely along a fifty-mile front in France. Field Marshal Paul von Hindenberg promised the war-weary homefront that he would be in Paris by April 1. He missed the target date.[3] But on May 31 the Germans reached the banks of the Marne, where they collided with the U.S. 4th Marine Brigade, and a savage fight erupted in Belleau Wood, on the road to Paris. The Marines halted the German advance but suffered the loss of nearly 7,800 men.

These and other heavy Marine casualties resulted in a shortage of combat personnel. Consequently, in August, only three months before the war ended, three hundred women were recruited to permit male clerical workers to go to the front. Officially, these women were listed as Marine (F) and popularly called Marinettes.

At the same time, the Army, too, was suffering tremendous losses, and General Pershing asked Washington to send 5,000 women volunteers to France to do clerical work and release men for combat duty. Instead, he was sent 5,000 unskilled, limited-duty, enlisted men who proved to be more of a handicap than an asset.

Germany surrendered on November 11, 1918, and Kaiser Wilhelm and his family went into luxurious exile in the Netherlands. More than 10,000 U.S. Army nurses had served abroad in France, Belgium, England, Italy, Siberia, and Serbia. Some had been wounded. Thirty-eight had been buried overseas in U.S. cemeteries, most of them victims of a deadly strain of flu.

Altogether, some 49,500 American women volunteered to serve in uniform during World War I. Nearly all of them sailed for home and returned to civilian life. A small group of Army and Navy nurses remained on active duty.

Global politicians hailed the bloody conflict as the "war to end all wars." But just to make certain peace would rule infinitely, on January 10, 1920, a League of Nations was established for the "peaceful settlement of international quarrels." Most major nations, including defeated Germany, became members. But not the United States. Americans wanted no part of "foreign entanglements."[4]

America rapidly dismantled its armed forces. There would be no future need for them. Two broad oceans and the League of Nations would protect the United States was the consensus. So during the 1920s, Americans felt comfortable in their cocoon, snugly isolated from the rest of the world.

Meanwhile, the War Department had become concerned about the demands of various women's groups that the United States totally abolish its "war machine." Consequently, Secretary of War Newton D. Baker created a small directorate called Women's Programs, United States Army, and appointed Anita Phipps as its head. She was to be the liaison between the Army and the women's organizations, and her mission was to convince them that the puny U.S. military was no threat to world peace.

Baker's scheme backfired. Instead of the female groups being placated by Phipps, they demanded that women be given greater roles in the services and that females be appointed as civilian aides to the secretary of war.

In the meantime, confusion reigned in the Women's Program. Because Anita Phipps's appointment had been something of a public-relations gimmick, she was never certain about her goal. So she began developing a plan for a Women's Service Corps (WSC) that called for 170,000 females to be mobilized in the event of war. The WSC would be an official component of the Army, and its members would be used in clerical and secretarial work as telephone operators, seamstresses, waitresses, cooks, couriers, and janitors.

In 1926, Phipps's grandiose plan was submitted to the War Department, where it was received by the generals with a total lack of enthusiasm. It languished until 1931, when the Army's chief of staff, Douglas MacArthur, a hero of The Great War, abolished Phipps's WSC plan as being of no military value.

In the spring of 1937, tousle-haired thirty-nine-year-old Amelia Earhart was preparing to go on a highly hazardous flight that no male had achieved: a 27,000-mile, east to west, around-the-world journey. Even before the pioneer aviatrix took off, her odyssey was cloaked in mystery that would later cause intense speculation that she had actually been on a military spying mission at the behest of President Franklin Roosevelt.

Earhart was known by many monikers: Queen of the Sky, Lady Lindy (after famed Charles A. Lindbergh), and Aviation's First Lady, among others. Her renown was worldwide. Famous movie stars, politicians, athletes, scientists, educators, and society lionesses clawed and scratched to be in her presence.

She was a close friend of Franklin and Eleanor Roosevelt and had dined with them in the White House several times. Once she had taken Eleanor for a moonlight airplane ride (leaving Secret Service bodyguards on the ground); and she had been known to have had late-night chats with the president in his study.

When only twenty-three years of age, Earhart set an airplane altitude record for women, and in 1932 her name exploded around the globe when she flew the Atlantic Ocean solo—five years after Lindbergh accomplished the feat. Spunky, keen-witted, and articulate, she was incensed because she became the target of scoffing and criticism that Lindbergh and other pioneer male aviators never had to endure.

In May 1937, Earhart, in preparation for the globe-circling flight, had her twin-engined, 10–E Electra airplane fitted with much larger gasoline tanks to give the craft a range of 4,500 miles. The Electra had a cabin designed to carry ten passengers, but she had the seats ripped out and, in their place, installed a large number of advanced scientific instruments. This alteration struck snooping newspaper reporters as odd: why was it necessary to fill the cabin with technical devices when all she would need for her flight would be the navigation device in the cockpit?

When asked about the instruments, Earhart would merely refer to her airplane as "my flying laboratory." But what she intended to "study" during her arduous journey would result in a debate and conjecture lasting infinitely.

On June 1, 1937, amidst heavy media hoopla, Earhart and her navigator, Fred J. Noonan, who had charted many courses for commercial airlines and was regarded as one of the best in his trade, took off in the Electra from the Miami, Florida, airport bound for San Juan, Puerto Rico, 1,033 miles away. From there the "flying laboratory" winged to Brazil, then across the Atlantic to West Africa, and on to Pakistan, India, Burma, Singapore, Australia, and New Guinea.

Early on the steaming hot morning of July 31, two months after leaving Miami, the Electra raced down a primitive landing strip at Lae, a town on the eastern tip of primitive New Guinea, and set a northeast course for Howland Island, a flyspeck in the central Pacific Ocean. This would be the most dangerous leg of the trek: a 2,556–mile flight. No one had ever flown this course before. But Earhart was an expert pilot, Noonan was one of the world's best navigators, and there were some 2,000 miles more of gasoline in the tanks than would be needed to reach Howland.

North of Howland was a vast expanse of the Pacific Ocean that was forbidden to foreigners, especially Americans. There the Japanese were constructing a heavily fortified string of atolls named Tarawa, Kwajalien, Eniwetok, Makin, and Saipan and a naval bastion on the island of Truk. It would later be learned that these strongholds were being built in anticipation of projected war with the United States.

Amelia Earhart and Fred Noonan left New Guinea behind. The sea was smooth, the visibility perfect, and the ceiling unlimited. After they had been in the air for eighteen hours, the U.S. Coast Guard cutter *Itasca*, waiting near Howland to send homing signals, received faint, fragmentary messages from the "flying laboratory."

Commander W. K. Thompson, skipper of the *Itasca*, was puzzled. The Earhart plane should have been approaching Howland, yet Lady Lindy's words were faint, muffled, and garbled. Thompson also was startled because the experienced fliers gave no position or bearing. Could it be that the Electra was nowhere near Howland Island?

Then the *Itasca* radio received no more signals.

Commander Thompson ordered the Howland runway cleared of dodo birds in anticipation of the Electra's arrival. At 7:42 A.M., Amelia's voice—high-pitched and jittery—broke the silence in the *Itasca* radio room: "Gas is running low. Only about thirty minutes left." How could that happen? Thompson reflected. The plane had enough fuel for 2,000 extra miles.

An hour later, the Coast Guard heard Lady Lindy's voice for the final time: "We are running north and south." Why north and south when the course should have been generally eastward?

Thompson fired off a message to San Francisco, from where it was relayed to Washington, D.C.: "Earhart unreported at 0900 [9:00 A.M.] . . . Believed down. Am searching area."

In Washington, Admiral William D. Leahy, chief of naval operations, instructed the commandant of the naval station at Honolulu to render "whatever aid you deem practicable in the search for Miss Earhart." That signal triggered a number of sub-riddles in the Case of the Vanishing Flyers.

A long-distance naval flying boat promptly hopped off from Honolulu, 1,900 miles to the northeast of Howland Island, to join the search. Flying at a high altitude and piloted by Lieutenant W. W. Harvey, the lumbering airplane had gone but a few hundred miles when it ran into a unique weather situation for the tropics: snow and sleet. After battling these harsh elements for nearly two hours, Lieutenant Harvey was forced to return to his Honolulu base.

In Los Angeles, meanwhile, Walter McMenamy, an amateur radio operator, gave new hope when he reported that he had picked up faint signals on frequencies assigned to the lost airplane.

At an airport near Oakland, California, George Palmer Putnam, Amelia's husband, waited anxiously in the radio room. There he opened a sealed envelope that his wife had given him before her departure on the journey. She had told him to read it only if she disappeared. It read: "Please know I am quite aware of the hazards. I want to do it—because I want to do it. Women must try to do things as men have tried. When they fail, their failure must be but a challenge to others."

What did Amelia mean by "I want to do it?" What was "it"—the global flight, or, as rumors would persist, a spying mission at the behest of President Roosevelt?

In the days ahead, the *Itasca* crew never saw or heard anything that would provide a clue to Earhart's and Noonan's whereabouts. Navy vessels were steaming toward the search area: the battleship *Maryland* and the aircraft carrier *Lexington* from California, and the Coast Guard cutter *Roger B. Taney* from Hawaii. For nearly ten days, these ships and seventy-six planes scoured 262,280 square miles of the blue Pacific. There was no sighting of the vanished fliers.

For months millions of Americans clung to their slim hopes that the aviation heroine would yet be found—just as it is done in Hollywood movies. But this was real life. There was no clue uncovered to the true fate of Earhart and Noonan.

Reports were rampant that Earhart had indeed been on an espionage mission to photograph and electronically inspect the Japanese bastions of Truk and Saipan after deliberately flying off course. Why else would the Electra have aboard all the special scientific equipment?

A second scenario held that Earhart was to have purposely crash-landed on a specific tiny island within the Japanese fortified belt. She had radioed the *Itasca* that she was nearly out of gasoline (even though she had fuel for an additional 2,000 miles). That was done, the theories went, so that Japanese electronic listening devices could pick up the message and add credence to her crash landing. This "emergency" would be an excuse for the U.S. Navy to ignore Japanese restrictions on foreigners and send a ship into the forbidden region to "rescue" the aviatrix and her companion—and inspect fortifications on the atolls.

Yet another theory was that the Electra had flown close to Truk or Saipan while photographing these strongholds and had been shot down by Japanese fighter planes, killing both Americans.

A fourth scenario had the Earhart plane shot down by Japanese fighters, crash-landing in the water, and the two Americans being captured. They had been taken to Tokyo, convicted as spies, and executed.[5]

Much later, Earhart's mother spoke to newsmen: "Amelia told me many things, but there were some things she couldn't tell me. I am convinced she was on some sort of government mission, probably on verbal orders."

Whether or not Amelia Earhart, a deeply patriotic American, was actually on a spying mission for President Roosevelt will probably never be known for certain.[6]

In the summer of 1939, two years after Earhart and Noonan vanished, General George C. Marshall, who had made a sterling reputation as a staff planner at General John J. Pershing's headquarters of the American Expeditionary Force in The Great War, was the new Army chief of staff. Only twenty-one years after the conclusion of that bloody conflict, billed by global politicians as the "war to end all wars," ominous black clouds again were gathering over Europe.

Convinced that war would soon break out and that the United States eventually would be sucked into the fighting, Marshall was deeply concerned about the Army's manpower—or lack of it. So he directed his staff in the War Department Building in Washington to conduct a study on the possible use of women.

When completed, the plan called for the establishment of a women's component modeled after the Civilian Conservation Corps (CCC) that

President Roosevelt had created to provide jobs for unemployed men and help "put America back to work" in the Great Depression era of the 1930s. Females would not be part of the Army, rather they would work with the Army as "hostesses, cooks, waitresses, canteen clerks, chauffeurs, and strolling minstrels."

3 ❖ "You Have a Debt to Democracy"

Less than twenty-four years after the final shot was fired in the "war to end all wars," a fearful world was struck by a blockbuster. On September 1, 1939, German dictator Adolf Hitler, who had seized power seven years earlier, sent his war juggernaut plunging into nearly defenseless Poland. France and England rapidly declared war against Germany. Poland was conquered in only six weeks.

In the United States, a Roper poll disclosed that 67 percent of the populace was opposed to taking sides in the European war. "Keep out of other nations' quarrels!" became the slogan across the land. However, on the morning of December 7, 1941, America's hope for remaining neutral went up in the smoke of Pearl Harbor. The United States, woefully unprepared and militarily weak, declared war on Japan. Then Germany and its ally, Italy, declared war on the United States. World War II had begun.[1]

Nine thousand miles west of California in the Philippines in January 1942, the 70,000 GIs and Filipinos of General Douglas MacArthur's ill-equipped and outgunned army were trapped by Japanese forces on Bataan, a harsh, forbidding peninsula on the main island of Luzon, near Manila. In the old War Department Building in Washington, an obscure one-star general named Dwight D. Eisenhower had been given the task of getting reinforcements, weapons, and supplies to Bataan. But he had virtually nothing to send, nor any means for getting it to the beleaguered force.[2]

By February the Battling Bastards of Bataan—as the abandoned soldiers called themselves—were steadily growing weaker and dwindling in number. With no means for resupply, they ate monkeys, cats, dogs, horses, mice, lizards, and iguanas. Quinine was exhausted, but some 500 malaria cases entered the two Army tent hospitals each week.

At one of these hospitals, U.S. Army Lieutenant Hattie Brantley, a nurse, was working countless hours tending to the flood of sick and wounded. Clad in heavy boots and wearing oversized coveralls that draped her slender frame, face caked with perspiration and dust, body numbed by fatigue, she stood outside one day and squinted into the sun as a flight of Japanese bombers circled overhead.

Brantley felt reasonably safe, because white bed sheets with huge red crosses were spread on the ground, plainly marking a hospital. Moments later, there were explosions. One bomb hit the nurses' and doctors' quarters. Another plunged directly into a ward of screaming patients. Brantley ran to the site and found bodies and pieces of bodies strewn about. One hundred and one American and Filipino patients had been killed in the wanton bombing.[3]

In March, with the Japanese mounting an all-out offensive to overrun Bataan, Lieutenant Earleen A. Francis, a thirty-one-year-old Army nurse from Jacksonville, Illinois, and nine other nurses boarded a PBY "flying boat" and headed for Australia, some 2,500 miles to the south. Francis was especially racked with emotion. Her husband, Lieutenant Colonel Garnet P. Francis, had been fighting on Bataan. Was he dead? Alive? Wounded? A prisoner? The couple had been married on Bataan by a chaplain during a brief lull in the fighting only a few weeks earlier. Then the bride returned to her nursing duties, and the groom went back to the front lines. They had not seen one another since.

When the PBY reached Mindanao, a Philippine island 600 miles south of Corregidor, Francis's PBY crash-landed, and she and the other nine nurses were captured by the Japanese. The nurses were shipped back to Luzon and put in the Santo Tomás internment camp in Manila.

Meanwhile, her husband, Garnet, had been captured on Bataan and transferred from the notorious Cabanatuan POW camp north of Manila, where thousands of American servicemen would die of Japanese abuse and brutality during the war, to Santo Tomás, which had once been a university. Colonel Francis presumed that his wife had been evacuated from the Philippines before Bataan fell.

Thinking that her husband was dead, Earleen Francis happened to run into him in Santo Tomás one day—and fainted.[4]

On April 9, four months after the Japanese had invaded the Philippines, the final bloody curtain fell on Bataan. Now the Japanese invaders focused on Corregidor, a small rock island perched in Manila Bay two miles off Bataan, where a stubborn force of GIs and Filipinos was holding on desperately in a hopeless situation, buying time for the United States to rearm.

Earlier, General Douglas MacArthur twice had been given direct orders by President Roosevelt to leave enemy-surrounded Corregidor and go to Australia to take command in the southwest Pacific. In a hair-raising caper, MacArthur was spirited away at night in a PT boat commanded by Lieutenant John D. Bulkeley, broke through the Japanese naval blockade, and reached Mindanao, from where MacArthur and his party were flown to Australia.[5]

Night and day the holdouts on Corregidor, short of weapons, ammunition, supplies, and food, were pounded by Japanese bombers and heavy artillery emplaced along the Bataan shoreline. At the center of Corregidor,

Lieutenant Eunice F. Young was one of the Army nurses laboring in a makeshift hospital burrowed into Malinta Hill, which rises to a height of 350 feet. Young, who had joined the service in 1939 when it had become clear to her that America would be at war soon, and the other nurses had established the hospital's operating room after the Japanese had invaded the Philippines.

The hospital was located in an offshoot of the main tunnel, which was crammed with a few thousand people, including Philippine civilians. The heat and humidity were stifling. Unwashed bodies gave off a horrendous odor. Huge black flies and cockroaches were everywhere. Despite these abominable conditions, the "Angels of Corregidor," as the nurses would be known, tenderly cared for the wounded patients. These young women moved from cot to cot, consoling the dying, calming the injured, administering injections, bandaging, giving water to those who were paralyzed, feeding those with no arms. Wearing GI coveralls or khaki shirts and slacks or skirts, the Angels often had to cover their faces and those of the patients with improvised masks of wet gauze as shields against the thick dust generated by bombs and shells crashing above them on Malinta Hill.

Eunice Young remembered: "We never seemed to be without wounded men waiting for surgery. We put in eighteen-hour workdays, seven days per week. Some nurses collapsed from exhaustion and shortage of food, and they, too, became patients."[6]

In late April, it was obvious to Major General Jonathan M. "Skinny" Wainwright, a tall, gaunt old cavalryman who was now the U.S. commander in the Philippines, that Corregidor was doomed. From his headquarters in Malinta Tunnel, he cabled Washington: "We are being subjected to continuous shellfire, the heaviest concentrations yet experienced."[7]

That day, two PBYs managed to elude the air and sea blockade and landed on Manila Bay south of Corregidor. After a medicine shipment was unloaded, thirty nurses, three civilian women, and seventeen military officers scrambled aboard. Then the aircraft skimmed across the bay and lifted off for Australia, where the nurses were to join MacArthur's army for his offensive back to the Philippines.

On Lake Lanano, Mindanao, some 600 miles south of Corregidor, the PBYs landed for refueling. Later, one of the airplanes, while taxiing into takeoff position, hit a submerged object, ripping a hole in one of its pontoons. Crew and passengers climbed out, and rapid repairs were made. However, the plane's load had to be lightened because of the damage. Several of the male officers, including a few West Pointers, pulled rank, bumping several lady nurses. These men got flown to safety and the nurses were left behind.[8]

On May 5, after an earth-shaking bombardment by hundreds of guns, waves of Japanese troops stormed ashore on Corregidor and soon overran the island. Along with thousands of American soldiers, Marines, and sailors, sixty-six Army nurses and eleven Navy nurses were captured. The women were imprisoned at Santo Tomás.[9]

Meanwhile, 1,500 miles east of the Philippines, the Japanese war juggernaut, which had been rampaging through much of the western Pacific, invaded Guam, a large island in the Marianas and a territory of the United States. Lightly defended, Guam fell in only five days. Among the Americans captured were five Army nurses, who were shipped to a prison in Japan.

Aware that the ill-prepared United States was literally fighting for its life and would have to fully mobilize, Congress, a week after Corregidor had fallen, authorized the establishment of a Women's Auxiliary Army Corps (WAAC), seeking to free able-bodied men for combat duty. Within hours, Secretary of War Henry L. Stimson, who had fought in France in what was now being called World War I, contacted thirty-seven-year-old Oveta Culp Hobby, a Texas newspaper executive, and asked her to take charge of the fledgling organization. She eagerly accepted and became America's first woman colonel.[10]

Hobby—bright, energetic, and articulate—had married William P. Hobby, publisher of the *Houston Post* and a former governor of Texas. She held several key positions at the newspaper before accepting a job in Washington as a $1–per-year director of the Women's Interest Section of the War Department's public relations office, in 1941, shortly before war broke out.

Colonel Hobby plunged into the demanding and frustrating task of building the WAAC from scratch. Often she met hostility rather than cooperation from the War Department. Male reporters at her first press conference bombarded her with irrelevant questions

"Can officer WAACs date men who are privates?" "Will WAACs underwear be khaki?" "What if an unmarried WAAC gets pregnant?"[11]

For months to come, newspapers and magazines carried stories about America's new "petticoat army, Wackies, and powder magazines." Despite the boos and catcalls, Colonel Hobby persevered, and within weeks she had recruiting, staffing, facilities, uniforms, and training programs operational.

Hobby set the tone when she addressed the WAAC Officer Candidate students at Fort Des Moines, Iowa, in July 1942. "You have taken off silk and put on khaki," the colonel said. "And all for essentially the same reasons—you have a debt and a date. A debt to democracy, a date with destiny."[12]

WAACs received their basic training at five army posts, and they soon were assigned to replace men as clerks, mechanics, typists, cooks, drivers, and in other capacities. One young WAAC wrote to her parents: "I wish I could think of some way to tell the gals back home what being in the service would do for them. Inside I can say I am doing something. I am helping. I shall continue doing all I can and be grateful."

An early volunteer for the WAAC, Pauline Krause, recalled that the Army Air Corps cadets at Gardner Field, California, were far from enthusiastic about the "invasion" of women soldiers:

> For weeks I drove an empty trailer transport. My job was to carry the male cadets from basic training classrooms to the air base. The fledgling pilots refused to ride with me, and instead, they trotted alongside the trailer rather than avail themselves of my service. Finally, one weary cadet realized that whether he trotted or rode made no difference to me. He broke the ridiculous impasse and jumped on the trailer with a sigh of relief. Soon, so did the rest of the cadets.

Two months after the WAAC was established, Congress, possibly at the behest of First Lady Eleanor Roosevelt, authorized a women's component of the Navy, which would be known as WAVES, an acronym for Women Accepted for Voluntary Emergency Services. Perhaps Mrs. Roosevelt's involvement had been generated by the fact that her husband, Franklin, had been assistant secretary of the Navy during World War I, had always been an enthusiastic sailor, and spent many vacations aboard the presidential yacht, a naval vessel, or his own boat.

In the Navy hierarchy in Washington, there was no great display of enthusiasm for the women's branch. One admiral told a few confidants that instead of women, he would have preferred "dogs or ducks or monkeys."

Appointed as first director of the WAVES was Mildred McAfee, who had been president of Wellesley College until called to serve by Secretary of the Navy Frank Knox, a former Chicago newspaper publisher. A native of Parkville, Missouri, McAfee was a graduate of Vassar College and received a master's degree from the University of Chicago. Like Colonel Hobby, McAfee, who held the rank of commander, was beset by hostility in the Navy Department, but she, too, built the organization in a short period of time.[13]

Not long after the birth of the WAVES, the other seagoing service, the Coast Guard, established the SPARS (short for *Semper Paratus* that branch's motto). Dorothy C. Stratton, with the rank of lieutenant commander, was appointed director. From the start, the SPARS had a recruiting advantage over the WAVES, although each wore similar uniforms. Pending construction of the SPARS' own facilities, recruits were trained at the ornate Biltmore resort hotel in Palm Beach, Florida.

Meanwhile, General Thomas Holcomb, commandant of the Marine Corps, was skewered on the horns of a dilemma. Men wearing the famous globe-and-anchor insignia were trained to fight, and Holcomb feared that the introduction of women into the Marine Corps would create confusion and major problems. Yet, after the Marines had taken heavy casualties at Guadalcanal in the Pacific in mid-1942, he knew manpower would be a major problem on the long and bloody road to Tokyo. So he asked Secretary of the Navy Knox to provide the Corps with "as many women as possible" to be used in noncombat roles "thus releasing a greater number of men for essential combat duty."[14]

Knox approved Holcomb's request, and plans were developed to establish the Marine Corps Women's Reserve (MCWR) in February 1943. Forty-seven-year-old Ruth C. Streeter was given the rank of major and appointed director. Enthusiastic and energetic, Streeter held both private and commercial pilot licenses. More than any of the directors of the women's components, she had first-hand knowledge of what the war was all about: Three of her four grown offspring were in the service, one in the Army and two in the Navy.

On September 1, 1942, First Lady Eleanor Roosevelt, in her widely read syndicated column, *My Day,* suggested that "women pilots are a weapon waiting to be used." When the influential First Lady spoke, official Washington listened.

Ten days later, Nancy H. Love was present at a news conference in Washington when Secretary of War Henry L. Stimson announced that she would be head of a new Women's Auxiliary Ferrying Squadron (WAFS). Members would be volunteers and all would be experienced pilots. As director of WAFS, Love would be based at New Castle Army Air Force Base near Wilmington, Delaware.

Love was twenty-eight years of age and the daughter of a wealthy Philadelphia physician. At the time of her appointment, she had been flying for ten years. Since 1936, she and her husband, Robert H. Love, had built a thriving aviation company in Boston, for which she served as one of the pilots. Nancy Love had been a pioneer of sorts, having safety-tested aircraft innovations for the U.S. Bureau of Air Commerce.

Soon, eager female pilots, one by one, began arriving at New Castle. They were a varied lot: heiresses (Woolworth's and Luden Cough Drops); one who had become the youngest licensed female pilot in the nation at age sixteen a half-dozen years earlier; a woman who had been inspired to fly in 1928 after reading an article by Amelia Earhart; and a former barnstormer who had some 3,000 hours of flying experience.

After a forty-day orientation period, Nancy Love's pilots began ferrying aircraft from factories to U.S. Army Air Corps bases around the nation. Meanwhile, Love had a surprise for her "girls"—official WAFS dress uniforms. Made by a civilian tailor she had located in Wilmington, the uniform consisted of a gray-green belted jacket, an open-collared light gray shirt, and gray-green slacks. "Groovy!" exulted one pilot, using a popular expression of the day. There was one catch: The women had to buy their own uniforms.

The WAFS were largely unknown to the general public. Even when hundreds of them would be ferrying airplanes across the nation, they were variously taken as Girl Scout leaders or, in Texas, as members of the Mexican army. Even though they wore their coveted wings, they did not look very military to civilians.

After flying P-51 Mustang fighter planes from California to Newark, New Jersey, four female pilots went to New York City for an evening of relaxation. They were wearing the standard summer uniforms of gabardine shirts and slacks. At Jack Dempsey's popular restaurant, they edged up to the bar and ordered drinks. The bartender glared at them. "No women in slacks!" he barked. "But these are our uniforms," they protested. Moments later, they were hustled out of the crowded restaurant.

Halfway down the block, they heard shouts: "Ladies! Ladies!" The manager of Dempsey's was running after them, having been alerted by an angry male Air Corps officer who had watched the episode. "Please come back," the manager pleaded. "We thought you were, er, ah, er, well you're wearing slacks." He had mistaken them for prostitutes. Hungry and thirsty, they agreed to return and spent the evening at Dempsey's "on the house."15

On another occasion, stormy weather caused four female pilots to make an emergency landing at Americus, Georgia. Leaving their aircraft in the hangar, they caught a bus into town to look for a hotel to spend the night. Soon after they began walking through the downtown area, a police car pulled up. Two of Americus's finest got out and ordered the women to come with them to the police station. One cop said sarcastically, " 'Ladies' in slacks are not allowed on the streets at night around here." He, too, had mistaken the pilots for prostitutes.

The women were locked up in a filthy cell. They protested that they were Army pilots in uniform. The police chief was unmoved. That would be merely another charge against them: impersonating military officers.

It was nearly 3:00 A.M. before the women were allowed to make a telephone call. They contacted Nancy Love and related their predicament. She demanded to speak to the police chief. He winced, holding the telephone receiver away from his ear. Ladylike and refined most of the time, Love had acquired a rough vocabulary. She read the riot act to the shaken police chief, impugning his lack of patriotism and charging that she would go directly to President Roosevelt about this outrage.

Minutes later the women were driven back to the airport. After dawn they lifted off in their planes, anxious to put as many miles as possible between themselves and Americus, Georgia.16

On September 15, 1942, only five days after the WAFS had been born, the War Department announced the formation of another Army Air Corps organization, the Women's Flying Training Detachment (WFTD). A day later, its leader, famed aviatrix Jacqueline Cochran, went to work on a paid basis—one dollar a year.

Cochran had been badgering the Army Air Corps for more than a year to recruit women pilots. A tough-minded, competitive, and outspoken woman, she had sent a sharply-worded letter to General Henry H. "Hap" Arnold, the Air Corps chief, urging creation of an all-female pilots organization commanded by a woman.

Jacqueline Cochran numbered several Air Corps generals among her friends, and she was on a first-name basis with them. She had started flying in 1932 and was the only woman to enter the McRobertson London-Melbourne race in 1934. That same year she became the first woman to compete in the annual cross-country Bendix Trophy Race. Much to the chagrin of her male competitors, some of whom would become Air Corps generals, she won the race.

Born in Pensacola, Florida, in 1913, Cochran had pulled herself up from a poverty-stricken early life to become head of her own highly successful national cosmetics firm, established in 1935. Respected by most men pilots, she was the kind of person who would fly into an Air Corps base at the controls of a B-17 Flying Fortress with a perfect three-point landing, dash into the operations center, and toss her coat to a colonel and tell him to hang it up. Then she would shake hands with the commanding general and other top officers who had dropped what they were doing to chat with her. An hour later she was back in the air and headed for her next destination.[17]

Jackie Cochran put out a call for volunteers for her new outfit. She was swamped with some 25,000 applicants, many of whom tried to beg or connive their way into a cockpit. She chose 1,830 of the most promising candidates, who had to pay their own way to Avenger Field in Texas, the nation's only all-female base.

These recruit trainees for the Women's Flying Training Detachment had experience piloting planes but had not logged nearly as many hours as Nancy Love's WAFS, who already were ferrying aircraft. In the first group of recruits were a Hollywood actress, a Reno blackjack dealer, a stuntwoman from Hollywood, a Chicago stripper, and a Kentucky nurse who made her rounds on horseback. Most noticeable was a member of the Florsheim shoe family who arrived at a nearby hotel with seventeen trunks and a trio of finely coiffeured Afghans.

During the first week the women were in training, more than 100 curious male cadets from the several training schools in the region suddenly developed engine trouble and had to make "forced landings" at Avenger Field. So the field commander ordered the base closed to all but genuine emergencies. Avenger Field, therefore, became known as Cochran's Convent.

On July 5, 1943, the War Department announced a reorganization of female components of the Army Air Force. All pilots in the WAFS and WFTD were now under the command of Jacqueline Cochran, whose title would be Director of Women Pilots. WAFS chief Nancy Love would continue as head of the ferrying division of the Air Transport Command. Cochran's new command would be called Women's Airforce Service Pilots or WASP.

The WASPs' job was to fly—and fly they did. During the war, they would log more than sixty million miles in the cockpits of every airplane in the Air Corps arsenal, from P-47 Thunderbolt fighters to the B-29 Superfortress. Through it all, they flew more miles than their male counterparts not in combat. And the WASPs would pay a heavy price: thirty-eight killed in the line of duty, thirty-two more injured.

In December 1944, like a bolt from the blue, the Pentagon announced that the WASP was being deactivated. The Army explained that it had more trained male pilots than it had airplanes, so they would take over the tasks the WASP had been handling. Eleanor McLernon Brown recalled:

> The time I had as a pilot in the WASP is one of my most treasured memories. Imagine the thrill of being chosen for training from among the thousands of other young women who applied. I wanted to serve my country and I wanted to be a pilot. When deactivation became a fact, it was a dismal experience, being told we were not needed any longer. But my pride in being a WASP will never diminish.

4 ❖ Secret Missions

A strange scenario was unfolding along 800 miles of coastline off French Northwest Africa just past midnight on November 8, 1942. An Allied radio station aboard a ship in the Mediterranean Sea, using the wavelength of a commercial transmitter ashore, was constantly calling out, *"Allô, Maroc!"* ("Hello, Morocco!"). In between, "The Star Spangled Banner" and the French national anthem, "La Marseillaise" blared out.

At 1:20 A.M., a voice came over the airwaves speaking in fluent French, identifying itself as that of Dwight D. Eisenhower, supreme commander of Allied forces. Actually, the radio-recording voice was that of Colonel Julius Holmes, a staff officer; Eisenhower's French was fractured at best.

In Eisenhower's (Holmes's) broadcast, he assured the French military commanders that the Americans were coming as friends and liberators, and he urged them not to resist. Hopefully, the invaders would land without bloodshed on either side.

In the blackness, hundreds of Allied ships, one of the largest fleets ever assembled up to that time, were slipping into position at widely separated points—off Casablanca, Oran, and Algiers. On board were thousands of American troops who would storm ashore at dawn to launch Operation Torch, the first major U.S. offensive since the Meuse-Argonne of World War I.

Eisenhower's plea was only partially heeded by the French. When the GIs landed, they were met with tenacious resistance in some locales and welcomed with open arms at others.

Only hours behind the vanguards, while shooting was still taking place at various points, a contingent of Army nurses went ashore with medical units. Their services were urgently needed: In four days and nights of fighting the bloodletting had been heavy. American forces suffered 837 wounded men, along with 556 killed and 41 missing.

Almost before the ink had dried on a cease-fire agreement, General Eisenhower began moving his Torch forces hundreds of miles eastward to Tunisia. The Allied plan was to trap German Field Marshal Erwin Rommel's *Afrika Korps* which was being driven westward in the direction of Tunisia by General Bernard L. Montgomery's British Eighth Army. It had gained fame as the Desert Rats.

The long trek by Eisenhower's units across the bleak and inhospitable terrain was slow and painful, made sluggish by a shortage of vehicles, cold weather, raw winds, and pelting rains that turned dirt roads into quagmires. Army nurses had to cope with the same hardships inflicted on the men during the long journey.

In Casablanca on December 22, five WAAC officers, thankful to be alive, went ashore from a British destroyer. They had sailed from England on a troop transport to take part in Torch, but their ship had been attacked and sunk by a German U-boat. Many lives had been lost. Two of the WAACs had been rescued from the burning vessel before it plunged to the bottom, and the other three were picked up from a lifeboat that they shared with a very seasick young male sailor.

Eventually, the five women boarded the British destroyer for the remainder of the trip. As the first WAACs to arrive overseas, the women were greeted at dockside by a delegation of high-ranking male officers.

Three weeks later, in mid-January 1943, the first contingent of WAAC enlisted women swung down the gangplank of a troop ship at Algiers, the teeming metropolis where General Eisenhower had established his headquarters in the stately St. George Hotel. Known since his boyhood in Kansas as Ike, Eisenhower had made a meteoric rise up the rank totem-pole, from being a staff colonel in Texas less than a year earlier to a four-star supreme commander. During the past few months, he had been converted from an opponent of women serving in the military to one of their principal advocates. After arriving in London in August 1942 to prepare for Torch, his conversion had taken place.

"I have seen [British service] women perform so magnificently in various positions, that I had become a booster of military women," Eisenhower would state.[1]

Once converted, Eisenhower had to "sell" most of his generals, many of whom were filled with misgivings and skepticism about women serving in uniform.

"What these men had failed to note was the changing requirements of war," Eisenhower would state. "The simple headquarters of a [Ulysses S.] Grant or a [Robert E.] Lee were gone forever. An army of filing clerks, stenographers, office managers, telephone operators, and chauffeurs had become essential, and it was scarcely less than criminal to recruit these from needed manpower when great numbers of highly qualified women were available."[2]

One of the staunchest die-hards against women serving in uniform was General George S. Patton, Jr., whose Western Task Force had captured Casablanca during the early stages of Operation Torch. Patton was the American battle leader the German high command feared most. "War is for *men!*" he would growl to his staff. Later, however, Patton's attitude seemed to soften. He said that one of his most valuable assistants was his WAAC office manager.

Back in Washington in late November 1942, Lieutenant General Brehon B. Somervell, the Army's supply chief, like Eisenhower, wanted to make wider use of women in the war effort. So he recommended that 500,000 females be drafted each year, using the same selective service apparatus that was bringing men into the armed forces. Somervell estimated that there were 11 million women available, and he proposed that the Army take 10 percent of them, leaving the remainder for other essential tasks in and outside of the military.

The United States had never drafted women, and behind-the-scenes contacts with leaders in Congress convinced Somervell that his proposal would be rejected overwhelmingly. Women in uniform would continue to be volunteers.

At the same time, Army Chief of Staff George Marshall also was exploring means for releasing more men to fight. In great secrecy, he authorized an experiment to see if women could be integrated into male antiaircraft-gun crews. There was ample reason for the clandestine nature of the field test. Even though women would not be involved in actually firing the weapon, Marshall feared a bad reaction from the populace should it leak out that women had been assigned to what could be regarded as a semi-combat type of operation.

The field test was conducted at two batteries protecting Washington, which Army leaders had been concerned might be a target of German bombers. Apparently the experiment was inconclusive, or perhaps the Army brass had second thoughts. Whatever may have been the case, the venture was quietly dropped.[3]

Meanwhile in December 1942, Stanton Griffis, an agent in Major General William J. "Wild Bill" Donovan's Office of Strategic Services (OSS), traveled to Finland to organize an espionage network in that small but strategically important country. A multimillionaire and close friend of Donovan, Griffis was shunned by the Finnish government on his arrival in Helsinki. The Nazis were using Finland as a base for operations against the Russian army, and the Finns were fearful of a full-scale occupation by the *Wehrmacht* (German armed forces). High officials in Helsinki, therefore, were reluctant to offend Adolf Hitler by an overt display of friendship with the United States.

Despite this obstacle, along with the fact that he was under Gestapo surveillance, Stan Griffis organized a spy network not only in Finland but also in neighboring Sweden, a neutral country and a hotbed of espionage for both the Germans and the Allies. One of his OSS agents in Sweden was an American woman, a former editor of *Vogue*, a popular magazine in the United States. She had been assigned to Sweden by the U.S. State Department as a "fashion attaché." Based in Stockholm, the vivacious woman was good at her State Department task and diligently promoted American clothing designed in Sweden. At the same time, she was extracting information from unknowing Nazi diplomats, who apparently were thrown off-guard by her charm and seeming total disinterest in global politics.

Another American woman, Therese Bonney, a free-lance writer, was recruited by the OSS not long after Pearl Harbor. Earlier, during the war between tiny Finland and the Soviet Union in 1939 and 1940, Bonney had established a close friendship with Field Marshal Baron Carl von Mannerheim, Finland's strongman, because of her sympathetic stories in the United States press. So in late 1942 Bonney was sent to Finland by the OSS with instructions to persuade the Finns to abandon their role as a "cobelligerent" (but not a full-fledged ally) of Nazi Germany.

Under cover of a reportorial assignment from *Colliers*, a large-circulation American magazine, Bonney reached Helsinki where she immediately was tailed by Gestapo agents. Nonetheless she managed to arrange a covert meeting with Baron von Mannerheim. Although she failed to convince the marshal to break openly with Adolf Hitler, she did obtain a wealth of intelligence about Finland's military apparatus and Nazi plans for prosecuting the war against the Soviet Union.

American diplomats always had looked on OSS cloak-and-dagger operations as some sort of satanic mumbo jumbo. In Stockholm and other neutral capitals in Europe, the assignment to U.S. embassies of OSS agents under diplomatic cover met with strong resistance from the tradition-bound, staid professionals of the State Department. Nevertheless, on her way back to Washington, D.C., to report to Wild Bill Donovan on her mission, Therese Bonney paid a short visit to the U.S. embassy in Stockholm to see a State Department official of long acquaintance.

Bonney disclosed nothing of her connection with the OSS, but subtlely asked her friend his opinion of Donovan's secret agency. Glancing around furtively as though Donovan had a spy on his tail, the diplomat confided: "I can always smell an OSS agent. We never give them any help."[4]

In July 1943, a battalion of WAACs, led by diminutive, spunky Captain Mary A. Hallaren, who had been an educator in civilian life, arrived by ship in England. As the first sizable unit of WAACs to be assigned to the European theater of operations, a galaxy of high military brass was dockside to greet the new arrivals.

The WAAC battalion had been brought to England at the request of Lieutenant General Ira C. Eaker, commander of the Eighth Air Force, who had led the first U.S. bombing raid in western Europe, on railroad yards outside Rouen, France, on August 17, 1942. Eaker had been convinced that the WAACs could take over most administrative tasks, thereby releasing large numbers of men to engage in combat.

A few fellow generals had urged Eaker not to ask for the WAACs, warning that the women would only disrupt administrative procedures. One general cautioned Eaker that he would be held accountable should the WAAC "experiment" fail. "I'm willing to take that responsibility," Eaker replied.[5]

At about the same time Eaker welcomed the women to England, President Roosevelt signed a bill that converted the WAAC to the Women's Army Corps (WAC). No longer was the female component an auxiliary; now it was integrated into the Army's regular chain of command. Oveta Culp Hobby was sworn in as director. Members of the auxiliary were given ninety days to decide if they wanted to join the WAC or be discharged. Nearly all of the officers and 75 percent of the enlisted women chose to sign up with the WAC.

Meanwhile in the Mediterranean, monumental events had been taking place. For five months, Eisenhower's Torch forces and Montgomery's Eighth Army had been slugging it out with the Germans and Italians who were trapped in Tunisia with their backs to the sea. Finally, on May 13, 1943, the resistance collapsed. A human deluge of 130,000 German and 120,000 Italian soldiers—more prisoners than the Russians had taken at Stalingrad—streamed into Allied enclosures. General Erwin Rommel was not among them; having seen the handwriting on the wall, Adolf Hitler had called him back to Berlin.

Two months later, on July 10, American and British forces landed by parachute, glider, and assault boats on the large island of Sicily at the toe of the Italian peninsula. Sicily was conquered in only six weeks, with most of the German and Italian forces being withdrawn across the two miles of water to the mainland. Hot on the heels of the fleeing enemy, Allied troops invaded southern Italy at several locations and began driving northward in bloody fighting in and among the mountain peaks.

American armed forces were suffering heavy casualties in the Mediterranean and in the Pacific, where General Douglas MacArthur's Army units and Admiral Chester W. Nimitz's Marines were island-hopping toward Japan, still thousands of miles away. These casualties would have to be replaced, so rear area installations were being combed for men to take over frontline duties. These men, in turn, would have to be supplanted.

Consequently in Washington, War and Navy Departments' manpower managers secretly began developing a plan to draft tens of thousands of women and arranged for a bill to be introduced in Congress. It never got past the House and Senate Armed Services Committees. "America is not ready to corral its young women into uniform against their will," one senator explained.

Colonel Oveta Hobby felt the issue was not dead, however. "What happens on the question of selective service for women depends on how long the war lasts," she told reporters.[6]

By New Year's Day 1944, there were 120,000 American women in uniform, most of them stationed in the United States. Integration of females largely had been accepted by most Army commanders, and with invasions scheduled for the spring in Normandy, Italy, and the Pacific, requests from overseas brass for more WACs skyrocketed.

General George Marshall, hoping to generate a far larger number of women volunteers, told the media that, outside of urgent family matters, joining the armed forces should take precedence over any endeavor. "It is important that the public understands the Army's urgent need for women to enable the military effort to go forward," Marshall emphasized.[7]

On December 31, 1943—New Year's Eve—Aline Griffith, a shapely brunette beauty who had been a model for Hattie Carnegie, the world-famous designer of fashionable women's hats, in New York City, strode to the registration desk in Madrid's ornate Palace Hotel. She had come to Europe on the Pan American Clipper, a huge flying boat, on a crucial mission for the OSS. Before leaving Washington, her controller had warned her: "If you fail, hundreds, even thousands, of American GIs could die!"[8]

The twenty-one-year-old Griffith had come to an especially dangerous place, for Madrid was infested with German spies, stringers, Peeping Toms, sleepers, strap-hangers, go-fors, cut-outs, and go-betweens. This large continent of Nazi agents operated without fear of arrest by Spanish police, for *El Caudillo* (leader) Francisco Franco had passed word to his government and military that they were to turn a blind eye toward German covert capers.

Against this large number of Nazi undercover operatives, the OSS had but eleven agents in Spain—twelve, counting Aline Griffith.

Back in September she had been recruited by an OSS official in New York after he learned that she was anxious for a job that would help the war effort, even though that would mean giving up a promising modeling career. A brother was aboard a submarine in the Pacific, and another brother was a fighter pilot based in England.

A week later, as instructed, Griffith reported to an ugly, prefabricated structure, known as the Q Building, in Washington. In a starkly bare room, an OSS official told her only that her code name was Tiger and she was not to confide to other OSS types in Washington her true name.

A day later, she was driven to a large, rambling old house thirty miles outside Washington. There she joined twenty-eight men, also OSS recruits. An instructor said the place was known as the Farm. In the days ahead she and the others were put through rigorous physical and mental courses designed to convert them into effective cloak-and-dagger operatives.

Then Tiger was sent back to the Q Building, where an OSS official code named Jupiter informed her that her assignment would be in Spain, a neutral country. Jupiter confided: "Two Allied invasions of the Continent are being planned. One is for the north [Normandy], and one for the south [France's Riviera]. OSS Spain will be responsible for the southern attack. The outcome of the war hinges on those invasions."[9]

After her meeting with Jupiter, Tiger was escorted down the hallway to an office where she met yet another official. "The job you have been selected for is vital," he said in almost a whisper. "A contact inside the Gestapo in Berlin informs us that Heinrich Himmler, the Gestapo chief, has one of his most capable spies operating in Madrid, running a network for uncovering Allied plans related to Operation Anvil [the Southern France invasion]. Your vital mission is to discover who that person is."

He added that the OSS mole in Berlin had provided the names of four people in Madrid, one of whom the agent believed was the person running the network. All moved on a level of international society, which made standard surveillance difficult, the official told Tiger. "We need an agent there—that's you—who can fit into that group."

Tiger's cover would be as an employee of an Oil Mission of the United States, a legitimate organization whose Madrid manager was cooperating with the OSS.

Now, after arriving in Madrid, Tiger reported to her job at the Oil Mission. An OSS agent, who had an office there and went by the code name Mozart, told her that he was the only one in Madrid who knew of her precise mission, code-named Operation Bullfight. There's no time to be lost, he stressed. The Southern France invasion was to hit about a week after D-Day in Normandy, probably in the spring.

Then Mozart handed Tiger a piece of paper and told her to memorize the four suspects identified by the Berlin mole: Countess Gloria von Fürstenberg, a friend of top Gestapo officials in Berlin who was living lavishly in Madrid with no obvious means of financial support; Hans Lazaar, press attaché at the German embassy in Madrid; Ramón Serrano-Suñer, Franco's brother-in-law and a friend of Adolf Hitler; and Prince Nikolaus Lilienthal, a Czech citizen who used a German diplomatic passport and was a friend of Heinrich Himmler.

Within days, Tiger rented an apartment on the Calle Monte Esquina—a luxury suite paid for with her OSS "hazardous duty" salary. She was told to expect "guests" on occasion—female agents who trudged across the towering Pyrenees Mountains along the Spanish-French border to bring military intelligence from the underground in Southern France.

Soon, Tiger felt like a full-fledged spy involved in a deadly game of wits. In her purse, she carried a small Beretta pistol and a cigarette lighter that was actually a camera. Also in her handbag were some "L" pills containing poison. If trapped, she could bite a pill and be dead in moments. She often carried a hatbox, and it held a larger "spy camera," a radio detector, chemicals, and wires—tools of the espionage profession. The intelligence she gathered was sent to Washington on a high-powered transmitter operated by OSS men in the attic of the U.S. embassy in Madrid.

Vivacious, well educated, and stylishly dressed, Tiger was rapidly accepted into Madrid's international social whirl. She was invited to lavish balls and dinners, meeting the créme de la créme of Spanish society, noting handshakes, winks, and nods among individuals, many of them suspected of being Nazi agents.

All the while, as instructed at the Farm, Tiger was forming a network of fifteen subagents, all of them women. She recruited a reliable Spanish woman, who found another woman, who in turn located still another until the network was completed. For security reasons, Tiger knew only the first woman; the others knew only two, except for the last one.

On April 6, two young, disheveled French women showed up at Tiger's apartment. They had crossed the Pyrenees with maps showing the location of coastal fortifications and artillery batteries along the Mediterranean in southern France. This vital intelligence was rushed to London where the two invasions were being planned.

Tiger was leaving for a weekend sojourn as a guest at the country estate of one of the four suspects, so she suggested that one of the couriers could use her comfortable bed. That night, an assailant slipped into the dark bedroom through a window and killed the sleeping French woman with a pistol shot through the head. No doubt the bullet was intended for Tiger.

One day, Prince Lilienthal, the Czech who was one of the four primary suspects, asked Tiger to rendezvous with him. They had known one another socially. Cautiously, she kept the appointment. Unaware that she was an OSS agent, he told her that he was on the U.S. embassy blacklist for his German sympathies, but he had a dramatic secret to pass on to the Americans. If he tried to communicate this information directly to U.S. officials, his family back in Berlin might suffer. He asked Tiger, who was not involved in espionage (he thought), to pass this secret to U.S. authorities.

Suspicious, Tiger asked him about his switch of loyalties. He replied that he had become disillusioned with Adolf Hitler, who, he was convinced, was taking Germany down the road to total destruction.

Then Lilienthal dropped his bomb. Through his contacts in Berlin, he had learned that Heinrich Himmler, the Gestapo chief, had informed a German general that he had a mole high in the U.S. intelligence apparatus in Madrid.

Tiger was shaken. If this report were true, was one of the OSS men she was working with a traitor? To which of her colleagues could she confide this shocking information? The one she chose might be the mole. In that case, she would soon be murdered.

5 ❖ A Conspiracy to Murder Hitler

In neutral Switzerland, a tiny, mountainous enclave surrounded entirely by Adolf Hitler's forces in France, Italy, Austria, and Germany, Allen W. Dulles did business in a building at Herrengasse 23 in the picturesque, medieval city of Bern, a hotbed of intrigue. The lettering on a small sign next to Dulles's front door stated "Special Assistant to the American Minister." But the sign was merely part of the games that those involved in international espionage play. Dulles, as nearly all of the hundreds of German and Allied spies roaming about Switzerland knew, was actually the OSS station chief.

Dulles was fond of tweed jackets and bow ties, wore rimless spectacles, and was seldom caught without his briar pipe—a stereotype of Hollywood's version of a kindly, middle-aged college professor. Despite his deceptively mild appearance, Dulles was tough-minded and cagey. A lawyer by trade, he had been posted to Bern during World War I, ostensibly as an employee of the State Department. Then he was doing the same thing he was doing a war later—collecting intelligence from inside neighboring Germany.

Dulles was fortunate to have arrived in Switzerland at all. In early November 1942 he had been in France on "legal work" when the Allies invaded North Africa and Adolf Hitler immediately sent troops to occupy all of France. Dulles managed to catch the last train to Switzerland.

On his arrival in Bern, Dulles's staff consisted of two other persons. But in this uneasy corner of Europe he began to weave his espionage network. With the Swiss border now sealed, he set about recruiting "talent" from among American citizens living in Switzerland. One of his early recruits was Mary Bancroft. She was the daughter of the publisher of *The Wall Street Journal*, a large, New York City-based newspaper. She was a fiery political liberal and Democrat—no doubt to the consternation of her conservative father. A comely brunette in her early forties, Mary had concrete opinions and seldom, if ever, was reluctant to express them.

Bancroft was engaged in free-lance journalism when Allen Dulles asked her to take a job in his Bern office analyzing German newspapers and magazines for the reports he telephoned almost nightly to OSS headquarters in Washington. It was the first step in plunging her into the murky yet intriguing domain of international espionage. Dulles had other things in mind to draw on her talents than digesting German publications.

Mary was a complex woman—restless, always seeking some new adventure. She lived in Zurich, where she sought out the noted Swiss psychiatrist, Carl Gustav Jung, because she was stricken by prolonged bouts of sneezing while at social affairs, mostly, Jung would discover, because she was bored.[1]

Bancroft saw Jung on and off for several months and was thought to have developed an affection for him, although he was twenty-five years older. One of his colleagues, a woman psychiatrist, did not share Jung's high regard for the outspoken American. Dealing with Bancroft, she said, was "like wrestling with a boa constrictor."[2]

Loquacious Mary Bancroft had never kept a secret in her life, as far as anyone was aware. But one night in his Bern quarters, Allen Dulles, puffing on his pipe, fixed Mary with a stare and said without a trace of humor, "Contrary to general belief, I think you can keep your mouth shut."

She was angered by his bluntness but kept listening. Dulles had a crucial job to be done, and there was no one else to do it, he said. He was going to assign the task to her. If she was unable to keep quiet about it, "Five thousand people will die," he added.

Bancroft was shaken—but moved. Her face turned pale. But she agreed to the assignment. No longer would her task be to thumb through German periodicals. Now she was a full-fledged OSS agent. Perhaps she had taken on the job out of patriotism, perhaps from a desire to get involved in an intriguing adventure. In his best cloak-and-dagger fashion, Dulles told her, "You will soon get a call from a Dr. Bernhard."

Mary didn't sleep well that night. Obviously she was going to take part in something big. But never did she dream that the task for which Dulles had chosen her would be of such a shocking magnitude: involvement in an undercover operation to murder Adolf Hitler.

"Dr. Bernhard" was the code name for Hans Bernd Gisevius. A bear of a man, six feet four inches and 260 pounds, he was an agent of the *Abwehr*, Hitler's secret service, and assigned to the Nazi consulate in Zurich. Gisevius, a lawyer, had joined the Gestapo in 1933, only to be ousted six months later because of his lack of enthusiasm for the Nazi cause. Then he became a member of the Berlin police, but he was fired for criticizing the SS, Hitler's elite army within an army.

In 1939, Gisevius joined the *Schwarze Kapelle* (Black Orchestra), a tightly knit secret group of prominent German military officers, government officials, church and civic leaders who were conspiring to "eliminate" Adolf Hitler. A short time later he became an agent for the *Abwehr* and was sent to Zurich where he became the eyes and ears of the German anti-Hitler conspiracy. He was posted at the German consulate under diplomatic cover as vice-consul.

In February 1943 Gisevius, at great peril to himself, sought out Allen Dulles. In a scenario reminiscent of a Hollywood spy thriller, the two men rendezvoused on a black night on the steps of the World Council of Churches building in Bern. The German told about the anti-Nazi group in Germany and how it hoped to throw the Fuehrer out of power and sign a separate peace treaty with the Western Allies to keep the Soviets out of Germany.

Dulles was impressed by Gisevius's sincerity and his reasons for seeking destruction of the Hitler regime. A few more covert meetings were held, and plans were worked out for Gisevius to furnish couriers for bringing secret information out of Hitler's headquarters in Berlin to Bern.

The OSS chief was eager to keep this intelligence bonanza flowing, and he figured the key to pleasing Gisevius lay in a book he was writing about his role in upsetting Hitler's applecart. The German desperately wanted it translated so that the book could be published in the United States the moment the war in Europe ended. Dulles promised to provide a skilled translator—cerebral Mary Bancroft.[3]

While working with the German on the book, Bancroft was given a second mission: In essence, she was to spy on Gisevius and report to Dulles everything that he said. She wondered how two men, who seemed to be rowing the same boat, could be so distrustful of one another. Soon she would learn that in espionage, no one takes anything for granted; participants were always on guard against treachery.

In June 1943 the telephone jangled impatiently in the Zurich apartment of Mary Bancroft. The caller identified himself as Dr. Bernhard and asked to come see her that same afternoon. When she opened the door, a hulking, forty-year-old man with a stiff Prussian bearing came into view. Mary was thrilled to know that this man with whom she was to work was a leader in the nefarious plot to kill Adolf Hitler. That meant that she, too, was playing a role in the dark conspiracy.

On this first visit, Gisevius brought 1,400 pages of his manuscript. More pages were brought to her in the weeks ahead. The translation was tedious, demanding, and exhausting. Their sessions invariably triggered spats and long discussions about philosophical matters. In time, the liberal American accepted the fact that the German was a hopeless right-winger, but she also was convinced that he was a sincere, Christian man who was putting his life on the line for his beliefs.

In early May 1944 Bancroft learned from Hans Gisevius that the Schwarze Kapelle was preparing yet another bold scheme to kill Adolf Hitler. Thirty-six-year-old Lieutenant Colonel Klaus Philip Maria Count von Stauffenberg, a German aristocrat who had lost an eye, an arm, and part of the other hand while fighting in North Africa, was to fly from Berlin to the Fuehrer's headquarters behind the Russian front for a conference. Von Stauffenberg would carry a bomb in a briefcase, set the timer, and place it at Hitler's feet while the participants were gathered around a conference table. Then he would use an excuse to leave the building and fly back to Berlin after the explosion.

Bancroft doubted if the plan would work. But she didn't express that view to her friend Gisevius, who was involved in ironing out details of the plot. Yet she felt a lofty sense of power. She doubted if any other American woman had even heard of the Schwarze Kapelle, much less the conspiracy's effort to wipe out the Nazi regime in one fell swoop.

Although officially recognized as noncombatants, Army and Navy nurses overseas sometimes found themselves in peril because of the shifting tides of battle. One of these instances came in January 1944 when an American and British force of 70,000 men landed far behind German lines in Italy at Anzio, a small port on the west coast. The plan was for the invaders to drive rapidly northward for thirty miles and capture the glittering prize of Rome.[4]

However, the Germans reacted rapidly and ringed the beachhead, only twenty-five miles long and four to seven miles deep, with troops and tanks, trapping the invaders.

The Berlin Bitch, as a German female propagandist was called by the GIs, taunted the Allied troops over Radio Berlin: "Hello out there, boys and girls at Anzio. How does it feel to be cooped up in the world's largest self-containing prisoner-of-war camp?"

In the Devil's inferno of Anzio, there was no "rear area." German artillery observers looking down on the bridgehead from the mountains around the beachhead could scan every foot of ground and call in deadly salvos. So crowded was the Allied-held territory that the four evacuation hospitals, housed in clusters of tents, were located along the shorelines next to supply and ammunition depots, communications posts, various headquarters, and other prime German targets.

Nearly 200 women of the U.S. Army Nurse Corps—the unsung heroes of Anzio—toiled around the clock to relieve the suffering and save the lives of wounded men. These nurses performed their duties while wearing steel helmets, fatigues, and combat boots. They faced danger as great as anyone else in the bridgehead.

Even though the hospital tents were clearly marked with red crosses on fields of white, artillery shells exploded regularly along the shoreline. While performing surgery and other duties, the nurses and doctors often heard the frightening rustle of a 700-pound shell from what the GIs called the Anzio Express, an enormous 280–millimeter railroad gun, just before it rocked the terrain around the hospital with a ground-shaking blast. At night, the Luftwaffe flew over, dropped parachute flares, then unloaded bombs along the shore.

Frontline troops had a name for the evacuation hospitals: Hell's Half-Acre. It was a place to be avoided. Sometimes the GIs concealed minor wounds to keep from being sent back to the tented medical centers. On occasion, wounded soldiers on cots in the hospital were hit a second or third time by shell or bomb fragments.[5]

The presence of female nurses served as a great morale booster for the fighting men at a time morale badly needed uplifting. So inspiring was the valor displayed by the women that an attitude developed among combat troops on the beachhead: "If they can do it, so can I."

When the Germans had collected sufficient strength from all over Italy, they launched a powerful offensive to wipe out the Allies. It appeared that the Germans were about to break through to the sea, so General Mark W. Clark, the U.S. commander in Italy, decided to evacuate the nurses to keep them from being captured. Then he had a change of mind. Pulling out the women could be a portent of disaster and spread panic among the hard-pressed troops.

At mid-afternoon on February 7, twenty-year-old Corporal Charles H. Doyle, a paratrooper, was reclining on his cot as a patient at the 95th Evacuation Hospital. His sensitive ears perked up as he heard a familiar roar in the sky. He could not see from under the canvas, but a Luftwaffe bomber was streaking over the beachhead, chased by Allied fighter planes. Perhaps seeking to escape his tormentors by gaining altitude and speed, the German pilot jettisoned his bombs. One or more of the explosives landed on the 95th Evac, killing twenty-three persons, including three women nurses, a Red Cross lady, several male medics, and a few patients. Corporal Doyle escaped unscathed.

One of those killed in the bombing was Lieutenant Colonel Blanche F. Sigman, chief nurse. Altogether, six women nurses died through enemy action on the Anzio beachhead, and sixteen others were wounded. The nurses who had been killed received Purple Hearts posthumously, and the wounded women were awarded the same medal. Four nurses received Silver Stars, the first American women to earn that decoration for valor.

The all-out German drive for victory was halted, and a few weeks later, the Allied force charged out of the beachhead and raced to Rome, which was captured on June 4, 1944.

Elsewhere in Europe, Lieutenant Agnes Mangerich and thirteen other Army flight nurses, along with several male medical technicians, were on an airplane bound for Bari, Italy, when the pilot had to crash-land in German-occupied Albania, in the Balkans. Violent storms and enemy gun-fire had disabled the craft.

With little food, Mangerich and the others trudged through the mountainous, rocky terrain eight hours a day, bound for an American camp on the Adriatic coast, 800 miles from the crash site. It was winter and bitterly cold; the group spent Thanksgiving, Christmas, and New Year's Day trekking through deep snow, stopping at any shelter they could find. The hikers suffered from infectious boils, body lice, and bouts with dysentery.

After sixty-two days, the exhausted marchers reached the camp, where they were greeted by soldiers armed with chicken, fruit, and chocolate bars. "I had only one thing in mind, however," Mangerich recalled. "I curled up in a sleeping bag in a little cave. Don't know how many hours—or days—I slept. Finally, someone tugged at me and said, 'The boat's here!' "

Although WACs and Army and Navy nurses were on active duty in many parts of the world, the law prohibited WAVES, SPARS, and Women Marines from serving outside the United States. Yet all contributed significantly to the war effort at home. At Cherry Point Marine Air Station in North Carolina, 80 percent of the control-tower operations were handled by women Marines. WAVES serving in naval aviation taught instrument flying, aircraft gunnery, and celestial navigation.

WAVES officers and SPARS officers, nearly all of them university graduates, were involved in finance, chemical warfare, and aerological engineering. At Norfolk, they helped install sophisticated radar on aircraft carriers and other warships.

For the first time, top-secret projects were opened to military women. Both the Navy and the Coast Guard utilized females in Long-Range Aid to Navigation (LORAN) stations, and WAVES were involved in a night-fighter training course. At a hidden communications center in Washington, D.C., WAVES officers spent countless hours staring at electronic screens, watching for "blips." It was boring, seemingly senseless work; the women had never been told the reasons for their job. When they were finally informed that each blip represented a U.S. ship being sunk, the task took on meaning and morale soared.[6]

WAVES Lieutenant Mary Osborne was assigned to a super-secret Naval Intelligence facility in Washington. Her job had its roots back in mid-1939, just before England went to war with Nazi Germany. British scientists had cracked the Enigma code, which was used by the German armed forces and diplomats to send wireless messages. Adolf Hitler and other leaders were convinced that the code was unbreakable.

Throughout the war, the British intercepted the German messages and gave the code name Ultra to all intelligence gathered from Enigma. British Prime Minister Winston Churchill had agreed to share the Ultra information with the United States, so Mary Osborne and her WAVES colleagues were receiving this information by wireless from England for transmittal to government and military leaders in Washington.[7]

On the other side of the world from Washington, D.C., in May 1944 the first contingent of WACs arrived in Australia, 2½ years after Pearl Harbor. They would serve under General Douglas MacArthur, who, after his escape from the Philippines early in the war, had established his headquarters in Brisbane.

Despite meager manpower and resources, ninety days after MacArthur had reached Down Under, he sent his troops northward to invade Japanese-held New Guinea, the world's second largest island, a land of jungles and swamps, scarcely changed from the Stone Age. For nearly two years, the Diggers (as the Australian soldiers were known) and the GIs had been fighting what MacArthur called a "hit-'em-where-they-ain't" campaign of speed and surprise. His troops leapfrogged Japanese coastal strongholds along the northern spine of 1,300–mile-long New Guinea. Fighting was as brutal and nasty as history had known.

Soon after their arrival in Australia, the WACs were shipped to Port Moresby, on the eastern tail of New Guinea, which is shaped like a squatting turkey. There the enlisted women were quartered within a barbed-wire compound under armed guard. They were "pardoned," the WACs complained, only to go to work or to social functions that had been officially approved. If a WAC had a date with a male enlisted man, the event had to be approved in advance. And the women had to be back inside the compound no later than 11:00 P.M.

Neither the WACs nor the male soldiers detailed to guard their compound were happy with the situation. No official explanation was given for the strict security measures. Some WACs thought the high command feared that the women might be raped by GIs who hadn't seen an American woman in a year and a half.

As MacArthur's forces battled their way along the torturous jungle road to Tokyo, his women soldiers followed. Later, he stated:

> I moved my WACs forward early after occupation of captured territory because they were needed and they were soldiers the same manner that my men were soldiers . . . They were eager to carry on as needed.[8]

The WACs and Army nurses had to cope with the same brutal environmental conditions as did the men in the primitive southwest Pacific: 100-degree temperatures; torrential rains; suffocating humidity; knee-deep mud; billions of mosquitoes; chiggers; poisonous snakes; leaches; tall grass that slashed human flesh like a razor blade.

While MacArthur's Army troops in the Southwest Pacific and the U.S. Marines in the Central Pacific were hacking their way toward Japan, much of the focus of the world was upon Europe where the Western Allies were about to launch the most gigantic invasion force in history across the English Channel and against Adolf Hitler's heavily fortified Atlantic Wall.

6 ❖ Lady Spies and a Blonde Guerrilla

In the early spring of 1944, staid old London, a city of three million people, was engulfed by an olive-drab tidal wave of American military men and women. It seemed that the young newcomers from across the Atlantic outnumbered the Londoners, whose cinemas, hotels, restaurants, dance halls, and pubs were swamped by GIs.

Londoners—indeed natives all over England, Scotland, and Wales—were perplexed by the habits of these Americans, who scrawled on rocks, on walls, in lavatories, and on seemingly unreachable places, "Kilroy was here!" The natives never found out for sure who Kilroy was, where he came from, what he did, or why anyone would be so awed by him as to write his name all around the British Isles.

At any given time, there were some half-million military men and women from about sixty Allied and neutral countries on leave in or posted to London. Among them were three female war correspondents: petite Betty Gaskill, who worked for *Liberty* magazine; Dixie Tighe, an attractive lady of some years who reported for the International News Service; and Judy Barden, a young woman who was employed by the *New York Sun*.

Although the women correspondents were not members of the armed forces, they certainly were that in spirit. Theirs was a potentially dangerous endeavor, covering the war from up close. And their uniforms were almost identical to those worn by U.S. Army nurses and WAC officers. Gaskill, Tighe, and Barden were angry and frustrated. The mightiest military endeavor in history, the cross-Channel attack against Adolf Hitler's Europe, was about to be launched, and the authorities would not permit them to cover the event by going along with the initial assault troops.

Charged up by professional pride and an understandable desire for equal treatment for their gender, the three women buttonholed Captain Barney Oldfield, an outgoing and congenial Army public-relations officer who had been saddled with the preposterous task of keeping fifty-eight media reporters—many of them prima donnas—happy and informed. These were the men and the women who wanted, or professed to want, to be in the "first wave" of the invasion. Their lure was looming front-page byline stories and establishing reputations that would endure for all time.

There were not enough available spaces on landing craft for all of the reporters to go ashore with the seaborne vanguard, so Oldfield, a qualified paratrooper and one-time press agent for a promising Hollywood actor named Ronald Reagan, was handed the toughest of all sales tasks: persuade some reporters that the surest way to get to the Far Shore first was to jump with the paratroopers.

A few male correspondents approached by Oldfield turned pale after it was suggested that they parachute into Fortress Europe. Oldfield recalled: "There was no whirlwind of enthusiasm for being among the first Americans to touch down behind the Atlantic Wall. Perhaps they had seen too many of those aerial photographs showing the pointed stakes that stood in every Normandy field, ready to impale Allied parachutists."[1]

Oldfield persevered and finally coerced a small number of correspondents to take a two-week crash course at a parachute school near Hungersford. Then a hitch developed. Word got back to the plush London hotels and bars that the school was being run by brutes and bone crushers. Oldfield remembered: "The picture painted by these reports suggested that Gestapo chief Heinrich Himmler himself and his thugs were planning on crossing the English Channel and enrolling in the parachute school in order to learn the latest techniques on sadism."[2]

Although a few male correspondents took the parachute course, most who had agreed to do so backed out. They would hit Normandy in invasion craft or by boat a few days later. Not so the women correspondents Betty Gaskill, Dixie Tighe, and Judy Barden. They demanded that they be allowed to take the parachute course and to jump behind German lines with the paratroopers.

Captain Oldfield tried to shadowbox with the three tenacious women, neatly sidestepping their inquiries and hoping that they would tire of the sport. Instead, they continued to take large bites out of a certain portion of the PR officer's anatomy. Oldfield sought out friends of the women in an effort to get them to call off the dogs. All was in vain.

Oldfield was skewered on the horns of a dilemma: If he didn't grant the female reporters' demand, he would be accused of sex discrimination. If the women were to be killed parachuting into France, he would be charged with being a cruel, callous, insensitive brute who had stupidly sent three members of the so-called weaker sex to their deaths.

Only a week before D-Day, Oldfield's thrust-and-parry tactics paid off. With a reasonable degree of grace, Betty Gaskill, Dixie Tighe, and Judy Barden agreed to go in by boat shortly after the initial assault. Oldfield resumed breathing.

As D-Day grew ever closer, General Eisenhower was burdened with pressures the weight of which few men in history have known. Each day, he had to make crucial decisions and referee disputes among the Allied generals in his command. Helping the supreme commander endure his trials and tribulations was a close-knit inner circle that included Lieutenant Kay Summersby. Since mid-1942 she had been his chauffeuse, aide, confidante, and occasional social companion. No women in World War II had been so close to the seat of power as was Summersby.

A tall, attractive woman in her early thirties, Summersby was divorced from her first husband and had met and was engaged to an American colonel when Eisenhower appeared on the scene. The colonel was later killed in action in Tunisia, during Torch.

Ironically, Summersby had become a member of Eisenhower's "inner circle" and was in French Northwest Africa when her fiancé met his death. After Eisenhower returned to London in early 1944 to take command of Operation Overlord, the invasion of northern France, he secured a WAC lieutenant's commission for Summersby.[3]

Allied security officers in London were confronted by a situation so delicate that not even Eisenhower himself could be advised about it. The target of the worry: WAC Lieutenant Kay Summersby.

For months Adolf Hitler and his *Oberkommando der Wehrmacht* (high command) had been frantically searching for intelligence that would pinpoint the time and place of the looming Allied assault across the English Channel. Frederick Morgan, the congenial British general who had been planning the invasion of France since late in 1943, stated ominously: "If the Germans have even a forty-eight-hour advance notice of [the Normandy landings], we could suffer a monstrous catastrophe!"

It was an open secret in Allied supreme headquarters that Dwight Eisenhower was infatuated with Summersby. Never was her loyalty, discretion, or integrity under question by security officers. Their worry was that she had been at Eisenhower's side almost daily for months and had heard top-secret matters being discussed. Perhaps she knew as much about the D-Day plans as nearly any Allied general, who often was provided only the information he needed to carry out his specific mission.

Security officers were haunted by several factors. What if Eisenhower and his ladyfriend were to have a falling out prior to D-Day? What, if anything, would be her reaction if she became a woman scorned? That prospect sent shivers up the spines of the security men. But there was nothing they could do about the situation—except to pray that Cupid continued to smile on the couple.

A second scenario that kept security officers awake nights was the possibility that Kay Summersby might be kidnapped by Nazi agents, who presumably were roaming southern England where the invasion was being mounted. She was well known to the *Abwehr* the German secret service agency that had 16,000 full- and part-time agents scattered around the world. The *Abwehr* knew that she had been a constant companion of the

Allied supreme commander for months and, therefore, would be a walking encyclopedia of D-Day information.

Kidnapping Summersby—who conceivably would be rushed to a house or building already in the hands of an undercover Nazi spy—would be a doable task. She often drove around London and elsewhere alone or in the company of another officer. Once in the hands of the Nazi agents, she could be made to spill D-Day secrets then "disposed of" at some lonely location in southern England.

An ear-splitting roar pierced the tranquility of the coast of Normandy. The racket echoed for miles across the turbulent English Channel. Six hundred Allied warships, their huge guns belching orange and black clouds, hurled salvo after salvo of shells toward German bunkers, artillery batteries, and strong points along the Atlantic Wall. It was 5:52 A.M. on June 6, 1944.

Operation Neptune, the assault phase of the invasion, had been launched six hours earlier when paratroopers and glidermen of the U.S. 82nd and 101st Airborne Divisions, along with the British 1st Airborne Division, had bailed out behind German fortifications. Casualties were heavy. Later, Captain Oldfield felt enormous relief that he had not caved in to the demands of the three women correspondents to bail out with the paratroopers. However, four days after the invasion began, there were women ashore: The first contingent of nurses waded onto the Normandy beaches, moved inland with their medical units, and began tending to the needs of wounded GIs.

On the night of July 20, Mary Bancroft, the OSS agent in Switzerland, was listening to the Swiss radio when the regular program was interrupted for a blockbuster disclosure. A bomb had been planted in Adolf Hitler's headquarters in East Prussia, but the Fuehrer had miraculously escaped with minor injuries. Some time later, the news said that loyal Nazi forces in Berlin charged into the conspirators' command post on Bendlerstrasse and arrested those inside. Most were shot before the day ended.

Much to her astonishment, Bancroft would learn that her German friend, Hans Gisevius, with whom she had been working, had slipped back into Germany and had left the conspirators' headquarters only minutes before the building was surrounded. He managed to survive by holing up in a friend's house in Berlin.

Fighting in Normandy was vicious. Adolf Hitler had ordered his generals not to give up a foot of ground. But early on the morning of July 25—D-Day plus forty-nine—the Allies broke out of the beachhead and charged eastward hell-bent toward the German border.

At the same time, General Eisenhower was preparing to launch the second of what he called in boxing jargon "my one-two punch"—an invasion of Southern France. Code named Operation Dragoon (formerly Anvil), the second invasion had been scheduled for a week after the Normandy D-Day, but a shortage of landing craft caused its postponement. Dragoon was designed to gain a beachhead along the fabled French Riviera, after which the combined U.S. and French forces would drive generally to the northeast and link up with the Allied armies breaking out of Normandy. Dragoon D-Day was set for August 15, 1944.

Meanwhile in Madrid, the OSS agent, Aline Griffith (code name Tiger), was still trying to unmask the Nazi agents whose mission was to uncover the secrets of the pending Southern France invasion. Time was running out. Late one afternoon in July, Edmundo, an OSS agent Tiger had been working with since her arrival in Spain, telephoned. In an excited tone, he asked if he could pick her up at midnight for an important job.

A few hours later the two agents were driving through the deserted streets of Madrid, and Edmundo halted the car before a building at 14 Calle Hermosilia. Only now did Edmundo make a comment on the mission. Someone had given him a tip. Both climbed out. The man pulled out his revolver; so did Tiger.

In seconds the front-door lock was picked, and the pair crept gingerly down a dark hallway, then up rickety stairs to the third floor to a door showing a thin crack of light at the bottom. Again the lock-picking. Edmundo slowly turned the knob and both OSS agents burst inside. Two figures moved. "Halt or I'll shoot!" Edmundo rasped.

In the corner was a huge radio transmitter, one capable of reaching all the way to Berlin. Then Tiger caught sight of a familiar figure—Countess Gloria von Fürstenberg. She stood there as if petrified, caught red-handed.

Fürstenberg admitted she was sending messages from the Gestapo chief in the German embassy in Madrid to Berlin. "I had to do it," she weeped, "to earn a few pennies to feed and clothe my children."

"Such a devoted mother," Edmundo hissed, knowing she had been living lavishly. "It tugs at my heartstrings."[4]

A few days later, Tiger was shocked to learn the identity of the OSS agent who was actually working for the Gestapo. His code name in the OSS was Pierre, a handsome, engaging, intelligent man with whom Tiger had socialized and worked with. Mozart informed Tiger that he had known for several weeks that Pierre, a Spaniard, was a double agent, so he had told him the Southern France invasion would hit at Marseilles. Then Mozart had him parachuted near Marseilles to advise the French underground—and Adolf Hitler—of the location of the Allied landing. There was one catch, Pierre would soon learn. He had been fed faulty information: Dragoon would not strike at Marseilles but along the Riviera, many miles away.[5]

Prior to the Dragoon invasion, the OSS parachuted spies far behind German positions along the Riviera. Some were women, mainly French nationals.

Men engaged in this dangerous game—a prolonged and agonizing death would be their lot if captured—did not have a monopoly on courage. Unlike the legendary Mata Hari of World War I fame, Allied female spies seldom, if ever, coaxed military secrets from high-ranking German officers in the intimacy of a boudoir. Rather women spies parachuting into Southern France had to depend, not on glamour and seductiveness, but, as with their male counterparts, on their courage, steel nerves, and resourcefulness.[6]

When the OSS recruited female espionage agents, the prospect was asked if she were willing to give her life for her country, if need be. Usually the answer was yes. Those who hesitated even for a moment were rejected by the recruiter.

In carrying out their espionage missions, female agents had one subtle advantage over the men: Because they were women, they could generally move more freely about the countryside without attracting as much suspicion as would males.

Among the OSS women agents was Virginia Hall, whose age was tactfully listed as "forty-ish." She had previously lost a leg in an automobile accident; but she badgered the OSS field directors in the Mediterranean to send her into Nazi-occupied France. Adding to Hall's peril, she was well known by the German Gestapo from previous sabotage missions.

On a dark night in March 1944, five months before D-Day for Dragoon, a lone airplane carrying Virginia Hall crossed the Riviera coast and droned deeper into Southern France. A green light showed in the cabin, a signal that her DZ (drop zone) was nearing. Hall gave a last-minute inspection of her chute, then stood in the open door.

Parachuting in itself is fraught with danger. A "streamer" (failure of the chute to open) could plunge her to her death in four seconds. If all went well, she would crash into the hard terrain with the impact of one jumping off the roof of a boxcar when a train was traveling forty miles per hour. Countless backs have been broken, skulls split open, legs and hips fractured.

Now the green light in the cabin turned red, and Virginia Hall leaped out into the dark unknown. Her artificial leg was tucked under one arm to prevent its damage on the heavy impact with the earth.

Despite her physical handicap, Hall was a human dynamo. She helped organize and train the French Underground and on occasion joined male colleagues to derail German troop trains, blow up bridges, and raid Nazi military facilities.

Between these actions, Hall frequented cafes and saloons where German soldiers spent their free time. With their tongues loosened by schnaps and calvados, the *Feldgrau* (field grey, the average German soldier) felt no restraint in discussing their units, their military duties, and defenses along the Riviera with the friendly, one-legged woman who seemed a mother figure to some of the teenagers.

Hall was in steady radio contact with OSS headquarters in London, a function that was particularly hazardous because of the almost constant DF-ing (electronic direction finding) by mobile vehicles operated by the German Gestapo and the Sicherheitsdienst (SD), the counterintelligence corps of Heinrich Himmler's dreaded SS (Schutzstaffel). For weeks Hall was on the go, often only one step ahead of the Gestapo.

After the Allies carved out a beachhead in Normandy, it had become clear to German intelligence, through electronic monitoring and information from left-behind spies in Italy and North Africa, that Eisenhower was massing forces for a second sledgehammer blow against Southern France. Actions against French "terrorists" and Allied spies behind the Riviera were greatly intensified as squads of Gestapo and SD descended upon the region known as the Côte d'Azur (blue coast).

One day, in a coordinated operation, the Gestapo and the SD struck—suddenly, massively, and with Teutonic thoroughness. Scores of Allied agents were trapped and arrested, all within a week's time. Despite the bestial treatment inflicted on those caught in the German net, Virginia Hall, and many other secret operatives, refused to abandon their posts and flee inland to the mountains as their associates begged them to do.[7]

Three weeks after the Dragoon landings, a dilapidated automobile of uncertain vintage was careening along a narrow, winding mountain road in the Ardeche region of Southern France. At the wheel was a former French Air Force pilot who, his three grim-faced passengers were convinced, thought he was still maneuvering the fighter plane in which he had fought the Luftwaffe in mid-1940 during the German invasion of France.

The Frenchman and two others were OSS agents. All were dressed in typical French wartime clothing—ragged, patched, wrinkled, ill-fitting. More sophisticated garb would have attracted the eyes of the Gestapo. They were on a secret mission to locate the 11th Panzer Division, which, U.S. commanders feared, might ambush Allied forces as they drove northward.

The fourth occupant was eighteen-year-old Stephen J. Weiss, a Brooklyn resident, who had landed with the 36th Infantry Division. He had become separated from his unit during the early confused fighting, found himself alone behind German lines, and hooked up with the three OSS agents.

Suddenly, while the car was chugging up a mountain, five members of the French Resistance, all armed with automatic weapons, broke out of some underbrush and leaped into the road. The French pilot screeched the vehicle to a halt. These underground warriors were looking for German army stragglers trying to flee northward in civilian clothing and Frenchmen suspected of having been Nazi collaborators, who would be instantly executed.

One Resistance man came to the car door and eyed the occupants suspiciously. The French pilot explained that they were OSS men and that baby-faced Stephen Weiss was from Brooklyn. Without another word, the underground leader motioned with his arm and a pretty, blonde woman emerged from the brush.

Wearing two German hand grenades in her belt and clutching a Schmeisser machine pistol, the woman began questioning Weiss in perfect English. Then she smiled broadly and informed her comrades that the car's occupants were authentic.

This was twenty-six-year-old Sarah Wilkins, an American who had been marooned in Southern France when the Germans occupied that region eighteen months earlier, in November 1942, and had been fighting with the French underground since that time. The Gestapo knew of her activities but had been unable to capture her. Why was she so certain that the men in the car were geniune? Because she, too, was from Brooklyn, and in quizzing Stephen Weiss, she discovered that they had lived in the same block.[8]

7 ❖ A Hair-Raising Escape

In mid-December 1944, Europe was gripped by the coldest winter in a quarter century. It appeared that Germany was near collapse, and generals at Allied headquarters in Paris were making bets on which day the war would end. Suddenly, three powerful German armies plunged into thinly-held American lines along a seventy-five-mile stretch of the Ardennes Forest of Belgium. Code-named Operation *Herbstnebel* (Autumn Mist), the mighty offensive caught the Americans by total surprise, and most of the GI units reeled back in disarray.

Tank-tipped German spearheads raced northwest for Liège, a city on the Meuse River only fifty miles away. With its huge stores of American fuel, Liège had to be captured if the swarms of German panzers were to roll on to Hitler's main goal, the port of Antwerp on the English Channel, another fifty miles away.

Also located in Liège were several Army field hospitals, where nurses, along with male medical personnel, had been plagued for several weeks by terrifying buzz bombs, Hitler's "secret weapon," about which he had boasted. Known to the Germans as the V-1 (V for Vengeance), the buzz bomb was a large, pilotless airplane filled with explosives, which would be sent aloft behind German lines and its engine would be set to cut off while over its target. Many of the lethal weapons had crashed to earth in Liège, killing and wounding thousands of civilians.

Often surgeries were taking place at the Army hospitals in Liège when the nurses and doctors heard the pulsating throb of an approaching buzz bomb. They held their breaths when the engine cut off, knowing that it was diving toward the ground. But the surgeries continued, and the nurses kept making their rounds in their wards to calm mutilated and frightened GIs.

Out in front in the German dash for Liège was a 4,000-man battle group of the 1st SS Panzer Division. The spearhead was led by twenty-nine-year-old *Obersturmbannfuehrer* (Lieutenant Colonel) Joachim Peiper. Handsome, well-bred, and resourceful, he brought to the Ardennes the experience of many months of heavy combat in Russia.

A Hitler favorite, Peiper received his orders for what his superiors called "the decisive role in the offensive." With its seventy-two tanks, Peiper's battle group was to rush along the narrow, winding roads of the Ardennes over a route specially chosen because it had fewer bridges than the other roads.

Having broken through the thin American defensive crust, Peiper plunged some forty miles deep into Belgium by December 17, the second day of the offensive, and his leading tanks had reached the village of Ondenval. Four miles to the north in the small town of Waimes, a team of the 47th Field Hospital was running a forward medical center in a school-house. Although busy with patients, one nurse, Lieutenant Mabel Jessop, felt twinges of anxiety. Along with other nurses, doctors, technicians, and orderlies, she was aware that something unusual was happening, for the rumble of artillery fire was almost constant—and not far away.

At midmorning, orders arrived to immediately transfer all patients to Malmedy, some seven miles to the rear. Another medical team of the 47th Field Hospital in nearby Butgenbach was told to follow. But the center at Waimes was to continue to function. Mabel Jessop tried to mask her concerns. Clearly, the Germans were coming. Were she and the others in her Waimes team considered expendable? At lunch, she had difficulty swallowing "the usual cold, tasteless mixture of canned hamburger and dehydrated potatoes."[1]

Jessop had hardly finished eating when word reached the medical team: Evacuate to the rear immediately! Patients and surgeons went first, driving generally southwest for two miles to the crossroads village of Baugnez, where the trucks and ambulances turned northward onto Highway N-23 and proceeded to Malmedy. Hard on the heels of the first convoy, a lone ambulance, crammed with Mabel Jessop and nine other nurses, headed out of town.

Nearing Baugnez, the ambulance was rocked by loud explosions. Peiper's tanks were shelling the road. The ambulance screeched to a halt, and the nurses scrambled out the rear doors and into a roadside ditch. Shells continued to explode on all sides. Typical of those finding themselves under fire for the first time, Lieutenant Jessop was convinced that the German gunners knew precisely where she was taking cover. She expected "to be blown up with the next blast."[2]

Some nearby male GIs, who also had jumped into the ditch, began crawling backward in the direction of Waimes, and the nurses followed. They were soon filthy with mud and slush. Glancing back over her shoulder, Jessop saw a frightening scene: Scores of German tanks were rumbling into Baugnez. She had no way of knowing that the insignificant hamlet would soon have its name in newspaper headlines across the Allied world.

A GI truck came along the road from the direction of Waimes. Frantically the nurses waved it down, told the driver what was taking place, climbed aboard, and headed back to the schoolhouse they had left barely an hour earlier. With other medical personnel, the nurses reopened the aid station, limited as were the facilities. They were still fearful of being captured, but they could not figure a way to get to safety with their incoming patients.

Meanwhile, back at Baugnez, Battery B of the U.S. 285th Field Artillery Observation Battalion, traveling in trucks, jeeps, and a command car, collided with Colonel Peiper's leading tanks. A shootout erupted, but the GIs were armed with only rifles and pistols, no match for the powerful guns of the panzers. Those Americans not killed were captured and herded into a field, 100 yards from the Baugnez road junction. There were approximately 130 GIs.

Passing along the road only sixty feet from the fearful prisoners were a few Mark IV medium tanks. Suddenly, a voice called out: "*Machen alle kaputt!*" ("Kill them all!"), and machine guns on the iron monsters began spitting bullets. There were screams, groans, and cries of agony. When the firing ceased, SS men trudged into the field and dispatched the wounded men with pistol shots to their heads. Almost miraculously, a few Americans survived. Later, they would crawl away to report the massacre."[3]

A few miles away in Waimes, Lieutenant Mabel Jessop, the other nurses, and technicians were unaware that their guardian angels had been watching over them. Had the medical group not been taken under tank fire as they neared Baugnez, its members no doubt would have been captured and shared the fate of the murdered GIs.

In midmorning of December 18, Mabel Jessop paused from her duties to go into a corridor for a cigarette. Peering out a window, she was startled to see two men approaching, weapons at the ready. One was wearing a German captain's uniform, and the other was in American uniform with sergeant's stripes and a 5th Armored Division shoulder patch.

Nearing the door, the "American" shouted: "Your hospital is under arrest! Everybody line up in the yard!" Only much later would Jessop learn that the Germans had infiltrated American lines with English-speaking soldiers clad in authentic GI uniforms.

The "American" ordered Jessop and the other medical personnel to climb into captured GI trucks and head back toward the German lines. Amid the confusion of loading, one of the 47th Field Hospital orderlies slipped away. On the outskirts of Waimes, he came upon three American halftracks, each mounting multiple .50-caliber machine guns. In moments the armored vehicles were clanking toward the schoolhouse. Seeing them coming, the German captain and the "American" sergeant took out in a run. Bullets chased them down the street, but they fled into some woods.

An hour later, a battalion of the U.S. 1st Infantry Division arrived in Waimes, and the nurses, patients, and medics were evacuated.

Throughout Belgium, in the Arctic cold and waist-deep snow, the most savage and largest pitched battle ever engaged in by American soldiers involved a half-million men on both sides. No quarter was asked, none was given. The brutal slaughter came to be known as the Battle of the Bulge. By GI guts and overwhelming airpower, Hitler's legions were halted short of Liège, but the killing continued throughout the Ardennes.

At an airfield at Liège on a day in late December, two male hospital orderlies were carrying U.S. Corporal John Phalen on a stretcher to an airplane ambulance parked on the runway. The craft would fly the seriously wounded GI to England for additional treatment. Phalen was happy to be leaving Liège. During the twenty-four hours he had been in an Army hospital there, buzz bombs had rained down on the city. One V-1 exploded near enough to rattle the small table next to his bed and collapse portions of the wall in his ward. He noted that the female nurses never left to take cover in the basement.

As the two orderlies at the airfield neared the flying ambulance to hoist Phalen's stretcher aboard, a siren abruptly split the dark winter sky just as three German ME-262 jet fighter planes swooped in and began a strafing run. The orderlies promptly dropped Phalen on his stretcher—in the center of the runway—and fled.

There Phalen remained, strapped to the stretcher, as the Luftwaffe jets strafed the runway. Streams of bullets from the spitting machine guns skipped off the concrete surface all around Phalen. Miraculously, he was not hit.

Standing in the door of the flying ambulance was a woman nurse, a first lieutenant, who saw the orderlies dash away. She shouted at them to come back and take Phalen out of the line of fire. In her extreme anger, she called the fleeing men names that Phalen thought were the exclusive property of frontline troops. The blue language was in vain; the orderlies continued running and disappeared from sight.

Now the Luftwaffe jets made a wide turn and were returning for a second strafing run. Again the machine guns spit out bullets that hissed past the prostrate Phalen. Then antiaircraft guns around the field opened fire. A direct hit was scored on one low-flying jet, which exploded, showering the runway—and Phalen—with sparks and debris.

When all the fireworks concluded, other orderlies came out and placed Phalen aboard the flying ambulance into the care of the still irate lady nurse. She would not permit the aircraft to take off until she obtained the names and serial numbers of the two men who had dumped Phalen like so much surplus meat in the center of the runway.

"I'll take care of those two yellow bastards when I get back from England," the otherwise ladylike nurse assured Phalen.

As the big aircraft revved its engines, taxied down the runway and took off, Phalen felt a surge of admiration for this flight nurse who could have gone to a safer spot than standing in the cargo door of an airplane under attack. He mused to himself, "Yellow bastards was one of the nicer things she called the two orderlies when shouting at them to come back and pick me up!"[4]

Meanwhile, the Battle of the Bulge had turned into a caldron of confusion. English-speaking German soldiers, dressed in authentic garb taken from POWs and riding in captured GI vehicles, were reported to be roaming the American rear areas, bent on murder, sabotage, and espionage. Some of these Teutonic infiltrators were said to be wearing civilian clothes, and all were armed with daggers and pistols. A GI didn't trust any American soldier unless he knew him.

Only a short distance from where the fighting was raging, a lone GI military policeman was manning a post along a road outside Aachen, an American-occupied German city on the Belgian border. It was a pitch-black night. His task was to halt all vehicles going into Aachen to determine if the occupants were genuine Americans.

When suspicious of a vehicle's occupants, the MP would ask questions to which only Americans would know the answer: Who did movie star Betty Grable marry? What baseball team are the Dodgers? Who is Popeye? What is the capital of Ohio?

Now, a lumbering command car, picking its way through the blackness, approached the Aachen checkpoint, and the MP asked for identity cards. Turning his cat's-eye flashlight on the first occupant's card, he called out in disbelief: "Frank McHugh! Not Frank McHugh from Toluca Lake, California?"

Stepping out of the vehicle, the figure replied, "Yep, that's me. Why do you ask?"

McHugh was a popular character actor in Hollywood movies and his face was known to countless numbers of Americans for his roles as a straight-faced comedian.

"I live only two doors from you on Navajo Street!" the excited MP replied.

"No kidding!" said McHugh, equally startled to come upon a neighbor at a lonely, black, and frigid outpost near a desolate German town.

"I sure am glad to see you," the MP kept repeating. "Real glad. I couldn't be happier about anything unless," he chuckled, "unless the young lady who lives next to you had shown up instead. You know—Mary Brian."

"Oh," said McHugh, putting on his familiar comic sternness, "so it's not me you're glad to see, it's Mary Brian?"

With the air of Aladdin about to rub his lamp, McHugh turned back to the command car where the dark silhouettes of several figures could be discerned. "Hey, Mary, there's a GI out here who wants to see you. I told him you'd been looking all over Europe for him!"

With that, Mary Brian, a beautiful Hollywood glamour girl of 4204 Navajo Street, got out of the car. Skeptical, the MP briefly flashed his dim light in the young woman's face, then let out a yip and tossed his helmet to the ground. He threw his arms around the shapely actress as though she were a mirage and might fade unless he held her tightly.

McHugh, Brian, and three others in the command car had been brought to Europe by the United Services Organization (USO), the civic group that provided entertainment to servicemen and -women at home and overseas. Now, Mary Brian quipped to the MP, only half in jest, that she didn't bargain for driving around in the dead of night near German lines when she had agreed to the European gig.

The unlikely Navajo Street impromptu reunion might have continued longer (if the MP had his way) had it not been for the voice of another woman calling from the vehicle to remind McHugh and Brian that they were to be at a First Army press camp in Aachen in fifteen minutes. The voice was that of June Clyde, also a Hollywood glamour queen.[5]

As the Battle of the Bulge raged, the Americans suffered such heavy casualties that Eisenhower ordered rear area units, including those in England, to be combed for able-bodied combat replacements. This procedure left a manpower void, so in January 1945 a battalion of black WACs was sent from the United States to England—the first black women to go overseas. In England they took over operation of a large military postal facility to replace men who had been handed rifles and shipped to the front.

Two years earlier the Army had been the first service to accept black women. They were assigned to segregated WAC units led by black female officers. Enlisted women lived in separate barracks, ate at separate mess tables, and took part only in segregated sports and social events. When on pass, they were expected to conform to the racial customs of civilians in a community.

Although black WACs had been sent abroad, Army policy still prevented black nurses from going overseas. One of them, Lieutenant Margaret Bailey, had joined the Army out of patriotism, even though she had her doubts. Opportunities for blacks in the Army, as elsewhere in the nation at that time, were strictly limited.

Because of the Army's segregation policy, Lieutenant Bailey, a native of Florence, Alabama, took her training at an all-black hospital in Montgomery, Alabama, and later treated only black soldiers at Army hospitals in the United States. When asked why she had joined the Army knowing what the conditions would be, Bailey always replied: "I think I can help the cause of the war. I am an American, too."[6]

Back in the United States, Congress, taking recognition of heavy American casualties in Europe and the Pacific, modified the law that had prohibited WAVES, SPARS, and Women Marines from serving abroad. Members of these services could now be assigned to U.S. territories overseas but not in foreign countries. Only volunteers were selected after being screened for performance, health, maturity, and emotional stability. Eventually, 1,000 Women Marines, 200 SPARS, and 4,000 WAVES were serving in Hawaii. Two hundred other SPARS were assigned to Alaska.

While the black WACs were getting acclimated in England, the Battle of the Bulge ended and Allied spearheads raced eastward across Germany to link up with the Soviet Army driving westward. Soon, Nazi Germany, which Hitler had pledged would last a thousand years, collapsed. In a red brick school building that served as Eisenhower's headquarters in Rheims, northeast of Paris, General Alfred Jodl, Hitler's closest military adviser, signed an unconditional surrender document. It was 2:41 A.M. on May 7, 1945.

After sixty-eight months of bloodshed and destruction a shaky peace hovered over Europe. But a cold war between the Western Allies and the Soviet Union was already simmering.

For tens of thousands of young American men—those seriously wounded, crippled, and mutilated—their war would go on. Theirs was a world gripped by pain, despondency, and hopelessness. A young medical technician, Corporal Peggy B. Moatz, recalled:

> My first day in the ward, I found a young fellow whose legs were paralyzed and he would not talk to anyone or go to therapy. I massaged his feet twice daily and exercised his legs, whether he liked it or not. Over his protests, I talked to him about his family and his girlfriend. By the time I was transferred, he was out of his shell and promised me he would go to therapy.
>
> About three months later, I saw a young soldier almost running on crutches toward me. "See what you've done!" he said, as he let his crutches go and fell into my arms. Yes, it was my one-time reluctant patient. He told me he was going to get married soon.

8 ❖ Two Spymistresses in Manila

While the global spotlight had been shining largely on the war against Adolf Hitler, halfway around the world in the Philippines, a war within a war had been raging for more than three years. It was an undercover war involving unsung heroines and heroes, mostly Americans and Filipinos. It was a vicious struggle against the Japanese occupiers, and the penalty for detection and arrest was excruciating torture, then an often prolonged and agonizing death.

When the Japanese invaded the Philippines in December 1941, a few days after the sneak attack on Pearl Harbor, thirty-three-year-old Margaret Utinsky was living in Manila with her husband, Army Captain John Utinsky. John and his unit were rushed to the nearby Bataan Peninsula, where the 50,000–man U.S. and Filipino force was beaten into submission a few months later.

When Margaret learned that her husband had been captured and died a few weeks later from starvation and abuse in a brutal POW camp in the Philippines, she decided to strike back at the Japanese. She would organize and direct an underground network on Luzon, the island on which Manila is located. But first, as an American, she would have to alter her identity.

Margaret Utinsky would vanish. In her place would be born a woman of another nationality and background. John Utinsky had been a native of West Virginia, but his ancestors had emigrated to the United States from the Baltics generations earlier. So Margaret became an instant "Lithuanian," Rosena Utinsky, who had been "born" in Kovno, one of the few Lithuanian cities whose name she could pronounce.

She adopted the code name Miss U and set about creating her underground network. That required two crucial things: money and members. After selling all of her personal belongings—rings, pearls, and bracelets—she accepted the services of a friendly Irish priest, Father John Lalor, to solicit funds from patriotic Filipinos.[1]

As time passed, Miss U, with the help of the priest (code name Morning Glory), recruited a sizable number of people. They were mostly foreigners sympathetic to the Americans—Spanish, Swiss, Irish, Chinese, and Italian, along with Filipinos. Also in her network was a group of Maryknoll sisters (code name Angels).

Middle-aged Elizabeth Kummer, recruited by Miss U, was among the handful of Americans permitted to roam Manila at will. Her husband, Max, was a German and had been Adolf Hitler's counsel in Manila until he had been booted out after bigwigs in Berlin learned that he had never joined the Nazi Party.

Elizabeth Kummer was acquainted with many Japanese officers. They trusted her because they thought her German husband Max was an ally. So from conversations with her Japanese "friends," she was able to warn Miss U when one of her covert operatives was under suspicion and in danger of being arrested by the *Kempei Tai*, the dreaded Japanese secret police.

Another key cog in Miss U's espionage apparatus was Mrs. Robert Yearsley, an older American who had lived in Manila for many years and was considered harmless by the Japanese authorities. She was blind. A cheerful, intelligent woman, she knew that it would be impossible to flee if her activities were discovered.

Mrs. Yearsley served as a sort of clearinghouse for messages going back and forth between members of Miss U's ring, American guerrilla leaders in the mountains, and GIs enduring the brutality of POW camps on Luzon. It could have been suicidal for Miss U to visit the Yearsley home, so Filipino boys, in the guise of doing household chores for the handicapped woman, would act as go-betweens, bringing and taking away messages.

Mrs. Yearsley also handled some of the underground's money. When one of her operatives needed funds, Miss U would telephone her "treasurer" and ask for a certain cake recipe—just in case the Kempei Tai had tapped their telephones. That was the signal for Mrs. Yearsley to send a young Filipino to her with a specified sum of money.

Much of the intelligence collected by Miss U and her network was carried by Filipino runners, men and women, to U.S. Army Corporal John Boone, who had escaped capture when Bataan fell, fled to the mountains northwest of Manila, and organized a guerrilla force. He had managed to acquire a radio transmitter, and he relayed the information from Miss U's network to General MacArthur's headquarters in New Guinea.

On September 28, 1944, Miss U was arrested by the Kempei Tai, apparently betrayed by a Filipino. Taken to Fort Santiago, an ancient prison, she was grilled mercilessly while being beaten and burned with the tip of lighted cigarettes. Each day, she expected to be beheaded, the fate of "terrorists."

After thirty-two days of imprisonment and torture, the Japanese, inexplicably, released Miss U—after she agreed to sign a statement that she had been well treated while in Fort Santiago. Within days, she was back directing her espionage ring. Then she received a tip from a Filipino working in a Japanese headquarters that the Kempei Tai was going to arrest her again.

That night, she slipped out of Manila and headed for the mountains, where she joined with the guerrilla leader, John Boone. Wearing a pistol on her hip, Miss U spent the remainder of the war fighting with Boone's irregulars.

In the meantime, another American woman, Dorothy Claire Phillips, established the Club Tsubaki, which became a favorite Manila night spot for Japanese officers and high civilian officials. The thirty-three-year-old woman let it be known that Club Tsubaki catered only to the Japanese. Consequently, she was hated by most Filipinos who considered her a traitor.

Club Tsubaki was packed every night with booze-swilling Japanese. Clad in shimmering evening gowns with plunging necklines, the proprietress circulated among the guests, laughing, teasing, flirting. On any given night, she would spend most of her time at the table of the highest ranking or most important Japanese.

Actually, Claire Phillips was a spy. Just before Pearl Harbor, she had come to Manila as a singer with an American touring musical company and married a sergeant in the Army. Like John Utinsky, he had been captured and died of starvation and brutality in a POW camp.

Knowing that she would have to conceal her identity as an American, Claire, with her olive skin, black hair, and flashing dark eyes, decided to become an "Italian," because that would make her an ally of the Japanese. She didn't speak a word of Italian but realized that neither did most of the Japanese. At considerable risk she bribed a young man, who worked as a translator in the Italian consulate in Manila, to obtain phony Italian identification papers for a Claire Fuentes. They showed that she had been born in Naples.

Phillips had a habit of concealing scraps of paper containing intelligence collected from members of her spy ring in her brassiere. Hence, one of them gave her the code name High Pockets, which stuck.

As the days and then the weeks stole past, Claire was anguished because she and her handful of Filipinos she had recruited were unable to obtain useful intelligence. Then she was struck by a wild idea: If she could not go to the Japanese, why not arrange for them to come to her. So she hit upon the idea of establishing Club Tsubaki.

Drawing on her show business background, Claire put on rousing floor shows every night, complete with a five-piece Filipino band and featuring five shapely, skimpily clad Filipino dancing girls. The Japanese patrons, most of whom had had plenty to drink by show time, watched goggle-eyed during the dancers' grotesque and sensuous movements. The guests became even more attentive when the show girls mingled with them after the show. All of the young Filipino women belonged to High Pockets' network, and each became skilled, as did the proprietress—in extracting useful military information from the Japanese officers.

The secrets collected from drunken Japanese would be of no value unless it reached General MacArthur's headquarters promptly. So High Pockets used the same communication technique as did Miss U: by carriers to Corporal John Boone in the mountains.[2]

On one occasion, High Pockets learned from an inebriated Japanese navy captain that his ship, loaded with ammunition, was going to sail southward for New Guinea at dawn. This revelation was rushed to Boone. Two weeks later, High Pockets received an exhilarating message: An American submarine had intercepted and sunk the Japanese ship.

Early on the morning of May 22, 1944, High Pockets was eating breakfast in her quarters at Club Tsubaki when four Japanese soldiers barged in and dragged her off to Fort Santiago. One of her female Filipino couriers had been caught with incriminating reports in her handbag. Under excruciating torture, the courier broke and named High Pockets and several key members of the espionage ring.

For many weeks, High Pockets was beaten with boards and fists. Her teeth were knocked out. Skimpily clad and bloody, she had to sleep on a cold stone floor in a cell. On occasion she had to watch female and male prisoners being beheaded in an effort to make her confess that she was operating an espionage network. Yet she never identified any of her operatives.

In February 1945, savage fighting was raging in Manila between MacArthur's forces and the Japanese defenders. Aware of the Americans' arrival, Margaret Utinsky, the underground leader code named Miss U, hitched a ride into Manila from the mountains, where she had been a guerrilla leader. On the outskirts of the burning city, a GI military policeman halted her vehicle. With a pistol on her hip, she dismounted.

"You can't go in there, lady," the MP said. "It's too dangerous."

"Too dangerous, hell," she snapped. "What do you think I've been doing for the past three years?"

Then Miss U realized the stupidity of her remark: This young GI knew nothing about her underground network or her guerrilla fighting in the mountains.

Rattled, the MP gave her permission to continue. As she walked away, he called out, "Lady, do you have permission to carry that pistol?"

Elsewhere in Manila, MacArthur's men rescued the other espionage network leader, Claire Phillips (High Pockets) from her dungeon before the Kempei Tai could execute her. She was but a pale shadow of her former vigorous self.[3]

Later, the United States government would award Margaret Utinsky and Claire Phillips the Medal of Freedom, the nation's highest civilian decoration. They were civilians in name only. Each had been involved in more hazardous actions than all but a few Americans who wore the uniform.[4]

Meanwhile, the awesome armed might of the United States was being mustered to invade Japan. Code-named Downfall, the operation would be larger than the Normandy invasion. MacArthur notified Washington that his forces could expect one million casualties before Japan was conquered. His supply officers requisitioned a few hundred thousand "body bags." Large numbers of additional military nurses and doctors were rushed to the Far East.

In early May 1945, fifteen B-29 Superfortresses of the 509th Composite Group began arriving on Tinian, a tiny island in the Marianas some 1,500 miles from and within bombing range of Japan. Commanding the unit was Colonel Paul W. Tibbets, Jr., who had seen action in Europe as a bomber pilot. He and only a handful of officers in the 509th knew that the unit had been selected to drop a powerful explosive device on a Japanese city.

Soon, the 509th became a target of curiosity among members of the other Superfortress squadrons on Tinian and nearby Saipan. They had been participating in mass raids on Japan for the past few months, but the newcomers never joined them. The curiosity heightened when Tokyo Rose, the silky-voiced propagandist on Radio Tokyo, "welcomed" the twenty-nine-year-old Colonel Tibbets and his men to Tinian.[5]

Besides Tibbets and a few others in the Marianas, none of the airmen knew of the role Jacqueline Cochran's WASP had played months earlier in testing the B-29, which had a wingspan forty feet wider, was twenty-five feet longer, and was twice as heavy as the B-17 Flying Fortresses and B-24 Liberators pilots had been used to flying.

Male pilots had been dubious about flying the Superfortress, not only because of its immense bulk but also because of a rash of engine fires that had broken out after the B-29s had been hastily manufactured. To help test these planes, Paul Tibbets, then a lieutenant colonel, recruited at Eglin Field, Florida, two WASP pilots, Dora Daugherty and Dorothea Johnson, both in their early twenties. Tibbets did not tell them of the engine fires.

After three days of intensive training, the two WASPs climbed into a Superfortress. On its nose, Tibbets had technicians paint the name *Lady Bird*. Then the B-29 lifted off for a long flight to a bomber base at Almagordo, New Mexico. Tibbets, it would be said, intended to demonstrate to doubting male pilots and crewmen that "even women" could handle the bulky bomber.[6]

For a week, Dorothea Johnson and Dora Daugherty flew male pilots and crewmen around the southwestern United States. The B-29 designers, meanwhile, apparently had worked out the kinks, and no fires broke out in the engines. Tibbets seemed to have accomplished his unspoken goal: inspiring confidence in the B-29 men who would soon be heading for the Pacific.

Soon the two WASPs were back at Eglin Field, knowing that they were among the only 100 or so humans who knew how to fly the Superfortress. The women also became convinced, in light of future developments, that they had played a role in bringing the war in the Pacific to a successful conclusion.

On August 5, 1945, a lone B-29 Superfortress, piloted by Colonel Tibbets, dropped what was later described to an awed world as an atomic bomb on the industrial city of Hiroshima, where 24,000 troops were stationed to oppose MacArthur's looming invasion. When the Japanese warlords, convinced that the bomb was the only one in the U.S. arsenal, ignored a surrender demand, a second nuclear explosion hit Nagasaki.

At noon on August 15, diminutive, myopic Emperor Hirohito, defying his general and admirals who planned to fight the invaders to the last man and the last bullet, took to Radio Tokyo to announce that the empire was capitulating.

Tumultuous victory celebrations were held throughout the Allied world. Now millions of American men and women began clamoring to go home, being discharged, and playing catch-up on civilian pursuits. On V-J Day, there were 57,000 Army and 11,000 Navy nurses, 100,000 WACs, 18,000 Women Marines, 86,000 WAVES, and 11,000 SPARS. Altogether, some 350,000 women had served their country in uniform during the war.

Every one of the tens of thousands of servicewomen had her own image of what she was going to do when she became a civilian. Some swore they would sleep for a month, getting up only for edible home-cooked meals. *House Beautiful* noted that WACs, WAVES, SPARS, and Women Marines were "starved for feminine frills and are expected to redecorate their bedrooms." The magazine solemnly added: "GI Jane will retool with ruffles."[7]

The discharged women proudly wore bronze lapel buttons showing a spread eagle and irreverently dubbed the "ruptured duck," a badge indicating honorable services in the armed forces. A flood of "Which Twin Has the Toni?" advertisements introduced them to the home permanents. Like the men, women veterans took out memberships in the "52–20 Club" named for the government unemployment pay of $20 for fifty-two weeks. Thousands enrolled in colleges under the GI Bill.

Newly minted veterans had thirty days to get out of uniform and into civilian clothes. Much to their dismay, the women discovered that the wardrobe they had left at home was now obsolete, replaced by a radical new fashion style called the New Look. A middle-aged Parisian, Christian Dior, had created outrageously luxuriant dresses. With their swirling skirts only inches from the floor (instead of at the knee), shoulders without padding and bosoms definitely with, they changed every fashion notion that America had observed for four years.

"The skimpy wartime look has fallen," said *Harper's Bazaar* in the autumn of 1945.[8]

In New York City, Anna Rosenberg, an envoy of President Harry Truman, complained about the New Look: "It shows everything you want to hide and hides everything you want to show."

Chic *Vogue* magazine had the answer for newly discharged service-women and females in general: "Throw out everything and buy a whole new wardrobe." For those who had been drawing pay of $50–$95 per month as WACs, WAVES, SPARS, and Women Marines, that advice from highly paid editors was far from practicable.

Then, three months after Dior had presented a New Look creation at $450 (equivalent to $4,500 in 1996) in Paris, American manufacturing ingenuity rushed to the rescue of newly discharged GI Janes, and other women as well. In New York, wholesale dress manufacturers began cranking out copies of Dior's creations. Using rayon instead of silk, four elegant flounces instead of eight—and high-speed electric cutters—the mass production geniuses produced a million New Look dresses within weeks. Now any woman veteran who wanted a creation of Paris, France, could get it in Paris, Arkansas—for $10.95.

One thing was certain: World War II had inalterably changed the viewpoints, goals, and aspirations of huge numbers of American women. An Army nurse put it this way, drawing on words from a popular diddy of the First World War: "How're you going to keep 'em down on the farm after they've seen Paree?"

In the months ahead, there was much controversy over the future role of women in the military. Colonel Westrey B. Boyce, who had succeeded Oveta Hobby as director in July 1945, believed that the WAC should be deactivated as rapidly as possible. Taking the same viewpoint were Captain Mildred McAfee of the WAVES, Captain Dorothy Stratton of the Coast Guard, and Colonel Ruth Streeter of the Women Marines.

Despite the opposition of all four leaders of the women's services, there were those in high places in Washington who felt that females could play a useful role in the armed forces after the war. Among the advocates was General Dwight Eisenhower, who had replaced the retired George Marshall as Army chief of staff. Confronted by thousands of skilled men being discharged, Eisenhower decided to keep the WAC on duty beyond its scheduled deactivation date in 1946.

Vice Admiral Louis Denfield, chief of Navy personnel, followed Eisenhower's lead and disclosed plans to retain women in the Naval Reserve for an unspecified length of time. Then the Marine Corps, a component of the Navy, followed suit. Only the Coast Guard discharged all of its SPARS by June 1946.

In postwar Washington, Congress was taking a new look at the administrative structure of the armed forces. Since 1798, the Department of War (which included the Army and the Air Corps) and the Navy had developed antagonistic rivalries that sometimes hampered operations. They competed vigorously for money from Congress. World War II had clearly disclosed the crucial need for unified direction. So after heavy bickering in Congress and sniping among the services, the National Security Act was passed and signed into law by President Harry Truman in 1947.

The law set up a unified military establishment, and the first secretary of defense was James V. Forrestal, a former president of Dillon, Read & Company, a Wall Street investment firm, who had been secretary of the Navy since 1944. Under Forrestal would be the secretaries of the Army, Navy, and Air Force (which had been granted separate status).

Soon after Congress unified the armed forces, the Cold War became heated. A Communist-inspired civil war broke out in Greece; a Communist coup took over Czechoslovakia; and the Russians blocked all rail, water, and highway traffic from the west, in violation of postwar agreements.

The blockade was an impudent effort by Premier Josef Stalin to drive the United States, Great Britain, and France out of West Berlin, which they had been occupying for three years. Refusing to be intimidated, the scrappy Truman launched Operation Vittles, a massive airlift, in June 1948. The airlift was a technical marvel. American and British planes brought in food, coal, petroleum, and other supplies to the more than two million people in West Berlin.

These crises caused Congress to study manpower needs in the event the United States would become involved in a war with the Soviet Union. There was heated debate in the House and Senate over the role of women in the peacetime military, and discussions intensified after the introduction of the Women's Armed Services Act, which would grant permanent status to females in the Army, Navy, Air Force, and Marine Corps.

The sticking point to passage was the fear by many in Congress that permanent status for women would eventually lead to their being thrust into combat. These concerns were allayed when wording was inserted that barred females from serving aboard ships and combat aircraft. Because defining ground combat was difficult, how women would be employed was left in the hands of the secretary of the Army—with the clear understanding that Congress was against females being directly involved on the battlefield.

Along with establishing permanent status for military women, the act also gave birth to the Women in the Air Force (WAF). Its first director would be Colonel Geraldine May, a soft-spoken, highly intelligent woman, who had been a social worker before graduating with the first WAAC Officer Candidate Class at Des Moines back in 1942.

Both the House and the Senate passed the Women's Armed Services Act, and on June 12, 1948, President Truman signed it into law.

One of the selling points to Congress had been that granting permanency to military women would lessen the need for reinstating the drafting of men to fill up the ranks. Twelve days after Truman put his signature on the bill, however, Congress renewed the selective service system in response to the widespread saber rattling by the Soviet Union and its satellite countries.

For nearly a year, Harry Truman and Josef Stalin stood eyeball-to-eyeball over the Berlin blockade crisis. In May 1949 the Soviet dictator blinked. He announced that out of humanitarian considerations the blockade was being lifted.

Although much of the Pentagon's and the White House's focus was upon the powder keg of Europe as the decade of the 1950s arrived, the most critical flash point was on the other side of the world.

9 ❖ Cracking a Man's World

A heavy rainstorm was lashing the Korean peninsula in the predawn darkness of June 25, 1950. Suddenly the black sky was illuminated by a yellowish glow from the muzzle blasts of hundreds of North Korean guns along the 38th Parallel, the dividing line between the Communist regime in the north and the democratic government of South Korea.[1]

Twenty minutes later the deluge of explosives lifted, and the quaint tone of bugles rang out—the signal for the massed North Korean forces to plunge across the parallel. South Korean troops were taken by total surprise. Without tanks, heavy artillery, antitank guns, or warplanes, they began to fall back. Within two hours, the retreat turned into a rout. It was every South Korean soldier for himself.

In New York, the United Nations Security Council called for an immediate end to hostilities and demanded that North Korea pull its forces back behind the 38th Parallel. Kim Il Sung, the Soviet-trained dictator of North Korea, ignored the order, and his army drove onward.

In Washington, President Harry Truman and the Joint Chiefs were gripped by a haunting specter: Was the North Korean invasion merely a strategic feint to draw U.S. attention away from Europe where the Soviet Union's powerful army might strike? If Kim Il Sung's aggression were left unchallenged, however, Josef Stalin could be emboldened to attack, Truman was convinced.

Consequently, two days after the North Korean army charged across the border, Truman, with the support of the United Nations Security Council, ordered General Douglas MacArthur in Tokyo to launch U.S. fighter planes and bombers in Japan against the Communist invaders. Then MacArthur was directed to rush troops from Japan to bolster the reeling and outgunned South Korean army.[2]

Less than twenty-four hours after Truman sent in U.S. ground forces, a C-54 transport plane landed at Kimpo airfield, a few miles southwest of Seoul, the capital of South Korea. Two planes were burning fiercely at the end of the runway. When the C-54 halted, out hopped four American newspaper correspondents, including Marguerite Higgins of the New York

Herald Tribune. She brought with her a reputation for using her good looks to get stories ahead of her male colleagues.

Higgins was the first American female to reach South Korea from outside the peninsula and, in the fluid battle situation, a candidate to be captured or killed. Although not an official military women, she looked, dressed, and acted like one and was subject to Army control.

One of her colleagues on the C-54, Frank Gibney of *Time* had tried to talk her out of making the trip. Korea was no place for a woman, he argued. However, she felt that she was equal in ability to any man and that she had proved herself as a correspondent in Europe in World War II.

In the parking area at Kimpo were thirty abandoned U.S. cars and trucks. Some still had keys in their ignitions. Each of the four correspondents "liberated" a vehicle. Maggie Higgins took a late-model Studebaker, a classy car at the time.

The tiny convoy headed for Seoul, toward the action. Masses of terrified refugees clogged the narrow road. Some cheered when they saw the Americans: No doubt the United States forces were on the way to repel the Communist aggressors. Higgins waved back, thinking "the poor fools don't know that we are only four correspondents armed with pencils."

That night, Higgins and her companions bedded down in Seoul. They had just fallen into an exhausted sleep when awakened by an American officer shouting, "They're in the city! Head southward for Suwon!"

Minutes later, amidst explosions, the three men correspondents were in one jeep, and Maggie Higgins and a driver were in a second jeep. In the blackness, the jeeps weaved through a torrent of refugees, but they eventually made it across the Han River that bisects Seoul east to west.

When the United States went to war in Korea, there were only 22,000 women altogether on active duty with the various services. One-third of them were nurses or medical technicians. Within four days of the first combat GIs arriving in South Korea, fifty-seven Army nurses landed at the port of Pusan on the tip of the peninsula. Twenty-four hours later the nurses were tending to battle casualties. In less than a month, there would be 100 military nurses in South Korea, a figure that would eventually reach 600.

Tens of thousands of GIs were pouring into South Korea, and they were organized into the U.S. Eighth Army under Lieutenant General Walton H. Walker, known to fellow generals as Johnnie because of his favorite Scotch. Short and stout, Walker was a tough, no-nonsense warrior who had been General George Patton's favorite corps commander in World War II. Walker disliked correspondents in general, and a few in particular. So it was no surprise that he would clash with the spunky Marguerite Higgins soon after he arrived in Korea.

Much to her consternation, Higgins was handed orders to get out of Korea, post haste. Johnnie Walker felt that a war zone was no place for a lady. She decided to beard the lion in his den and, on the morning of July 18, bustled into his headquarters at Taegu.

Higgins managed to get almost to Walker's office because no one recognized her dirty face and her khakis and helmet liner. Just another GI. Then a public-relations officer spotted her and said, "I'm taking you to the airstrip, right now, even if I have to call some military police."

"Am I under arrest?" Higgins asked.

"Don't pull that stuff. I know your publicity tricks."

A few hours later, Higgins landed in Tokyo and found that MacArthur, who usually didn't interfere with administrative decisions made by his commanders, had rescinded General Walker's order, and she went back to South Korea on the next plane.

The savage fighting in mountainous Korea increased in intensity after November 1950, when powerful Chinese Communist forces in Manchuria crossed the Yalu River into North Korea to aid Kim Il Sung's hard-pressed army, which had been driven back into its own territory. Casualties among the Communist armies were enormous, but American and South Korean troops also were hard hit.

Captain Anna McGoff Robie, an Army nurse, recalled: "In January 1951, while serving with the 14th Field Hospital, we were awakened by a loud thumping sound and looked out to see thousands of North Korean and Chinese prisoners marching by. In a month's time, we had 30,000 patients— all very dirty and full of lice. We nurses were sprayed twice weekly with DDT. It was three months before we had showers. We used helmets as water basins."

Since the war had erupted, the Pentagon refused to assign military women, other than nurses, to South Korea. Service chiefs kept to themselves the reason: the possibility that MacArthur's force might be wiped out or captured. No one in the Pentagon wanted to be responsible for the fate of American women if they fell into the hands of the Communist soldiers with their documented track record for brutality against POWs. As for the Army nurses, their skills were vital, so their destiny would have to be risked.

In Washington, meanwhile, President Truman had become disenchanted with his secretary of defense, Louis Johnson, who had been a partner in a prestigious West Virginia law firm. Truman wrote: "Louis began to show an inordinate egotistical desire to run the whole government . . . He tried to use the White House press men for blowing himself up and [tearing] everyone else down."[3]

At Truman's request, Johnson "resigned" in September 1950 and was succeeded by George Marshall, the World War II Army chief of staff, who had been in retirement on his Virginia farm. Although the White House had decided to double the size of the armed forces to three million men after the fireworks broke out in Korea, Marshall felt that there was an inadequate reservoir of military manpower to meet the demands in Korea and commitments in Europe, while maintaining a sufficient reserve in the United States.

Consequently, Marshall requested Truman to present the name of Anna Rosenberg to be assistant secretary of defense for manpower. Marshall had known her for several years, and her views carried great weight with him. He felt confident that she would help resolve the manpower pinch. Rosenberg's greatest obstacle to Senate confirmation was the fact that she was a woman trying to crack the man's world in the Pentagon.

Born in Hungary in 1901, Rosenberg had been brought to New York as a child. By the 1920s she was working in the field of industrial and labor relations. In the 1930s, during the early days of President Franklin Roosevelt's New Deal, she served on several regional boards involved with the National Recovery Administration (NRA), a government body that was anathema to conservative members of the Senate.

While World War II was in progress, Roosevelt in 1944 and Truman in 1945 sent Rosenberg to Europe to study the Army's manpower problem. There she earned the friendship of an influential figure, Supreme Commander Dwight Eisenhower. On the basis of her work in Europe, Eisenhower later helped get her two prestigious civilian awards, the Medal of Merit and the Medal of Freedom.

After Truman submitted Rosenberg's name to the Senate, Marshall was eager for a quick confirmation so that she could plunge into her duties. When she appeared before the Senate Armed Services Committee on November 29, 1950, however, hostile lawmakers confronted her with a flood of media reports that she had been a Communist and belonged to several Communist-front organizations. She vehemently denied the charges. Two witnesses testified that they had personal knowledge that Anna Rosenberg had been involved in Communist activities "up to her neck."

It seemed certain that Rosenberg's confirmation was doomed. Then the Senate Armed Services Committee began receiving numerous letters from those in high places, urging her confirmation. Among the writers were Dwight Eisenhower, CIA Director Walter "Beetle" Smith, Nelson Rockefeller, and Eleanor Roosevelt.[4]

After an exhaustive nationwide search, agents of the Federal Bureau of Investigation located another Anna Rosenberg, who was living in California. She allegedly admitted that she had been involved in a Communist-front organization in New York.

George Marshall felt that FBI Director J. Edgar Hoover had made a special effort to help and telephoned to thank him. Then he wrote a highly laudatory letter on Hoover to President Truman and sent a copy to the FBI chief.[5]

Typically, Hoover was careful not to get involved in any action that might be construed as "political" in nature. "Quite frankly, I regarded our efforts in this case as part of the routine operations of the FBI," Hoover replied.[6]

With the twin clouds of suspicion and confusion dispersed from above Anna Rosenberg's head, the Senate Armed Services Committee, on December 14, voted unanimously to confirm her, and the full Senate followed suit.

Assistant Secretary of Defense Rosenberg took over her duties with typical vivacity. Her tiny frame was always stylishly clad. Her high heels beat a rapid staccato on the floors of Pentagon corridors. Most defense officials cooperated with her. A few welcomed her with all the enthusiasm they might muster for the arrival of a mumps epidemic.

Coincidental with Anna Rosenberg being sworn into the high-level post, female groups, backed by a few supporters in Congress, were putting the heat on the Pentagon to expand roles for women in the armed forces. Most outspoken was Margaret Chase Smith, who had been sent to the Senate by Maine voters in 1949, becoming the first women to be elected to that legislative body without a previous appointive term.

In a sharply worded letter to George Marshall, Senator Smith demanded to know: "If you have any actual plans for utilizing far more women in the [Korean] war effort, what are they?"[7]

Presumably Smith's letter was shuttled along to Anna Rosenberg, and it energized her efforts to get more women into uniform. She had been warning Marshall of a looming manpower shortage as casualties continued to pile up in Korea and rear-area units there were being combed for able-bodied replacements. In turn, those sent to the front would have to be supplanted.

At Rosenberg's urging, Marshall established the Defense Advisory Committee on Women in the Services (DACOWITS), described as a blue-ribbon panel of fifty prominent women who were appointed to three-year terms. Among the members were the directors of the Army, Navy, and Marine Corps women's services in World War II, professionals from the business field, academicians, and those from politics, the arts, and the legal profession. Chairing the committee was Mrs. Oswald Lord, who had had previous experience as head of a similar Army panel.

DACOWITS' designated function was to heighten the recruitment of women by making the public aware of the military's needs, to allay any qualms parents might have about their daughters joining the armed forces, to enhance the image of military women, and to make recommendations to the secretary of defense on improving the quality of life for women in the armed forces.

On September 18, 1951—a year and three months after the Korean war erupted—DACOWITS held its first meeting. Colonel Mary Hallaren, director of the Women's Army Corps, spoke for the services in laying down the needs of the female branches. Hallaren had a distinguished record in World War II and had commanded the first battalion of Women's Army Auxiliary Corps (WAAC) to arrive in the European Theater of Operations.

Known affectionately as the "Little Colonel," the five-foot Hallaren was energetic, bright, and outspoken when the occasion demanded. Before

World War II she had been a teacher and lecturer for women's groups. Now, at the DACOWITS meeting, Hallaren pointed out that "every woman means one less [male] draftee. There's just one objective to keep in mind above all others, however; the services cannot sacrifice quality to fill a [recruiting] quota."[8]

A month later, Anna Rosenberg announced that the Department of Defense, in conjunction with DACOWITS, was going to launch a massive advertising and public-relations campaign to recruit an additional 72,000 women to the armed forces. This would boost the number of females from 40,000 to 112,000 by July 1952, a ten-month span.

On November 11, 1951, President Harry Truman personally kicked off the drive. Millions of dollars and much ballyhoo was expended on the project. An appeal was made to the patriotism of the targeted segment of the population with such slogans as "America's Finest Women Stand Beside Her Finest Men."

The recruitment drive fizzled. By the fall of 1952, a year after the promotion had been launched, only some 6,000 women had joined up, far short of the 72,000 target. For the Women's Army Corps, the campaign was a disaster. Targeting an expansion to 32,000 from 12,000 members, the WAC lost ground during the recruitment program, slipping to less than 10,000.

It became clear that the Pentagon chiefs and DACOWITS had totally misread the mood of the American people. More than 300,000 women had been recruited in World War II, so the service leaders apparently had assumed that attracting one-fourth of that number to join up now would be a simple task. Civilians had been fired up with patriotism in World War II, but now, only six years later, most had had their fill of armed conflict, international crises, and, in many cases, of the military as a whole. Nor did young women have any desire to become involved in a war in a godforsaken locale halfway around the world for some vague cause which they (and most civilians) were unable to comprehend. Moreover, despite the advertising blitz, the armed forces, with their low pay scales, poor living conditions, and marginal benefits, could not compete for quality women with the private sector in a vibrant economy.

Members of DACOWITS were deeply disappointed that more women had not rushed to the colors. Dr. Eli Ginzberg, who had conducted a series of studies on women in the work force for the National Manpower Council, warned DACOWITS and the directors of the female military branches, "This country has still not accepted women in the military as a normal part of its life . . . Recruiting women in the absence of compulsory service is difficult and costly. One cannot turn the country on its head in order to get a few more women into the uniformed services of the United States."[9]

After the Korean War ground to a halt in 1953 and a shaky truce was implemented, the Pentagon began a phase-down, reducing the number of

Americans in uniform from 3.7 million to 2.9 million. Women's total strength dropped from a peak of 48,700 in late 1952 to slightly more than 35,000 by June of 1955.

For most of the following decade, the women's services evolved into what a high-ranking WAC officer called a "beauty contest." An obsession with personal appearance took precedence over military aspects. Training programs were loaded with courses to improve a woman's bearing, not for military purposes, but to make her more ladylike. She was taught how to apply makeup properly and what shades of lipstick and nail polish would blend best with her uniform.

Hair styles were required to be fashionable but consistent with the uniform. Large bouffants and beehives were *verbotin*. Short, "mannish" styles were recommended, but not so short that they gave a "lesbian appearance." Recruits were taught nothing about firing weapons or living in the field, but they were told that wearing hats and gloves were hallmarks of the military lady. They underwent a mild degree of physical training, but only to keep their figures firm and trim, rather than as a technique to build endurance and strength.

Remarked one WAC: "I've known Campfire Girls more rugged than we are!"[10]

By the early 1960s it had become fashionable for an admiral or general to have an attractive woman junior officer as an aide—a status symbol. Pretty women were handpicked for front office jobs as secretaries and receptionists in the Pentagon and at high-command headquarters.

In January 1966, Jack Anderson, a widely-read syndicated columnist, charged that the United States military women were soft and totally unfit to go to war. Instead of being the "soldiers in skirts" of World War II, he claimed, the women had been converted into "typewriter soldiers," far more concerned with the art of facial makeup than the art of war. "More attention is being paid to the rise and fall of hemlines than to the ebb and flow of battle lines," Anderson declared.[11]

This "typewriter soldiers" status seemed to be accepted by the directors of the women's services. In May 1967, Colonel Barbara Bishop, head of the Women Marines, said that females should not try to make comparisons between the roles of men and women in the armed forces because so much greater demands are asked of males. "It behooves every woman to remember she is not going to be asked to put her life at stake [in battle] as the men are," Colonel Bishop explained.[12]

Meanwhile in the 1960s, the United States armed forces were steadily being sucked into a morass of jungles, swamps, and rice paddies in an ancient land halfway around the world. The place was named Vietnam: Few Americans had ever heard of it.

10 ❖ An Ordeal in Southeast Asia

There were no banners. No bugles. No presidential speeches proclaiming crusades "to make the world safe for democracy" or a day which "shall live in infamy." No United Nations resolutions or stirring Congressional declarations. But on March 8, 1965, America was at war when two Marine battalions landed at Danang, a port on the eastern coast of South Vietnam.

A month later, the leathernecks (as they were known) were reinforced by two more Marine battalions that established a base at Phy Bau, forty-five miles north of Danang. In June, the 173rd Airborne Brigade reached the country, and by October, some 150,000 U.S. troops were in Vietnam.

President Lyndon B. Johnson had ordered the heavy military buildup to prop up the collapsing government of South Vietnam after a series of United States presidents had pledged to defend the tiny nation against aggression by the Vietcong (Communist guerrillas) and the troops of North Vietnam, a Communist country backed by the Soviet Union.

The Pentagon called the conflict a limited conventional war, but the grunts (as Army foot soldiers called themselves) and the Marines soon were confronted by a situation that would pose both danger and moral dilemmas. Vietnam, in essence, was a guerrilla war with no front lines. Civilians and the Vietcong looked and dressed alike. One couldn't tell the good guys from the bad guys (or gals). One could only tell for certain when someone suddenly fired at you—and often it would be too late. So the American fighting men rapidly became suspicious of all Vietnamese.

Even as the war steadily escalated, leaders in the Pentagon were reluctant to ship servicewomen to Vietnam. However, by late 1965, some 650 American women, including civilians working for the armed forces, were "in country." Three hundred of these women were Army, Navy, and Air Force nurses, all of whom were officers and had to be twenty-one years of age. Their tour of duty was normally one year. Most Navy nurses lived and worked on two hospital ships, the *Repose* and the *Sanctuary*, which sailed off the coast of South Vietnam. Air Force nurses cared for the badly wounded on evacuation sites to the Philippines, Japan, Okinawa, or the United States. Army nurses worked in facilities classified as field, surgical, or evacuation hospitals, and MASH (Mobile Army Surgical Hospital).

On the average, the military nurses, most of whom belonged to the Army, were a few years older and more highly educated than the grunts and leathernecks who fought the Communist soldiers. The women were largely middle-class, Caucasian, often deeply religious, and idealistic. All were volunteers. Many had been inspired to serve by a line from President John F. Kennedy's 1961 inaugural address: "Ask not what your country can do for you, ask what you can do for your country."

One of the first Army medical units to reach Vietnam, in the fall of 1965, was the 85th Evacuation Hospital, commanded by Colonel Harold Murphree. Soon after their arrival, General William Westmoreland paid the unit a visit. He was dismayed to discover that the local Army commander had located the unit in tents several miles from Qui Nhon, a coastal city far north of the U.S. command hub of Saigon. That region was so heavily infested with Vietcong that the grunts (GI combat soldiers) called it "Indian country."

Concerned about the safety of the fifty female nurses, the doctors, and the patients, Westmoreland ordered the 85th Evac to switch locations with an engineer battalion in Qui Nhon. The switch became a logistics nightmare. Just as it began, the hospital was flooded with wounded men from the U.S. 1st Cavalry Division, which was involved in a savage fight in the Ia Drang Valley. While parts of the hospital moved inside Qui Nhon, parts had to remain behind to care for the influx of patients.

Colonel Murphree was a skilled neurosurgeon, and most of his time was spent in the operating room. While the piecemeal move of the unit was being made and occasional shells were plopping around the vicinity, Murphree conducted a delicate brain surgery on an officer who was a nephew of one of the Senate's most influential members, Richard Russell of Georgia.

Because of the surgery demands, Murphree in effect turned over day-to-day administration of the 85th Evac to his head nurse, Lieutenant Colonel Mary Donovan. A small, gray-haired veteran of many years in the Army, with a pixieish sense of humor and a twinkle in her eye, she was on her final tour of duty before retirement. Although the torrid heat severely impacted her health, Donovan refused to accept that fact and continued with her long work hours.

Although experienced in the medical field, few, if any, of the nurses in Vietnam were prepared for their introduction to war. They were brought an endless horror show of mutilated bodies of American boys, most not long out of high school. Each nurse would have one particular case she would never forget, one wounded man who symbolized for her the frightfulness and futility of war: the shrieking, hysterical grunt who arrived at the emergency room carrying the headless body of his closest pal; a GI so incinerated that he looked like a burned marshmallow; a teenage soldier without arms or legs, blinded, but still with his nose and mouth and screaming for the nurses to kill him.

"The injuries are unprecedented," said Major General Byron L. Steger, the Army's chief surgeon in the Pacific, "because this war is fought largely with small arms, booby traps, punji sticks, and claymore mines. Nearly all inflict multiple wounds of the most vicious, mutilating kind."[1]

Lieutenant Lynn Laabs, a twenty-two-year-old Army nurse, echoed that sentiment. "Sometimes it's quite depressing," she said. "The wounded soldiers are all too young and they suffer such horrible pain. But I want to be here. I want to work hard for them. And at the end of the day, I know I've done something, or at least I've tried."[2]

Nearly exhausted, the nurses would reach the end of their standard twelve-hour shifts only to have helicopters bring in more wounded GIs. Working in the emergency room of an evacuation hospital, Lieutenant Cissy Shellenbarger described her ordeal as "a gruesome, painful, and exhausting experience that would stay with most of us [nurses] for the rest of our lives." She added: "Nothing really prepared you for it. I never got to a point where the horribly mutilated bodies of young men didn't bother me."[3]

Major Marsha Jordan, an Air Force flight nurse with the 56th Air Evacuation Squadron, remembered:

> I never had a patient die on the plane, but came close several times. We were able to take appropriate means to keep them alive. The ones that were not so severely injured would be supporting their buddies. They'd joke and kid around and I'd get involved in that. One Marine had had one arm and both legs amputated, and he was blind. Only twenty years old. He was going back to a girlfriend and his family, and he couldn't wait to get home. His spirits were high, and his buddies were helping him. I think he was just feeling lucky that he was alive.

In early 1966 General Westmoreland gained the wrath of a large group of female Army nurses. Intelligence had informed him that a regiment of North Vietnamese regulars were heading into the Highlands near Ban Me Thout and bitter fighting seemed certain. So he ordered the 3d MASH (Mobile Army Surgical Hospital) to move to the vicinity of the expected clash. As was always the case, he wanted a hospital located only a few minutes from the battlefield to increase the chances of wounded GIs surviving. Because of the clear-cut danger that loomed ahead, Westmoreland directed that the women nurses remain behind. Through their commanding officer, they complained strongly, but the general stuck to his decision.

Back in the United States, some military women, other than nurses, were volunteering to be sent to Southeast Asia, but most requests were turned down. A WAC lieutenant complained to syndicated columnist Jack Anderson: "There's a war going on in Vietnam, but you have to be a civilian to be assigned there. Women are fighting in the jungles with the Vietcong, but we aren't allowed to dirty our dainty hands!"[4]

There were WAC officers convinced that a "gentlemen's agreement" between the Joint Chief in the Pentagon and the commanders in Southeast Asia was keeping military women out of the war zone. If there had been such a conspiracy, it was broken when General Westmoreland, a veteran of three wars and commander of U.S. forces in Vietnam, urgently requested the Pentagon to send a few WAC officers and ten enlisted women to expedite the mountain of paperwork that was threatening to engulf his headquarters in Saigon.

The first contingent of WACs arrived at Tan Son Nhut airport outside Saigon in the fall of 1966. They climbed on Army buses and realized that there was peril involved in their assignment. Wire mesh covered the windows of the bus. The mesh, they were told, was to prevent Vietcong from pitching grenades into the vehicle on the road to Saigon. A short time earlier, the Vietcong had set off a bomb in the main terminal of the airport.

In the weeks ahead, other commanders in Vietnam asked the Pentagon for WACs, mainly to handle secretarial chores, and the number of female soldiers in country would be about 160 within a few months. Some of the WACs were quartered in the Majestic Hotel, a five-story structure in downtown Saigon.

One evening not long after the first group of WACs arrived in Saigon, a tremendous explosion rocked the Majestic. Men and women soldiers in the building threw themselves to the floor or stood up and asked excitedly: "What in the hell was *that!*"

Replied a native restaurant waiter: "Vietcong."

As the hotel's occupants cautiously peeked outside, sirens began to wail as fire engines and ambulances rushed to the scene. Directly across the street from the Majestic and moored to the bank of the Saigon River was a popular floating restaurant. Men and women, bloody clothes ripped to shreds, were stumbling across the gangplank that connected the restaurant to the shore. Nine Americans were among the thirty-one persons killed in the bomb explosion.

A day later, a WAC who had been in the Majestic wrote home that this had been "my first taste of combat." It was a misconception held by activists wanting women to be converted into warriors. This WAC had been *adjacent* to danger; she had not been *involved in combat*.

In Vietnam, WACs were allowed to serve in only two locations judged to be relatively immune to enemy attack despite occasional Vietcong bomb explosions—Saigon and a large new Army base at Long Binh, fifteen miles northeast of the city. A Pentagon colonel explained: "The American people aren't prepared to have their young women shipped home in body bags."

In Washington, Colonel Barbara Bishop, director of the Women Marines, was urging the Pentagon brass to have her officers and enlisted personnel assigned to Vietnam. Since the Marine Corps founding in 1775, the leathernecks had prided themselves on being the "first to fight." Now the men were battling in Vietnam, but only sixty-five women Marines were allowed to serve overseas, mainly in Japan and Okinawa.

Colonel Bishop's tenacity paid off. On March 18, 1967, Sergeant Barbara J. Dulinsky climbed off a transport aircraft at Bien Hoa Air Force Base, thirty miles from Saigon, and became the first woman Marine to arrive in Vietnam. Others followed. Most were assigned to secretarial and administrative tasks at the headquarters of the Military Assistance Command, Vietnam (MACV).[5]

Eventually, thirty-six women Marines would serve in Vietnam and adjoining Thailand. In theory, all had volunteered, because none objected when they received orders to go to Southeast Asia. Sergeant Bridget V. Connally was asked why she had volunteered. She replied: "Who volunteered? I received my orders in the mail!"[6]

In June 1967, the Navy announced that Lieutenant Elizabeth G. Wylie had been assigned to the staff of the Commander, Naval Forces, in Saigon, thereby raising the hopes of other WAVES that they might be sent to Vietnam. But soon their wishes were dashed. Because of the small comparative ratio between the numbers of WAVES and the size of the Navy contingent on shore in Vietnam, the Navy brass decided not to send significant numbers of women to Southeast Asia. Only two or three WAVE officers were in Vietnam at any one time; no enlisted women were permitted to go.

All the while, Colonel Jeanne M. Holm, director of Women in the Air Force (WAF), was growing more frustrated and angry. Photos and stories of military and civilian women serving in Vietnam were being plastered across the pages of newspapers and magazines, and WAF officers and enlisted women were being excluded from Southeast Asia. Holm, who had enlisted with the WAC as a truck driver in World War II, was convinced that there was a "male conspiracy" between the Air Force Personnel Center in the Pentagon and the top commanders in Southeast Asia to keep WAFs out of the theater.[7]

Holm and other WAF officers felt that the principal obstacle to deploying females in Southeast Asia was General William W. "Spike" Momyer, commander of the Seventh Air Force. Momyer, a nonemotional, logical, and pragmatic officer, was a "suspect" because of his hard-nosed demeanor and reputation for not wanting women in his command. Holm decided to beard the lion in his den, so she flew to Vietnam.

Much to her astonishment, Holm found General Momyer to be cordial, pleasant, and open-minded. He agreed that WAF officers could be assigned immediately to some locations in Vietnam and that enlisted women might be stationed there in six months when the critical housing shortage would be eased.[8]

Holm's tenacious politicking with the brass paid off. A few weeks later, in June 1967, Lieutenant Colonel June H. Hilton, along with five enlisted WAFs, stepped down from a commercial airplane at Tan Son Nhut air base for duty at MACV in Saigon. In the months ahead, some 600 WAFs would be assigned to Seventh Air Force headquarters and to bomber bases.

Holm was disappointed, however. She was convinced that many times that number of WAFs could have carried out useful tasks in Southeast Asia had the Air Force "gotten its act together."[9]

An especially frustrating bone of contention among military women who served in Vietnam was what they perceived to be, with considerable merit, the double standards subtlely applied to their morals. Lieutenant Lynda Van Devanter, an Army nurse, remembered:

> If the guys wanted to screw ninety-seven prostitutes in a day, it was to be expected. "Boys will be boys." Every PX (post exchange) stocked plenty of GI-issue condoms. However, if we wanted to have a relationship, or to occasionally be with a man we care deeply about, we were not conducting ourselves as "ladies" should.[10]

While the conflict was steadily escalating in Vietnam, advocates of increased roles for women in the armed forces received a monumental boost back home. Prodded by DACOWITS, leaders in the Pentagon asked Congress to repeal the "glass ceiling" that limited the number of women in the services to only 2 percent of the total numerical strength, thereby reducing promotions for female officers and preventing the elevation of women to general and flag (admiral). The highest rank a female could hold was colonel or its Navy equivalent, captain. DACOWITS felt that if the women's services had their own general or admiral, these components would gain more professional respect from Congress and the public, attract larger numbers of quality recruits, and junior officers could aspire to higher career goals.

In October 1966, Representative Otis G. Pike introduced a bill that would demolish the glass ceiling for women, and hearings began in the House. The media labeled the legislation the "lady generals and admirals promotion bill."

That description was faulty, Assistant Secretary of Defense for Manpower Thomas D. Morris testified. The Pentagon's objective, he explained, was to "eliminate any distinction between men and women officers in regard to ceilings on grades [and] limitations of numbers who can occupy certain grades."

Morris added: "There is no plan to establish any quotas between men and women in each of the officer grades. We seek parity only in respect to recognizing merit and performance."[11]

Other Pentagon officials told the committee that the military's endorsement of the bill was not intended to alter the traditional role of women in the services, nor was its support to be construed as paving the way for women to be assigned to combat units, as some critics in Congress and the media had charged.

"We believe that the nation still adheres to the concept that combat, combat support, and the direction of our operating forces are responsibilities of male officers," Thomas Morris explained. "The utilization of women for duties which they can perform as well or better than men, is fully compatible with this reality."[12]

The House hearings were brief and devoid of controversy. The committee reported the bill out favorably, meaning it was recommended for passage by the full House. But the Eighty-ninth Congress adjourned before a vote could be taken.

Sensing victory, DACOWITS abandoned its function of making legislative recommendations to the secretary of defense and instead set its sights directly on members of the Ninetieth Congress, which convened late in January 1967. Women military officers met regularly with DACOWITS Chairwoman Agnes O'Brien Smith to hatch grand strategy. Although regulations prohibited direct political involvement by active-duty personnel, the Pentagon turned a blind eye and a deaf ear toward this flagrant violation.

DACOWITS members descended upon Capitol Hill and button-holed senators and representatives, urging passage of the bill. Some women had close ties with the Johnson White House, where they lobbied intensely. Other DACOWITS members had connections with influential newspaper publishers, editors, and columnists, most of whom plugged for legislation to remove the glass ceiling. Military women—active-duty, retired, and reservists—flooded Congress with letters and telephone calls.

Consequently, after Otis Pike's bill was reintroduced, it sailed through the House in April and was sent to the Senate. Some in the media conjectured it might run into opposition. But it soon became evident it would pass easily after Senator J. Strom Thurmond, a World War II combat veteran, staunch conservative, and an influential member of the Armed Services Committee, became the measure's strongest booster.[13]

In May, the bill cleared the Senate and was delivered to the White House. It was a foregone conclusion that President Johnson would sign the legislation.

On November 8, 1967, six months after the bill reached the White House, a media extravaganza was arranged for Johnson's signing the measure into law. With a large phalanx of television and still cameras, along with scores of reporters, arrayed before him, Johnson, blinking in the glare of klieg lights, took his seat at a table. On his right were the uniformed directors of the women's services, members of DACOWITS, and female civilian leaders. On his left were Vice President Hubert H. Humphrey, members of the Cabinet, congressional bigwigs, and the four beribboned chiefs of the Army, Navy, Air Force, and Marine Corps.

It had been said of Lyndon Johnson that he never went to the toilet without first considering the political ramifications of the ritual. Now he apparently sensed a chance to gain great political mileage with many women. Taking pen in hand, the president cast a quick glance at the Joint Chiefs and remarked: "There is no reason why we should not one day have a female chief of staff—or even a female commander-in-chief."[14]

Johnson's prognostication drew beams of approval from the women officers and members of DACOWITS. There was no visible outpouring of enthusiasm from the Joint Chiefs.

DACOWITS had scored a landmark triumph.

By early 1967, two years after the Marines had first gone ashore at Danang, some 465,000 American troops were bogged down in Vietnam. GI casualties were piling up at an alarming rate. Back home, draft boards were calling up larger numbers of young men. Congress was being bombarded by letters from parents demanding that other means be found for supplying soldiers for the Vietnam meat-grinder. On university campuses, massive rallies protesting U.S. involvement in Southeast Asia were proliferating. Students were publicly burning draft cards in defiance of the law.

Lyndon Johnson now was confronted by a knotty problem: The draft was due to expire in June 1967, so what could he do to make his forthcoming request for an extension more palatable to the House and Senate? Speaking to a joint session of Congress, the president stressed that he planned to greatly augment the number of women in the military, the first increase in size since the Korean War fourteen years earlier. He hoped to have thousands more females in uniform by 1970. The inference was plain: These women would reduce the number of men being inducted.

As in America's past, Washington's interest in expanding roles for women in the armed forces had been energized by a crisis of war.

11 ❖ Lady Generals and Lady Birds

Until mid-1967, polls had shown that 80 percent of the American people backed the Johnson administration's effort to halt Communist aggression in Southeast Asia. But slowly, almost imperceptibly, much of the homefront began looking at the war as hopeless, with no victory in sight. Concerned by the loss of popular support at home, Lyndon Johnson launched a sophisticated public-relations campaign to convince Americans that great progress had been made toward achieving U.S. goals.

Called the Success Offensive, the promotion was spearheaded by Walt W. Rostow, a Johnson confidant, an old hand on the Washington political scene, and chief of the White House Psychological Strategy Committee. Media were peppered with press releases, speech transcripts, statistics, graphs, charts, and official statements—all with the theme, "We are winning the struggle in Vietnam."

Even Vice President Hubert Humphrey, a dedicated dove, spoke out. Appearing on NBC's *Today* show, Humphrey observed enthusiastically, "Territory is being gained. We are making steady progress."

Then the superstars of the Success Offensive took center stage: General William Westmoreland and Ambassador to South Vietnam Ellsworth Bunker were brought back to Washington. While the television cameras whirred, Westmoreland emphasized in a speech at the National Press Club: "We have reached an important point where the end begins to come into view."

The Success Offensive seemed to be attaining its objective. The We-Are-Winning bandwagon was rolling. Then, suddenly, in January 1968, a wheel came off the bandwagon: The Communists launched their surprise Tet offensive.

Although Tet had been a battlefield disaster for the Communists, it reaped huge rewards for them. In the United States, much of the major media portrayed Tet as an American debacle. So large numbers of the populace, not just the "peaceniks" and campus agitators, soured on the war. Even if U.S. victory were possible, was it worth the cost of blood of young Americans?

Demonstrations across the land took on increased intensity and were joined by many who had earlier supported U.S. goals in Southeast Asia. So President Johnson, much to the surprise of even his own staff, took to television and announced that he would not seek reelection that fall. Later, the Democrats nominated his vice president, Hubert Humphrey, in his place to oppose the Republican standard bearer, Richard M. Nixon, who had been vice president under Dwight Eisenhower.

The presidential contest was heated. Its central theme was the war in Vietnam. Locked in a nip-and-tuck race, Nixon, aware that student and other deferments had caused many Americans to seriously question the fairness of the selective service system, sensed a chance to score heavily with the electorate. On October 17, 1968, only three weeks before voters would go to the polls, Nixon declared that, if elected, he would "take a new look at the draft." He doubted the wisdom of "permanent conscription in a free society," and said that after U.S. military involvement in Vietnam concluded, he would end the draft and find other means to fill military manpower needs in peacetime.[1]

Nixon won the November election, gaining 301 electoral votes to 191 for Humphrey. As he had promised, soon after being sworn into office in late January 1969, he established the President's Commission on an All-Volunteer Force (AVF) and appointed Thomas S. Gates, a former secretary of defense, to be its chairman.

The fifteen-member panel included two former Allied supreme commanders, the director of the National Association for the Advancement of Colored People, three university professors, two business executives, economists Alan Greenspan and Milton Friedman, and the vice president of the National Council of Negro Women.

After ten months of work, in January 1970, the Gates commission sent its report to President Nixon. It proposed an All-Volunteer Force of 2.5 million men. No mention was made of women. The key to the success of the AVF seemed simple: Compete with the private sector for manpower by offering volunteers attractive benefits.[2]

Three months later, on April 23, President Nixon, in an address to a joint session of Congress, announced that as a result of the Gates commission report, he would establish an All-Volunteer Force as soon as conditions in Southeast Asia permitted.

Within days, the Pentagon created the Central All-Volunteer Task Force to develop a strategy for making the concept workable. Headed by George A. Daoust, Jr., deputy assistant secretary of defense for manpower and utilization, the panel proposed attracting volunteers through higher pay, more-comfortable living conditions, bonuses for special skills, allowances for dependents, and other inducements.

Unlike the Gates commission, Daoust's group realized that the armed forces, in the wake of the Vietnam war, might find it difficult, or impossible, to attract sufficient male volunteers to fill the ranks. So a contingency option was developed for meeting personnel shortages by greatly increasing the number of women and employing far more civilians.

Daoust's plan called for the armed forces to double the number of females within five years, so there would be some 180,000 women on active duty by 1977. Because most of its components were trained for combat, the Marine Corps would be required to increase the strength of its small women's contingent by only 40 percent.

In Saigon on March 23, 1968, William Westmoreland received a telephone call from General Earle G. "Bus" Wheeler, the Army chief of staff in the Pentagon. President Johnson, Wheeler said, had just announced at a news conference that Westmoreland would be the new chief of staff effective on July 3, 1968, when Wheeler retired.[3]

Soon after Westmoreland took over his new job in the Pentagon, he recommended to the secretary of the army that the heads of the Army Nurse Corps and the Women's Army Corps be established as general officers. The service secretary concurred. So on June 11, 1970, American history was being made in Washington, thirty-six months after Congress had removed the long-standing ceiling on promoting women to the highest military plateau.

Colonel Anna Mae Hays, who had served for twenty-eight years and in three wars in the Army Nurse Corps, stood before General Westmoreland. After pinning the star of brigadier general rank on each of her shoulders, Westmoreland, to the surprise of Hays, bussed her on the mouth. It was the first known instance of one American general kissing another general.

Minutes later, Westmoreland pinned brigadier general's stars on Colonel Elizabeth Hoisington, also a veteran of three wars. "Now," Westmoreland said, "In accordance with a new Army custom . . ."

A few days after the star-pinning session, Katherine "Kitsy" Westmoreland, the general's wife, found herself at the hair stylist beside the newly-minted general, Anna Mae Hays, a widow. Kitsy was known throughout Army circles for her clever wit. "I wish you would get married again," she said. "Why?" the puzzled Hays asked. "Because," Kitsy replied, "I want some *man* to learn what it's like to be married to a general."[4]

A short time later, Air Force Colonel Jeanne Holm, a twenty-nine-year veteran, was promoted to one-star general. And in July 1972, Captain Alene B. Duerk, chief of the Navy Nurse Corps, became the sea-going service's first rear admiral. Five more years would pass before the Marine Corps elevated Colonel Margaret Brewer to brigadier general.

American women had finally reached near the top of the military profession and blazed a path for many others to follow. But none had excelled merely by her own efforts. Rather she had achieved general or admiral rank on a solid foundation of perseverance, dedication, and courage displayed by tens of thousands of women going back to World War I days, more than a half-century earlier.

In 1972, the National Organization for Women and other feminist groups, along with their supporters, were pressuring Congress to pass an equal rights amendment (ERA) to the Constitution. Critics held that the Constitution already guaranteed equal rights for women. Advocates argued that despite these guarantees, women did not always receive equal treatment.

Conservative members of Congress wanted the ERA to include provisions that prohibited women from being drafted into the armed forces or assigned to combat duty. NOW and other feminist groups feared that these exemptions would weaken the amendment. Only by women having the "opportunity to fight" would they gain true equality, ERA backers asserted.

Senate debate over draft and combat exemptions in the ERA was heated. Senator Birch Bayh, a liberal Democrat, asked: "If a woman wants to volunteer [for combat], should she be treated any differently than a man?" Indeed she should be, snorted Senator Sam Ervin, a folksy, conservative Democrat. "Women have no place on the battlefield," he declared.[5]

In March 1972, with the draft and combat exemptions for women struck from the bill, the ERA passed the House and Senate handily. Senator Ervin found, much to his amazement, that fifteen senators, who earlier had been in favor of the exemptions, jumped ship and voted for passage.

ERA supporters now had seven years for thirty-eight state legislatures to ratify the amendment for it to become the law of the land. These boosters had no way of knowing that the removal of the draft and combat exemptions would one day doom the ERA.

Elsewhere in Washington in 1972, Admiral Elmo R. Zumwalt, the chief of naval operations and a Nixon appointee, began firing a litany of Z-Grams to the fleet, drastically altering traditional regulations and customs. In what many old salts regarded as a dangerous threat to Navy cohesion and discipline, Zumwalt greatly relaxed wearing apparel and personal grooming. Navy men now could wear their hair to shoulder length, grow beards, sport long sideburns, and dress casually while on duty.

Zumwalt believed in practicing what he preached. He, too, grew long sideburns, and admirals and other officers began referring to him as "Sideburns" Zumwalt. They were puzzled over why the conservative commander in chief, Richard Nixon, himself a World War II Navy officer, had not intervened. They speculated Nixon had "put on blinders" because he would be up for reelection in the fall of 1972, and his political handlers had advised him not to inject himself in Navy administrative decisions that were controversial and might cost him votes.

Zumwalt also lowered the bars that kept Navy women from serving in the engineers, the chaplain corps, and in certain shore units. And in 1973, six women became the first naval aviators to earn their wings. The media called them the Lady Birds.

One of those to graduate in the first coed class, Lieutenant Barbara A. Rainey, was assigned to fly transports hauling passengers and cargo. She soon became disillusioned, convinced that most of the men who had graduated with her were logging more hours in the air and getting choicer assignments.

"The patterns of male pilots to advance as naval officers are established," Lieutenant Rainey said. "But with us [women], it hasn't really worked out yet." Five years after gaining her wings, she would decide to resign from the Navy.[6]

Apparently the Army did not want to lag behind the Navy. So after a special committee studied the feasibility of opening its aviation program to women, the Army chief of staff approved the idea. Lieutenant Sally Murphy became the first woman helicopter pilot in the Army when she graduated with the first coed flight training class.

Unlike the Navy, Air Force, and Marines, the Army was not restricted by law from using women in combat, a fact that bothered many members of Congress. So the advent of women pilots, especially those flying helicopters, ignited questions on their future roles. Although the Army's helicopter pilots were assigned to support units, the ebb and flow of battlefield situations could result in women flying choppers being involved in the middle of heavy fighting, many in Washington feared.

Even the Army's female helicopter pilots were divided about the eventual possibility of being in combat. Lieutenant Nancy K. Carter, whose stepfather had been a World War II fighter-plane ace, was the first woman to rappel from a Chinook helicopter, an act not devoid of danger. "I'm very proud of my country," Carter said. "And if Congress says, 'You're going into combat,' fine, let's go, right along with my male counterparts."[7]

With regard to men wanting to protect her, she added: "I don't need it. I can hold my own."[8]

Lieutenant Deborah Rideout, also an Army chopper pilot, disagreed. She felt having females in a combat environment could result in a certain amount of problems in a unit because "deep down inside, I think every woman—even the toughest Tug Boat Annie—wants to be protected."[9]

12 ❖ A Painful Homecoming

While the war was raging halfway around the globe in Vietnam, Pentagon leaders were hit by a series of lawsuits filed by military women who claimed that service policies discriminated against them on the basis of sex, and, therefore, they were being deprived of equal protection under the law. Instigating and orchestrating most of the legal actions was the American Civil Liberties Union (ACLU).

In the spring of 1970, twenty-three-year-old Navy Seaman Anna Flores was assigned to an air station in Florida when she became pregnant. Her boyfriend was a Navy enlisted man. The couple planned to marry, but in the meantime Flores miscarried. Then her commander took action to have her discharged, even though she was no longer pregnant, pointing out that to do otherwise would "imply that unwed pregnancy is condoned" by the Navy.[1]

Taken in tow by a battery of ACLU lawyers, Flores, on August 24, asked the U.S. District Court in Pensacola, Florida, to prevent the Navy from discharging her for having been pregnant. Such an action would be discrimination, the ACLU charged, because the sailor who impregnated her was allowed to remain in the service.

Pentagon bigwigs were confronted by a rash of media stories sympathetic to Flores. Even though she had standing behind her the considerable wealth and clout of the ACLU, she was portrayed as a lone young woman fighting the male chauvinists in the Pentagon and their discriminatory policies. Consequently, Navy leaders capitulated and allowed Seaman Flores to remain on duty.

In the wake of media questions about her future chances for promotion and whether subtle retaliations would be set in motion, the Pentagon felt compelled to issue a public statement: "This incident should not affect her future eligibility for duty assignments, promotions, or reenlistment for which she is qualified."[2]

At about the same time, Captain Susan R. Struck, a twenty-six-year-old Air Force nurse stationed at a base in Washington state, became pregnant. In accordance with regulations, the service began proceedings to discharge her. But she refused to go and appealed to a lower court, which ruled against her. Struck appealed to a higher court. Although Air Force brass planned to see the litigation through to its conclusion, service lawyers believed that Struck would eventually win. So she stayed on active duty.

Along with the litigation over Pentagon pregnancy policies, there were legal actions filed to eliminate the regulation in which married military women were required to prove that husbands and/or offspring were dependent upon them for in excess of one-half of their support to be entitled to extra dependency allowances, family housing, and other benefits available to men in the services. In December 1970, Ruth Bader Ginsburg of the American Civil Liberties Union filed a class-action suit in federal court on behalf of Air Force Lieutenant Sharron Frontiero, arguing that the denial of equal benefits for women was sex discrimination.[3]

The lieutenant had married Joseph Frontiero, a civilian, in 1969, a year after she had joined the Air Force as a physical therapist. While she was working at the hospital at Maxwell Air Force Base near Montgomery, Alabama, her husband was enrolled in college and receiving $205 per month under the GI Bill, which provided financial benefits for veterans.

In her argument before a three-judge federal court, attorney Ginsburg contended that there was family housing available at the air base, but that Lieutenant Frontiero was forced to live elsewhere at her own expense because she was a woman and her husband was not recognized as a dependent by the Air Force. Moreover, Ginsburg declared, the lieutenant was being discriminated against because her husband was not eligible for medical services available to the wives of male officers.

After the federal judiciary ruled against Frontiero, Ginsburg appealed to the Supreme Court, which ruled that it was unconstitutional for the armed forces to require a female member to prove that a husband or minor children were dependent upon her for over one-half of their support unless an identical action was required of men. The armed forces were given the option of providing the same entitlements to women or revising regulations to require men to prove the dependency of their wives and offspring.

"It is the most far-reaching and important ruling on sex discrimination to come out of the Supreme Court yet," said Ruth Ginsburg. "It will spell the beginning of reforms in hundreds of statutes which do not give equal benefits to men and women."[4]

In complying with the Supreme Court decision, the Pentagon issued a directive stating that military women were to be treated equally with men in matters regarding dependency, and that the word "wife" would be replaced by "spouse."

Perhaps the thorniest issue involving the status of women in the military was the Pentagon's long-standing policy of discharging women, whatever their rank or length of service, if they gave birth to or adopted a child or had personal custody of a child. Armed forces leaders felt that child-care demands greater responsibility on the part of the mother than it does of the father.

On rare occasions, waivers were granted to mothers, especially when they were nearing retirement after twenty years of service. But the applicant had to provide substantial evidence that her child could be adequately cared for while she was on duty and that motherhood would not diminish her military capabilities.

In February 1970, Major Lorraine R. Johnson, who had served in the Army Nurse Corps for thirteen years, challenged that traditional policy. She filed suit in a California federal court to keep from losing her commission in the reserves.

In 1967 she had married a local teacher and a year later gave birth to a son. Except for a short time, she worked as a civilian nurse and participated in monthly drills at the Army Reserve Training Center in Santa Ana. However, she was advised by the Army that it had rejected her request for a waiver and that proceedings were being initiated to separate her from the service.

In her lawsuit against the Army, Major Johnson stated that she had eight years to go before retirement, that she was "ready, willing, and able" to carry out her duties, and that she stood to lose $16,000 in future reserve pay if she were discharged. Moreover, she pointed out that the Army would be deprived of a qualified nurse who had devoted thousands of hours instructing medical technicians in intensive care.[5]

The court issued a temporary injunction to prevent the Army from discharging the major and to give Army lawyers time to prepare their case. Rather than to try the matter in court in the white-hot glare of media scrutiny, however, the Army dropped its plan to discharge Major Johnson.

Perhaps as a face-saving device, the Army continued to require waivers from military mothers for the next few years, but nearly all requests were routinely approved.[6]

Meanwhile, momentous events were taking place in Paris, France, where Henry A. Kissinger, President Nixon's chief foreign policy adviser, and Le Duc Tho, North Vietnam's emissary, had been holding peace negotiations for several months, since August 1972. Kissinger had convinced South Vietnam's President Nguyen Van Thieu to accept a cease-fire agreement, which was weighted heavily on the side of the Communists, after Nixon had made a solemn pledge that the United States would hurl its full military power against the Communists should North Vietnam try to use the truce to gain a military advantage.[7]

Bolstered by Nixon's assurances, Thieu reluctantly signed a cease-fire agreement on January 27, 1973, along with the United States, North Vietnam, and the Vietcong. The pact provided for the withdrawal of all U.S. and allied forces from Vietnam and the return of all prisoners—both within sixty days. It permitted the North Korean Communists to leave 150,000 troops in South Vietnam.

As soon as most American troops and airpower departed, the Communists, having achieved their goals, broke off the Paris peace talks and launched a heavy offensive against the out-manned and outgunned South Vietnam army. Masses of Soviet tanks rumbled off the docks in Haiphong, the major seaport in the North. At this crucial point, the U.S. Congress began to disengage America totally from Southeast Asia. Funds to South Vietnam were cut off. A loyal ally was doomed.

For America's veterans, homecoming was often a painful experience. Those who had answered their country's call and served with dedication and honor were the targets of verbal and sometimes physical abuse. Among them were many of the 5,600 nurses who had performed their duty in Southeast Asia during the long war. As was the case with the men, some of the nurses—long afflicted with loneliness, extreme tension, interminable hours, and incessant exposure to death and mutilated bodies—had become victims of a tragedy of the war: alcohol and drug addiction.

When the transport plane carrying Lieutenant Charlotte Miller, along with other nurses and male soldiers, neared the Seattle airport, they broke out with shouts of joy. Scrambling from the aircraft after it rolled to a halt, the returnees kneeled and kissed the ground. Minutes later, their euphoria vanished when snarling citizens hurled obscenities and fruit at them as they walked through the terminal building.

"It really made me wonder why did I go," Miller declared. "If I had the choice right then I would have gone right back to Vietnam. At least I'd have been among friends."[8]

Like all the women, Miller had gone into the military voluntarily. "I requested Vietnam," she said. "It seemed like the right thing to do. If our men were over there, the least I could do was go over there and help. I'm proud of my accomplishments. If I had to do it over, I'd go again."[9]

Lieutenant Cissy Shellenbarger, who had served as an Army nurse at a field hospital in Nha Trang, had a similar experience. When she arrived by airplane on the West Coast wearing her customary combat fatigues and boots, military officials advised her to change into civilian clothes before leaving the base. "I didn't dare wear my Army uniform or tell people I was an Army nurse or that I had served in Vietnam," she remembered.[10]

Like the men veterans, untold numbers of military nurses came home from Vietnam suffering from anxiety, insomnia, nightmares, flashbacks, and even thoughts of suicide. When one female Army nurse was stricken by severe depression, she sought the counseling of a civilian psychiatrist, who, it developed, did not have the foggiest grasp of the impact of her traumatic experiences. When she began telling him about the horrors she had seen almost constantly in Vietnam, he replied casually, "Never mind all that. Tell me about your childhood."[11]

Many returning nurses who had been involved nonstop with life and death matters had no patience for the trivial pursuits in civilian hospitals. One nurse who had been under rocket attack at Danang remembered:

> For twelve months in Vietnam, I made decisions about whether someone was going to live or die. Then I got into this [civilian] hospital and was told I could not hang a pint of blood unless a doctor was standing there. I kept getting called in by the head nurse, who said, "You've really got an attitude problem. You're no longer in Vietnam." Like, who do you think you are?[12]

Most military women coming home to a country that didn't want to acknowledge them were wracked by bitterness. "I'd been waiting and waiting to get back to The World," recalled an Army nurse. "But when I got back all I could think was 'I want to live in Nam.' Life in the United States seemed superficial and indulgent."

Lieutenant Lily Adams, who had been stationed in the 12th Evacuation Hospital at Cu Chi, was so upset by the angry glares she received from many civilians after returning home that she burned the uniform she had worn so proudly—and then threw her medals in the trash.

Unlike most American nurses, Army Lieutenant Mary Stout, who had been stationed at the 2nd Surgical Hospital at An Khe, had someone with whom she could communicate—her husband, Carl. He had fought in Vietnam as an infantry lieutenant while she was serving there. Mary Stout recalled:

> I was more frightened in this country than I ever had been in Vietnam, even when we had mortar attacks and rockets going off. Carl and I were leaving for Wichita, Kansas, to enter college when we heard about a ROTC instructor in Syracuse whose house had been fire-bombed. I was frightened of the antiwar protesters. It wasn't safe here. This was supposed to be my home, and if you'd gone and served your country, it wasn't safe here.[13]

Vietnam veterans were still streaming back home when, on July 1, 1973, Secretary of Defense Melvin Laird announced the creation of the All-Volunteer Force. Almost from the beginning, the AVF concept ran into major problems. America had demoralized and unjustly vilified her own armed forces, and patriotism had hit an all-time low. Angry at their leaders in Washington, angry at the American people who had demonstrated in the streets on behalf of the brutal Communist enemy and praised Ho Chi Minh, thousands of career officers and noncommissioned officers—the backbone of any army—quit in disgust. Few men drafted during the Vietnam war reenlisted; they, too, wanted out. Overall experience and competence were at low ebb. Should the mighty Soviet armed forces strike in Europe or elsewhere, the United States could have been in big trouble.

Meanwhile, Pentagon manpower managers, whose careers were at stake should the All-Volunteer Army concept fall flat on its face, projected a need to recruit 365,000 men each year to maintain a total force whose targeted strength had been reduced to 2.1 million. However, by mid-1973, it became clear that despite financial and other inducements, young men in droves were steering clear of recruiting offices.[14]

As a result of the looming crisis, Congress established a Special Committee on the Utilization of Manpower in the Military. Three months later the panel released a report that castigated Pentagon leaders:

> We are concerned that the Department of Defense and each of the military services are guilty of "tokenism" in the recruitment and utilization of women. We are convinced that in the atmosphere of a zero draft environment, women could and should play a more important role.
>
> We strongly urge the Secretary of Defense and the service secretaries to develop a program which will permit women to take their rightful place in serving our armed forces.[15]

At the same time, the Senate Armed Services Committee recommended raising the total strength of women in the armed forces as high as 20 percent. The committee stated that its suggestion was based on the assumption that women joining up in far larger numbers would continue to be better educated and more intelligent (based on entrance examination scores) than male recruits.

Aware that the Pentagon was gripped by potential manpower shortages, the Defense Advisory Committee on Women in the Service, which had largely been silent during the long, bloody struggle in Southeast Asia, now was inspired to become far more aggressive in demanding revolutionary changes in the armed forces to integrate much larger numbers of women—and in much higher plateaus of responsibility.

Leading the DACOWITS charge on the Pentagon was Sarah McClendon, a feisty Washington-based correspondent for a newspaper chain. "This group has got to become an *action* group!" she told members.[16]

McClendon, outspoken and intelligent, had been a WAC officer during part of World War II, so she felt that she had at least a grasp of the military. She complained, with considerable merit, that the main handicap of DACOWITS was that its members knew virtually nothing about the armed forces. So she began agitating for the Pentagon to replace members whose three-year terms were expiring with retired women officers who were attuned to McClendon's goal of a U.S. military with a large percentage of female soldiers, sailors, airmen, and Marines.

An intramural hassle erupted in DACOWITS when the combative McClendon demanded that the group's sessions, which had been held behind closed doors for nearly thirty years, be opened to the public and the media. The few remaining traditionalists vigorously opposed the suggestion, fearing that the meetings would turn into forums for the broad dissemination of the feminist agenda for the armed forces through the media.

At this point, the feminist Center for Women Policy Studies leaped to McClendon's support, filing a suit in federal court to enforce her demand. After the judicial body ruled in favor of the Center, DACOWITS' meetings, as predicted by some members, became three-ring circuses in which an array of feminists testified before the committee. They lambasted the Pentagon for not being sufficiently active in stamping out what they perceived to be "overt discrimination" against military women. Broadcast and print media focused almost entirely upon the complaints of the feminists who testified.

At the same time, leaders of the National Organization for Women (NOW) were making their own pitch for the public spotlight. They declared that females in the armed forces were being discriminated against because they were not allowed to receive decorations for valor on the battlefield, awards that were important to promotions.

NOW didn't comprehend that soldiers do not *receive* combat decorations, rather they *earn* them, often by feats requiring strength and enormous endurance.

Meanwhile, a new feminist superstar burst onto the Washington scene. Patricia Schroeder, who had been elected to the House of Representatives from Colorado in 1972 at the age of thirty-two, quickly lobbied her way onto the Armed Services Committee. She promptly branded it the "Ol' Boys Club" and designated herself as the panel's gadfly.

It was a powerful perch for newcomer Schroeder: The Armed Services Committee controlled about 40 percent of the federal budget, and when one of its members spoke, the brass in the Pentagon listened. Schroeder—bright, energetic, and articulate—let it be known that she was the champion for women seeking a greater role and "equal opportunities" in the armed forces, including combat assignments.

Schroeder had graduated with honors from the University of Minnesota and obtained a degree from Harvard Law School. Then she headed West to be general counsel for Planned Parenthood of Colorado. Almost from the day she was seated on the Armed Forces Committee, she announced that she was eager to "expose" what she perceived to be the "waste and folly of defense spending" and divert the excess dollars to increased welfare programs. And she denounced what she claimed to be a "cooperative relationship" between the committee and the Pentagon. The proposed 1974 billion-dollar military authorization bill was "frivolous," a "boondoggle," and a "colossal waste of money," Schroeder declared.

Her relentless attacks against maintaining a strong defense hardly endeared her to the Pentagon leaders. "Doesn't that crazy Harvard broad know the Soviet Union has built the mightiest peacetime war machine that history has known?" growled one general privately.

The congresswoman's verbal clashes with crusty F. Edward Hébert, a conservative Democrat and chairman of the Armed Services Committee, were often the topic of lively Washington cocktail-party conversations. Hébert had been city editor of the *New Orleans Times-Picayune* when elected to the House thirty years earlier, and he had ascended to head the committee through seniority in 1970.

Schroeder was unimpressed by Hébert's long stint in the House. In one barb hurled at him, she declared, "The wisdom allegedly acquired by mere political longevity can easily be overestimated." Hébert fumed.

Stinging from Schroeder's relentless sniping, Hébert refused to approve her appointment to the United States delegation going to a Strategic Arms Limitation Talks (SALT) conference in Geneva, Switzerland. "I wouldn't send you to represent this committee at a dog fight!" the chairman told her.[17]

Schroeder had cultivated like-minded feminist friends in the State Department, which neatly skirted Hébert by waiving the rule requiring the chairman's approval of all nominations to traveling delegations on military matters. Schroeder made the trip to Geneva.

Schroeder's critics, of which there was no shortage, claimed she was an insatiable "publicity hound." One story that made the rounds in Washington told about the time she and a bevy of members of Congress flew to a foreign country on a junket. When the aircraft was about to land, a freshman in the House asked an old-timer: "What's the protocol for getting off the plane?" Reflecting for a few moments, the other replied: "The protocol is not to get trampled by Pat Schroeder when she makes her dash for the television cameras."

13 ❖ Clash over the Service Academies

For two years by the spring of 1974, F. Edward Hébert, chairman of the House Armed Services Committee, had been deflecting repeated efforts by colleagues to pass legislation permitting women to enter the service academies at West Point, Annapolis, and Colorado Springs. Since their founding, these institutions had been male only. In May, Hébert, under heavy pressure from within and outside of Congress, called hearings on an academy integration bill introduced by Republican Representative Pierre "Pete" du Pont, scion of a wealthy Delaware family.

The hearings were bound to generate fireworks. Both sides on the controversial issue had already mobilized and were prepared for the clash. Curiously, the directors of the four women's services were equally divided on the thorny issue.

"We don't need to send women to the [Military] Academy to get sufficient qualified women into our officers' program," said Brigadier General Mildred Bailey of the Army. "The armed forces should be able to spend more time on national defense and less time on items like this that we don't need."[1]

Captain Robin Quigley of the Navy agreed. "The [Naval] Academy exists for one viable reason, to train seagoing naval officers and to give the Marine Corps a hard core of career regular officers," Quigley explained. "There is no room, no need, for a woman to be trained in this mode, since by law and by sociological practicalities, we would not have women in these seagoing or warfare specialties."[2]

Brigadier General Jeanne Holm of the Air Force held a different point of view. "I would like to see women in the [Air Force] Academy in the not too distant future," she declared.[3]

There was no doubt where the Pentagon brass stood on the issue: They were strongly opposed to it. Two weeks before the hearings were to convene, Under Secretary of Defense William P. Clements sent a letter to Hébert detailing the department's objections to du Pont's bill. Clements argued that the service academies trained men for combat and sea duty, from which women were barred by law, and that most, but not all, graduates served on ships or were assigned to fighting units. Moreover, he added, the armed forces were getting all the female officers they needed through the Reserve Officers Training Corps (ROTC), which had been opened to women two years earlier.

At about the same time, the secretaries of the Navy, Army, and Air Force released statements, also signed by the uniformed chiefs, opposing the admission of women to the academies for the same reasons put forth by Under Secretary Clements.

During the hearings by Hébert's committee, the Air Force Academy superintendent, Lieutenant General Albert P. Clark, focused on the daily life of the cadets: "The environment is designed around the stark realities of combat. The cadet's day is filled with constant pressure. His life is filled with competition, combative and contact sports, rugged field training, use of weapons, strict discipline, flying and parachuting, and demands to perform to the limit of his endurance mentally, physically, and emotionally.

"It is the type of training that brings victory to battle," Clark continued. "It is my considered judgment that the introduction of female cadets will inevitably erode this vital atmosphere."

Army Secretary Howard H. Callaway took a similar line. "Admitting women to West Point will irrevocably change the academy. The Spartan atmosphere, which is so vital to producing [combat] leaders, would surely be diluted," he stressed. Navy Secretary J. William Middendorf II agreed: "Unless the American people reverse their [negative] position on women in combat roles, it would not be in the national interest to utilize the expensive education and facilities of the Naval Academy to develop women officers."[4]

Also testifying for keeping the academies all-male was Jacqueline Cochran, head of the WASP in World War II and, along with the late Amelia Earhart, America's best-known woman pilot. She said that her experience in that global conflict convinced her that "women have no business in combat" and that academies train leaders to fight. Putting women in combat was "ridiculous," she emphasized.[5]

Now the other side rolled out its heavy artillery. Representative Patricia Schroeder said that the bureaucracies in government are customarily slow to react to changing circumstances, such as accepting women at the academies. Women should go to the academies for the same reason men go there: to pursue military careers. And she castigated Pentagon leaders for "fighting the issue" when the equal rights amendment (ERA) would soon become law and admitting women to the academies would be inevitable.[6]

Representative Fortney H. "Pete" Stark, who had earlier nominated a female to the Naval Academy, testified that women should be taken into the academies "with haste and without question." In a curious twist of logic, he said that "we need them there . . . far more than they need the academies."

Another member of the House, Donald Fraser, expressed anger over the fact that he had nominated a woman pilot to the Air Force Academy and that her application had been returned without being considered. "How cynical that while we make an effort to recruit [far more] women into the forces . . . we are denying them access to the best educational institutions in their professions," Fraser said.

Most of those testifying in favor of integrating women into the academies argued simply that it was a matter of equality, of giving females the same military opportunities as men. However, Representative Charles B. Rangel declared, "If fighting must be done, women should join men in doing it."[7]

The often raucous hearings continued on and off until adjournment in August, nearly four months after they had begun. It appeared that women in the academies was a dead issue, especially after President Richard Nixon had endorsed the Pentagon's position. Behind the scenes, Chairman Hébert had privately assured the military brass that the Armed Services Committee would not report an academies coed bill out to the full House.

Almost simultaneously with the adjournment of the House hearings, an electrifying event rocked Washington, and much of the nation, an episode that soon would have a dramatic impact on the women in the service academies issue. In the wake of a tangled web of high-level high jinks that the media had dubbed with the umbrella catchword "Watergate," President Richard Nixon resigned on August 9, 1974.

Replacing the disgraced chief executive was Gerald R. Ford, who had been a highly popular congressman with members of both parties on Capitol Hill. Earlier, Ford had been designated to replace Vice President Spiro Agnew, who had resigned after disclosures that he had taken kickbacks.[8]

Ford told a national television audience that "our long nightmare is over" and that he had pardoned Richard Nixon so that the nation, torn apart by Vietnam and by Watergate, could begin healing. "May our former president, who brought peace to millions, find it himself," the new occupant of the Oval Office said.

A soft-spoken man blessed with great tact, Ford had been a center on the Michigan University football team in the mid-1930s. During World War II, he was a Navy officer in the Pacific. Advocates of women being integrated into the service academies would find that the new president was far more receptive to their cause than Nixon had been.

On August 12, only three days after Nixon resigned, the commandant of the Coast Guard dropped a bombshell on the Pentagon. He announced that in July of the following year the Coast Guard Academy would begin integrating women, concluding a 100-year males-only tradition. Although military in nature, the Coast Guard in peacetime is a component of the Treasury Department and not directly connected to the Pentagon.

Located on the banks of the Thames River in New London, Connecticut, the Coast Guard Academy had an average enrollment of about 600 cadets. Unlike West Point, Colorado Springs, and Annapolis, the Coast Guard Academy does not receive its students by congressional appointment. Rather, qualified applicants compete for entrance in annual nationwide examinations.

The announcement by the Coast Guard put pressure on wavering members of Congress to integrate women into the other academies. The heat grew more intense when the U.S. Merchant Marine Academy, located on the south shore of Long Island Sound at Kings Point, New York, disclosed that it, too, was accepting qualified female applicants. The Maritime Administration, an agency of the Department of Commerce, operates the academy, which was founded in 1942.

In January 1975, F. Edward Hébert, one of Washington's most powerful foes of integrating the service academies, became the central figure in a heated, behind-the-scenes dispute in the House Democratic Caucus. Many liberals in his own party had been unhappy with Hébert's pro-Pentagon stance, and they succeeded in bouncing him from the Armed Services Committee chairmanship. He was replaced by Melvin Price of Illinois.

Soon, an all-out push began in Congress to get women into the academies. In April, Representative Samuel Stratton, an ardent booster of sex integration, flaunted legislative protocol by skirting both the Armed Services Committee and its military personnel subcommittee and tagging an amendment onto a Department of Defense appropriations bill then being considered by the full House. Stratton's amendment would require the three service academies to open their doors to women.

Members of the House and Senate in favor of integration were skewered on the horns of a dilemma. The function of the academies was to train officers for combat; but few in Congress were eager to repeal their own laws barring women from combat units. Anxieties of those in Congress were alleviated, however, when a scheme evolved to split the academies' responsibilities between preparing officers for combat and also for careers in the armed forces. That convoluting resolution of the knotty issue permitted senators and representatives to sidestep whether women should be thrust into combat.

On May 26, 1975, the House voted overwhelmingly, 303 to 96, to admit women to the Air Force, Naval, and Military academies. Just over two weeks later, the Senate, whose members were skittish about going on record on such a politically explosive issue, endorsed the amendment by a voice vote. Then President Ford signed the legislation. Female cadets and midshipmen would enter the three academies in the fall of 1976.

In the meantime, halfway around the globe, the final bloody curtain was falling on America's abandoned ally, South Vietnam. On March 12, 1975, during an all-out Communist offensive to crush the South Vietnam army, a majority in the U.S. Congress voted a special resolution cutting off military aid to the Saigon government.

Less than a month later, on April 10, Ho Chi Minh's Soviet-built tanks smashed through a wrought-iron gate of the presidential palace in Saigon, and all resistance in Vietnam ceased. Over the radio station, a spokesman for the (Communist) Provisional Revolutionary Government announced that Saigon would henceforth be known as Ho Chi Minh City.

Communist "moles," who had lived double lives in Saigon for years, began to surface. Some of them had stayed in the same downtown hotel that had been home for many American military women prior to the U.S. withdrawal. Thu Nhan, a free-lance photographer who had occasionally been employed by the Associated Press during the war, arrived at the wire service offices and stunned an old friend, bureau chief George Esper, by admitting "I have been a [Communist] revolutionary for ten years. My job in the Vietcong was liaison with the [American] media."

American correspondents who had covered portions of the war were shocked to learn that another trusted colleague, Pham Xuan An, was a colonel in the North Vietnam intelligence service. During the conflict, he had worked as a reporter for *Time* magazine, whose editors had been unaware of his true identity. Perhaps Pham was the slickest Communist spy. He had had free access to U.S. and South Vietnam military bases and cultivated numerous contacts high in the armed forces of both the U.S. and South Vietnam.

In 1976, a year after Saigon fell, feminists had taken control of DACOWITS, the group George Marshall had authorized twenty-five years earlier to counsel the Pentagon on how to attract larger numbers of qualified women into the military. Now, DACOWITS had evolved into an anti-Pentagon lobby with its own agenda for the armed forces.

Prodded by the scrappy journalist, Sarah McClendon, DACOWITS demanded that "laws now preventing women from serving their country in combat . . . be repealed." Then the panel took aim at the Veterans of Foreign Wars, claiming that the organization was "hostile" to women and discriminated against them. A formal request was made by the committee for the Pentagon to immediately cut its ties with the VFW.[9]

In its campaign for revolutionary changes in the armed forces, DACOWITS focused on physical standards that the committee felt were holding back the progress of female personnel. "According to medical science, it is commonly known that women are shorter and have other physical differences [than men], but women have proven they have the capabilities to do a given task in the military if given a chance," DACOWITS advised the Pentagon.[10]

In secluded nooks in the Pentagon, male officers scoffed at the DA-COWITS conclusions. Did the committee mean that *all* women could perform *all* jobs, including those involving combat, as well as or better than men? Or did the panel mean that *some* women could carry out *some* tasks as well as males? And, the men officers asked one another, did it require "medical science" for DACOWITS to grasp what was "commonly known"—that males and females have physical differences?

DACOWITS next called on the Pentagon to reevaluate the physical requirements for personnel in hundreds of jobs "to ascertain if height and weight are valid requirements for performance." It was suggested that physical standards could be replaced with "other job qualifications," such as high school academic records and the armed forces entry examinations— areas in which females generally exceeded male performances. "If these academic standards replaced physical ones, they would prove that women would make better soldiers and sailors," DACOWITS maintained.[11]

By January 1976, going into the fourth year of the All-Volunteer Force, larger numbers of women were being inducted. Now there were 109,133 females in the military, or 5 percent of the AVF's total strength. Now the United States had 44 percent more women in uniform than twenty other major nations combined, including the Soviet Union. Most of the U.S. women were in the Army, the largest component by far in the AVF. Many were stationed at locales around the world, wherever the United States had military commitments.

14 ❖ First Crisis for the Coed Army

During the early months of 1976, tension was mounting steadily along the Demilitarized Zone (DMZ), the strip of heavily fortified ground stretching east–west across the waist of the Korean peninsula. Although the Korean War had concluded twenty-three years earlier, no peace treaty had been negotiated and many thousands of U.S. troops were still on guard in the South.

Through electronic snooping, U.S. intelligence learned that North Korean dictator Kim Il Sung had modernized his 650,000–man army and that the Soviet Union had supplied it with some 2,000 modern tanks. Even more alarming, satellite photos disclosed that 50,000 of Kim's troops were massed just above the DMZ, only thirty miles from the South Korean capital of Seoul.

This intelligence seemed to indicate that a Communist invasion of the South was a distinct possibility. If the powder keg exploded, it would be the first real test for the All-Volunteer Force, which, in South Korea, had many hundreds of women in its ranks, many of them in combat-support units not far from the DMZ.

Both North Korea and the combined U.S./South Korean forces manned observation posts at a trapezoid of ground some 750 yards square around the village of Panmunjom. This patch of real estate was known as the Joint Security Area (JSA) and was supposed to be neutral, with either side having access to it.

Over the years, the JSA had become covered with a thick growth of trees, and one of them, a forty-foot poplar, was blocking the view of a U.S. observation post. So Lieutenant Colonel Victor S. Vierra dispatched a ten-man squad of GIs, armed only with pistols, to escort five South Korean workers who were to trim the lower branches of the poplar.

Early on the morning of August 18, 1976, the tree-trimming party, led by Captain Arthur G. Bonifas, went to the site. A few minutes after the workers began pruning the branches, a North Korean truck charged up in a cloud of dust and out jumped two Communist officers and nine enlisted men, all heavily armed (in violation of the armistice).

Lieutenant Pak Chol, the senior North Korean officer, was a veteran of countless DMZ "incidents" and hassles with the American and South Korean soldiers. Pak bolted up to Captain Bonifas and "ordered" him to cease the work. Bonifas, through an interpreter, refused. Pak shouted that any more trimming would bring "serious trouble," a threat the Americans had heard many times before.[1]

Within minutes, sixteen armed North Korean soldiers arrived, and now thirty Communists surrounded the Americans and South Koreans. It was clear the provocation had been carefully choreographed. Lieutenant Pak was waving his arms and screaming that any more tree-trimming would mean death. Moments later, Chol screamed: "Kill! Kill!" Wielding crowbars, clubs, axe handles, and metal pipes, the Communists charged. Bonifas and Lieutenant Mark T. Barrett were bludgeoned to death, their skulls crushed. Other GIs were badly injured.

A twenty-man UN Quick Reaction Force, which had been assigned to monitor the tree-trimming from a distance, rushed forward and the Communist group fled.[2]

General Richard Stilwell, commander of U.S. forces in Korea, and his chief of staff, Major General John K. Singlaub, agreed that a measured response to the cold-blooded murders of the American officers was essential. So Operation Paul Bunyan was developed to forcefully assert U.S. rights in the neutral JSA and to impress upon the Communists that such brutal aggression could result in serious consequences for them.[3]

"That damn tree must come down!" Stilwell told Singlaub. Both men were combat veterans of three wars, and both had been with the OSS and CIA in espionage roles.

Within minutes, it was clear to all U.S. and South Korean forces that a crisis was at hand and war could be imminent. Along with their male comrades, American women soldiers, many of whom had infants and young children to care for, were ordered to report to their duty stations immediately in full combat gear, including weapons. It appeared that for the first time in U.S. history large numbers of females might find themselves as participants in combat in the event North Korean tanks broke through the battle line along the DMZ.

Only later would General Singlaub learn that his order had not been obeyed by all women soldiers. Most of them did report to their posts, but some abandoned their duty stations, which were relatively near to the DMZ, and headed southward, away from the looming violence. Other female soldiers asked for transfers to the rear or off the Korean peninsula. Getting involved in a shooting war was not what they had envisioned when they joined the Army. Singlaub rejected their requests, and also turned thumbs down on a male officer's suggestion for a mass evacuation of all military women.

Singlaub had other headaches. Hundreds of civilians, who had replaced GIs in maintenance and supply depots, requested immediate transportation out of Korea. Civilians could not be ordered to stay. Furious, Singlaub told his personnel officer, "Don't spend a single U.S. government dollar on plane tickets for the bastards. If they want to go so badly, they can pay their own way."[4]

In a few instances, male sergeants, with otherwise outstanding records, were shaken by the imminence of violent conflict, not for their own safety but for that of their wives or girlfriends. So some men soldiers left their posts during the early hours of the alert to search for their loved ones to take them to safer areas to the rear.[5]

Early on the morning of August 21, five days after the two American officers had been murdered, a task force of 813 U.S. and South Korean troops began moving toward the JSA. At the same time, artillerymen stood by their pieces with hands on the lanyards. In far-off Guam, B-52 bombers took to the air and headed in the direction of Pyongyang, the North Korean capital. Forty aircraft were launched from the carrier *Midway* to vector northward. Heavily armed helicopters clattered up and down the DMZ.

At precisely 7:00 A.M., the task force arrived at the JSA and took up defensive positions. Two engineer teams with chain saws moved up to the poplar tree and felled it with a few deft strokes. Then the force withdrew without a shot having been fired.

Combining clout with prudence, the show of force produced dramatic results. At noon that same day, the North Korean Communists requested an urgent meeting of the Military Armistice Commission, the American and North Korean group that had been convening at Panmunjom in fits and jerks since 1953. At the session, a North Korean colonel read a message from Kim Il Sung, who expressed regret over the murder of the two U.S. officers. In the future, Kim added, he hoped the two sides could get along in a spirit of cooperation.

Later at a critique with sergeant majors about the measured U.S. response to the Communist provocation, Jack Singlaub was told by a black noncom, a veteran of Vietnam fighting, "General, when my outfit reported for duty, two of the women held babies in their arms. Now ain't that a hell of a way to go to war!"[6]

Singlaub did not disagree with the assertion.

In the United States in August 1976, the first twenty women arrived at Williams Air Force Base in Arizona to begin undergraduate flight training, more than four years after the Navy had accepted females into its pilot ranks. Air Force tradition called for a trainee to be pitched fully clothed into a large tank of water after a solo flight in a jet trainer. Captain Connie Engel became a celebrity of sorts when she landed after her solo and male classmates tossed her into the tank. She was the first woman to be accorded that unique recognition.[7]

Some nine other women trainees took the plunge into the water, then all of them moved up to flying the T-38 Talon, earned their wings, and were assigned to noncombat units. Lieutenant Christine E. Schott, the first Air Force woman to solo in a Talon, had hoped to become a fighter pilot, although her main goal was to be an astronaut. She was assigned to pilot a C-9 Nightingale "flying ambulance" with a medical airlift squadron at Scott Air Force Base in Illinois. Other women graduates began flying jet refueling tankers and weather reconnaissance aircraft. Much to her dismay, Captain Connie Engel remained at Williams as a flight instructor.[8]

Three years after the birth of the All-Volunteer Force, Army brass in the Pentagon became concerned about the shortage of recruits. After viewing the blood and gore of the battlefield that television had beamed into their homes nightly during the Vietnam war, young men were not tearing down the doors of recruiting stations. Short of resuming the draft, a political hot potato and not likely to occur, the Army of the future would have to absorb nearly six times the number of women as had been the level during the draft era, Pentagon analysts estimated.

Consequently, Army researchers were sent scrambling to collect facts for a study about the role of military women throughout history. Digging deeply, the researchers found evidence of two all-women units. King Gezo of Dahomey, West Africa, had maintained three regiments of female warriors, numbering some 9,000 troops in all, in 1851. Gezo's women were said to have fought bravely, but in a clash with a force of male Egba fighters, the Dahomey women were virtually wiped out.

During World War I, the Army researchers noted, the Russians were allied with France and Great Britain in fighting the German army. In 1917, a Czarist woman, Madame Bachkarova, recruited strong females for a combat unit she called the "Battalion of Death." The madame's approach was partly motivational: She figured that the presence of women soldiers in the front lines "would challenge the Russian men and inspire them to fight more bravely."

However, the Battalion of Death apparently had not been engaged in the fighting. Rather, when bread riots by hungry peasants broke out across Russia, the all-female outfit was assigned to guard the palace of Czar Nicholas II, who soon was forced to abdicate his throne.[9]

During World War II, the Soviet Union, fighting desperately to stem the onslaught of Adolf Hitler's military juggernaut, mobilized 800,000 women, or 8 percent of a total force of twelve million by the end of the conflict. Most women served in combat-support units, others were in mixed-gender combat outfits, some belonged to guerrillas behind German lines.

After the war, the Soviet propaganda machine spread tales about the exploits of women pilots against the German Luftwaffe. On one occasion, according to Soviet sources, two Russian female fighter pilots tore into a flight of forty-two German bombers. During the running battle, the story went, the pair of women shot down four bombers and caused the surviving thirty-eight bombers to turn tail and flee for home before they reached their target.

More than 300,000 women served in the German *Wehrmacht* (armed forces) in World War II, but only as auxiliaries. Even when the Third Reich was on the brink of extinction in 1945 and Adolf Hitler drafted seventy-year-old men and thirteen-year-old boys, handed them bazookas, and sent them into the front lines, German women were not called upon to fight.

Tens of thousands of women in these German auxiliaries were captured by the Russians at the end of the war. Many were severely beaten, starved, sexually assaulted, put into brothels for Red Army soldiers, or executed.

In 1948, three years after the close of World War II, Israel was at war with its Arab neighbors bent on wiping out the tiny new nation. As a matter of survival, the *Hagana*, the Israeli defense organization, drafted thousands of women. A relatively small number of them, known as the *sabra*, fought side by side with the men in the early stages of the war. Since that time, the *sabra* has been depicted as both glamorous and ruthless in battle, traits that were pure fiction.

Actually, in less than a month after the outbreak of the Israel/Arab war, the women were pulled out of the front lines after it had become evident to the Israeli high command that sexually integrated units were suffering far higher casualties than were the all-male outfits.

In 1949, soon after Israel signed a series of peace agreements with Syria, Egypt, Lebanon, and Transjordan, females were removed altogether from combat units. Tamar Eldar Avidar, attaché for women's affairs at the Israel Embassy in Washington, explained that the policy change had been primarily based on the government's deep concern that women in combat areas would be captured, tortured, and sexually abused by the enemy.[10]

Since Israel's war of independence, women are still important members of the army, but they have been trained separately in the *Chen*, a Hebrew acronym for women's corps, which translates into "charm." Conscription has been and is universal, but the government is liberal in granting exemptions for religion, health, marriage, motherhood, and general unsuitability. Therefore, only about half of eligible eighteen-year-old women actually serve in the military.

Although women receive weapons training in the *Chen*, most of them serve mainly in support roles such as parachute riggers, intelligence analysts, teletypists, nurses, social workers, secretaries, and weapons instructors. Their role, as had been traditional with United States women since early in World War II, was to free men to do the fighting.[11]

Israeli women do not fly airplanes, nor do they serve on ships. Many jobs requiring heavy physical strength are not assigned to them. They do not serve in locales where isolated showers for bathing are not available, nor do they pull duty in inclement weather. They are evacuated from potential combat areas during alerts.

A special unit of women, the *Nahal*, is assigned to protect frontier settlements, and they routinely carry weapons. Orders are for women of the *Nahal* to take to the bunkers in the event of attack and wait for male military units to rush to the scene to engage in whatever fighting, if any, is required. Neither the commanders nor the *Nahal* women themselves take their participation in the military seriously. Armed with old, obsolete weapons, they joke about one another's marksmanship, or lack of it, during periodic target practice.

An Israeli general explained the reason women are kept out of the front lines, even when the life of the tiny nation surrounded by enemies is at stake: "A woman's just not built for fighting, physically or mentally. I don't think women should fight, not because they're soft, but because their purpose in life is to tend to the next generation."[12]

Major General Yoram "Ya Ya" Yair cited an incident during the 1973 Yom Kippur War as an example of why women should not be in direct combat and how their presence unhinges the male bonding so crucial to success on the battlefield. When a woman at the Golan Heights front was wounded, the men who witnessed the event were traumatized, Yair said.

"It is not a question of whether she was ready to die on the battlefield," he stressed. "The question was, was the company of men ready for it? Or did it change their ability to keep going the moment they heard the agonizing scream of a woman? And we train our soldiers to keep going [during an attack]."[13]

An unspoken factor in the Israeli military leaders' objections to women in combat is the thought of their women being captured, tortured, and sexually assaulted by the Arab enemies. "For Israelis to imagine an Israeli woman being a prisoner of war is unbearable," said Reuven Gal, a military psychologist.[14]

Asked by a visiting U.S. Army major about the wisdom of using women in combat, an Israeli colonel replied: "*You* can perhaps afford such experiments. *We* have to take war seriously!"[15]

Among the Israeli population there has been and is no controversy about assigning women to combat units—90 percent of the females oppose the idea.

Meanwhile, the U.S. Army Research Institute was handed the job of testing the effectiveness of forty different combat-support companies in field conditions. The units were to use varying percentages of women soldiers up to a maximum of 35 percent.

Code named MAX WAC, the exercises began in October 1976, just as the Jimmy Carter-Gerald Ford presidential election campaign had reached its greatest intensity. More than fifty officer observers fanned out to posts across the United States to watch sexually integrated military police, signal, maintenance, and transportation units perform in the field.

These outfits often work in close combat support, so soldiers were required to carry rifles and bazookas, operate machine guns, and blacken faces to go on night patrols in the rear areas, a sometimes risky task in fluid situations in wartime. Observers were stunned by the unexpected good results of the exercises. They did not know that local commanders had finessed the situation by the simple expedient of leaving their women soldiers back in the barracks while the men were in the field.

Psychologist Cecil D. Johnson, chief of the Army Research Institute, explained later that unit leaders had been leery about sending women out to camp with men, inferring that females might be subjected to unwanted sexual abuse.[16]

When the Army insisted that entire integrated units had to be field tested, additional exercises were conducted. In its official report, the Institute listed some curious incidents. One male commander had ordered a large tent with a stove in it to be set up for a certain woman lieutenant. Sergeants had an especially difficult assignment because of a "role conflict between being a male and being a non-commissioned officer" responsible for leading their squads and platoons. "They assigned men and women to do a job," the report stated, "but allowed the women to stand by while the men did the work."

MAX WAC turned up many other disturbing aspects of the sex integrated experiments. Women had much trouble with tasks requiring physical strength, a fact that came as no surprise to Army professionals. And the female soldiers complained about the lack of privacy for their most intimate body functions and about inadequate sanitation facilities. Until MAX WAC, the report concluded, most of the women had never regarded their jobs as being part of warfare.

At the same time the MAX WAC experiment was taking place, hundreds of young women were preparing to make history. In the fall of 1976, they would enter the Naval, Air Force, and Military Academies, the first women to "invade" the traditional all-male bastions.

15 ❖ "Your Mission Is to Win Our Wars"

Critics of Congress' decision to open the doors of the Naval, Air Force, and Military academies to women were large in number and vocal. Especially outspoken were retired officers who claimed the military had become the politician's toy, a way to accommodate special-interest groups without losing the support of constituents back home, a test tube for social experimentation.

Members of Congress who had argued stridently for the sex integration of the institutions downplayed any suggestion that this change might lead to female graduates being assigned to combat jobs. Representative Samuel Stratton, who had introduced the amendment, declared that the academies did not train officers exclusively for combat, that only 90 percent of current academy graduates had served in combat assignments.

The point Stratton failed to mention, however, was not that "only" 90 percent of the academy graduates had served in combat or combat units, but that 100 percent had been prepared to do so—physically, mentally, and emotionally.

Even while the controversy was simmering in Washington and elsewhere in September 1976, 157 young women arrived at the Air Force Academy, located on a 17,878–acre site on a plateau in the foothills of the Rocky Mountains, seven miles north of Colorado Springs, Colorado. The institution is the newest of the service academies, having been dedicated in 1955.[1]

This first contingent of women were the elite, having been carefully screened and selected from 1,039 applicants. Many had been star athletes on their high school female sports teams. Eighty-four percent had been in the top 10 percent of their high school class academically, and 79 percent had been named to the National Honor Society for scholastic achievement.[2]

The women doolies (recruits) would live and work here for four years in a close, pressurized environment where they would be outnumbered fifteen to one by male cadets. These teenagers—if they survived the demanding and often grueling regimen—would merge into womanhood in an isolation resembling a tour of duty on a deserted island in the Pacific.

Under orders from Congress to make the coed system work, Air Force Academy officials had had more than a year to plan for the revolutionary change. Although the law specified that only "minimal essential adjustments" be made to allow for "physicological differences," the academy developed double standards that often bore no relation to the nomenclature of the two sexes.

On arrival, the male doolies were hustled into barber shops, from which they emerged virtually bald, a traditional ritual designed to impress on them that they were no longer civilians and now were subject to strict military discipline. Female doolies were taken to hairdressers and given stylish trims.

All of the women were assigned to living spaces on the sixth floor of Vandenberg Hall. Earlier, an academy planning committee had concluded that women would respond better to "positive motivation" than to the traditional harsh discipline to which male doolies were subjected. Therefore, the sixth floor was off-limits to men. There the women functioned under the mild tutelage of female lieutenants who had been carefully selected as Air Training Officers to act as role models.

On the floors below in Vandenberg Hall, the bald-headed male doolies were abused and hazed by upperclassmen, who sometimes burst into the newcomers' rooms in the middle of the night. It was a rough initiation intended to develop an officer who one day would be an effective combat leader; fight this nation's wars with skill and tenacity; and, if need be, endure brutal prisoner of war camps.

Double standards became more obvious in the physical fitness program, a crucial component in the academy routine. Doolies were required to run 600 yards in a specified time, and perform an array of broad jumps, pull-ups, and push-ups. Few women had the strength or endurance to compete. So a new system was improvised for them: They were allowed more time for the run; they did far fewer push-ups, and if they could hang on a crossbar for twenty-five seconds in lieu of pull-ups, they were considered to have passed the physical fitness tests.[3]

Many women lagged on long, rigorous marches, fell out on group runs, and were unable to negotiate some obstacles on the assault course, which was later modified to make it easier for them to compete. Most of the females succeeded in the physical training because their poor performances were accommodated by academy policy.

Most of the male doolies had entered the academy with an open mind about women as classmates. However, the double standards caused many of the men to resent the presence of females. Shielded from even mild hazing by upperclassmen and not participating in much of the daily academy life, the women would never earn acceptance by the men.[4]

Angering male cadets was what they regarded as the failure of academy officials to admit that sex integration had created severe problems. Even the existence of double standards was denied to the media. A "few minor adjustments" had to be made, reporters were told, and alterations in routines were "insignificant."

Lieutenant General James R. Allen, the academy superintendent, irritated most of the male cadets when he repeatedly made public pronouncements on how magnificently integration was working. One upperclassmen declared: "The guys at West Point and Annapolis know their 'supes' didn't want girls, but our 'supe' doesn't back us!"[5]

Anger among the men intensified when General Allen told the *Denver Post*: "The only problem we've had is finding there's no way to hold the women back to equal effort. They've been working harder than the men."[6]

After a survey disclosed that 70 percent of male cadets were opposed to having women at the academy, the administration had researchers try to conceive means for developing greater acceptance of females by the men. "Are certain tasks in basic training or some of the athletic competitions really central to the primary goals of the Air Force Academy?" the researchers conjectured. If not, those activities should be eliminated because "as males observe that young women do not perform well in some [of those] areas, there is an immediate decline in favorable orientation toward women."[7]

Other research recommendations focused on wiping out "sexism": admit more women; accept fewer "traditionally-minded" men; and make the "entire academy milieu less military, less discontinuous from the rest of society."[8]

Two thousand miles east of the Rockies that fall, administrators at the Military Academy were grappling with the same vexing integration problems. West Point, as it is commonly called, is steeped in Army tradition, going back to March 1802, when Congress established the institution on the banks of the Hudson River fifty miles north of New York City.

Other officer programs are capable of producing combat leaders, but West Point had always guaranteed it, made it the reason for its existence, as eloquently described by General Douglas MacArthur in his final speech to the cadet corps in 1962:

> Your mission remains fixed, determined, inviolable—it is to win our wars. Everything else in your professional career is but corollary to this vital dedication. All other public purposes will find others for their accomplishment; but you are the men who are trained to fight; yours is the profession of arms.

Prior to academy integration, Lieutenant General Sidney B. Berry, the West Point superintendent, had been strongly against the change. Now, he had accepted it with the stoicism of a dedicated soldier. "We have our orders," he told a group of West Point alumni. "Now it is our responsibility to implement them to the best of our ability."[9]

One of the first changes at West Point to accommodate women was in physical fitness programs. Classes in boxing and wrestling had long been staples. These one-on-one encounters toughened the men and taught them how to survive in life-or-death fights on the battlefield. Because women were given less-strenuous substitutes for these classes, they never had bloody noses. The men knew that war was about bloody noses.

It was not lost on male cadets that double standards meant lower standards. Aware of the men's attitudes, the West Point administration eventually created a euphemism for double standards: equivalent training. This meant, it was explained, that equal *effort* rather than equal *accomplishment* was expected from all cadets.

A first-classman (senior) dryly observed: "I guess it won't make any difference if we win the next war, just so we *tried!*"

West Point's annual Enduro run required a cadet to cover 2½ miles wearing combat boots and helmet, while carrying a rifle, poncho, rucksack, and other gear. Because the run was a combat-training function, academy officials debated whether to excuse females from participating or to impose an equivalent standard.

It was decided that women would take part, but their performances would not be used as a basis for determining who received the coveted Recondo (reconnaissance/commando) patch, a traditional award for achievement in the event. Forty-two percent of the women completed the run within the specified time frame, but Recondo patches were awarded to 73 percent of the females. Eighty-nine percent of the men passed the test, but only 75 percent of them received the patch. Male cadets were not happy.[10]

A couple of hundred miles south of West Point, the first group of women midshipmen reached the U.S. Naval Academy, which lies on 1,100 acres along the banks of the Severn River at Annapolis, Maryland. George Bancroft, secretary of the Navy under President James K. Polk, established the institution in 1845. The historic mission of Annapolis (its common designation) is to turn out qualified Navy ensigns and Marine Corps lieutenants.

Journalists and television crews descended upon Annapolis like, in the words of a male upperclassman, "a swarm of boll weevils in a cotton field," to interview the female midshipmen. The interviewees expressed their opinions freely. But if a male, during an infrequent interview, were to state his views about women at the academy that strayed from the official line, his stay at Annapolis could be jeopardized.

A story in the *Washington Post* that lionized the women midshipmen quoted two males at the tag end. The men had mentioned that the presence of women was weakening the brigade. Moreover, they thought the females would not be able to measure up as good combat officers. Within hours, the two men, who had made their observations while imbibing at a bar in town, were reprimanded and invited to resign from the Naval Academy.

An upperclassman, Jeff Bush, who had been a sergeant with the elite Marine First Reconnaissance Battalion prior to his appointment to the Naval Academy, expressed the viewpoint of most males:

> When I first heard women were going to come, I didn't care that much. I was curious, if anything. I was a little worried that they might not get a chance to prove themselves. But it's been the other way around. The academy has used a lot of pressure to establish women as stripers [midshipman brigade officers]. The scary thing is that it's creating a presumption that women can command troops. The whole thing has become like a fairy tale. And it's the operating military that's in for the biggest hurt.[11]

Bush, who planned to return to the Marines as a lieutenant after graduation, added: "I don't get too excited about much around here anymore. The place has lost a lot of spark for me."[12]

Jeff Bush and other upperclassmen were convinced that the stress environment that for decades had developed combat leadership was rapidly deteriorating, mainly because women were largely immune from such discipline. One first-classman was reprimanded by his company commander because he had "upset" a female. After having corrected her table manners several times (long a customary procedure for plebes), he ordered her to eat with oversize utensils at her next meal. Returning to her room, the woman broke out in tears and her roommate hurried to the company commander and protested such "brutality." Actually, it had been a mild sanction. Then the first-classman was called in and told to cease harassing the woman. Had this episode occurred in the past, both plebes, not the first-classman, would have been disciplined.[13]

Until women came to the academies, the men wrote "peer evaluations" of their classmates, a highly significant means for measuring leadership traits. In evaluating his classmates, each man was stating, in essence, how he felt the others would one day react in life-and-death situations in battle. Developing leadership was the mission of the service academies.

This anonymous and accurate peer evaluation system prevented academy officers from selecting favorites among the student body and pushing them for stripes, that is, leadership posts in the corps. There had been no known instance of the secret process backfiring against minorities: A black cadet had been brigade commander in 1970. Yet academy officers apparently feared that peer evaluation would discriminate against women cadets, so the procedure was scuttled.

Many critics of the integrated academy claimed that combat leadership was being downgraded in favor of an overemphasis on academics, especially social sciences and the humanities, with fewer courses in military and hard sciences. James H. Webb, Jr., a 1968 graduate of the Naval Academy who had seen heavy fighting in Vietnam as a Marine platoon leader, summed up the view held by most active-duty and retired male officers:

> Harvard and Georgetown and a plethora of other institutions can turn out intellectuals *en masse*; only the service academies had been able to turn out combat leaders *en masse*. If academics were the test of leadership, Albert Einstein, who couldn't even work a yo-yo, would have been a five-star general and chairman of the Joint Chiefs of Staff. And General George C. Marshall, who graduated last in his class academically but first in leadership at Virginia Military Institute, would have been a clerk.[14]

Not surprisingly, women cadets held a different view of their pioneer role at the tradition-bound Military Academy on the banks of the Hudson. One member of the 1976 plebe class, seventeen-year-old Carol Barkalow, had decided at the conclusion of her junior year in high school that she wanted a military career. She had been highly active in sports—and enjoyed the discipline, the comradeship, and the physicalness—and in helping her teammates.

"I also wanted to serve my country," Barkalow said. "For me, the answer was the Army. My guidance counselor told me that West Point was starting to accept women."[15]

As plebes, Barkalow and the other females were required to greet the male upperclassmen "Good morning, sir." "Too often, we'd hear back, 'Mornin' bitch!'" she said. "I was naive, I guess. I thought they would just accept us."

By the time Barkalow's class graduated, the men's attitudes had begun to mellow somewhat. The women's attitudes had changed, too. "If we weren't feminists when we went in, we were when we came out," she declared.[16]

16 ❖ A New View in the Pentagon

Inauguration Day in Washington emerged crisp and clear. Late that morning, the gleaming platform in front of the Capitol was packed with relatives of President-Elect James Earl Carter, Jr., Supreme Court justices, leaders of the Senate and House, and assorted other political types. A large battery of television cameras was arrayed in front of the platform. Some 100,000 bundled up and shivering party faithful thronged onto the lawn and the makeshift bleachers. It was January 20, 1977.

In Carter's honor (he was a Naval Academy graduate and served on active duty for seven years in peacetime), the Marine Band played the *Navy Hymn*. Walter Mondale, a former senator from Minnesota, was sworn in as vice president by, at his own request, House Speaker Thomas "Tip" O'Neill, a rough-and-tumble politician who had learned the tools of his trade in Boston.

Then it was Carter's turn. "Are you ready to take the oath of office?" Chief Justice Warren Burger asked him at precisely 12:03 P.M. While Carter's wife Rosalynn held the family Bible, he placed his hand on it. "Congratulations," murmured Burger after the oath. Jimmy Carter, a peanut farmer from the hamlet of Plains, Georgia, became the 39th president of the United States.

Then the new president, his family, and an entourage of the Washington elite took their places on the reviewing stand to watch the traditional Inauguration Parade wend its way along Constitution Avenue, which was packed with humanity on both sides. Among the marching units was a squadron from the newly integrated Air Force Academy, and as it passed, President Carter saluted the cadets with a toothy grin.

Carter did not know that officials at the Air Force Academy, aware of his advocacy for expanded roles for women in the military, had "stacked the deck," in the words of male cadets. After the integrated squadron had been selected, word arrived that the unit would have to be reduced in size for the parade. Several cadets were chopped off the squadron—none of them were women.

Academy officials then arranged the marching formation to place the women in conspicuous places—in the front row and on the left flank where they would be plainly visible to President Carter. This procedure was in violation of Air Force regulations that specified the shortest persons were to march in the rear.

Carter, who had described himself as "very liberal" on "human and civil rights," was a staunch advocate of the equal rights amendment passed by Congress and being hotly debated in state legislatures across the land. For twenty-two months, he had stumped tirelessly to win the Democratic party's presidential nomination over several far more widely known candidates. Campaigning as an "outsider" against President Gerald Ford in the general election of November 1976, Carter persuaded a scandal-weary, politically cynical electorate that he was the man to occupy the White House in the post-Watergate era. "Trust me!" had been his constant theme.

In 1943, two years after graduating from high school, Carter had entered Annapolis and graduated in the top tenth of his class a few months following the conclusion of World War II. After a short stint of battleship duty, Ensign Carter transferred to the submarine service and, in 1951, he was assigned to the nuclear submarine program, then aborning at Schenectady, New York, where he studied nuclear physics and engineering at Union College.

For as long as he could remember, Carter had aspired to become the chief of naval operations. In 1953, however, he abandoned his goal and resigned from the Navy to "go back [to Plains] and build a more diverse life." Twenty-four years later, fifty-two-year-old Jimmy Carter far exceeded his dream of being chief of naval operations: Now he was commander in chief of the armed forces.

Less than twenty-four hours after taking the oath of office, Carter fulfilled a key campaign pledge: He signed Executive Order Number 1. Supporters equated the action to Abraham Lincoln's signing of the Emancipation Proclamation. Opponents described it as almost an act of treason. With one deft stroke of his pen, Carter had pardoned the draft dodgers of the Vietnam War.

More than 2,000 men who had fled to foreign countries to take safe refuge until the danger passed were now free to return home. The order also covered some 10,000 men already convicted on breaking the law, an additional 2,500 still under indictment, and an unknown number who had evaded service by simply not registering for the draft.

Carter also asked Pentagon leaders (who would include his own appointees) to review the cases of 88,700 men who had received less than honorable discharges for deserting or going AWOL with the aim of possibly upgrading their discharges. Finally, the new president promised a study of the estimated 173,000 men who received undesirable discharges that had been dispensed during the Vietnam War years.[1]

The ink barely had dried on Carter's executive order than his action was vigorously attacked by the Veterans of Foreign Wars, the American Legion, the Disabled American Veterans, and other groups whose members had worn the uniform. These organizations claimed that Carter's action was an affront to all American men and women who had done their duty by serving in Vietnam.

Carter's action triggered acrimonious debate in Congress. Conservative Senator Barry Goldwater said "this is the most disgraceful thing that a president has ever done."[2] Liberal Senator Edward N. "Ted" Kennedy, whose late brother, former President John F. Kennedy, had seen action as a PT-boat skipper in the Pacific during World War II, praised Carter for his "major, impressive, and compassionate step toward healing the wounds of Vietnam."[3]

While campaigning against Gerald Ford, Carter had repeatedly stressed his all-out support for the growing feminist movement. "I am fully committed to equality between men and women in every area of government," he had declared. "Government" includes the armed forces.

Soon the Carter Pentagon was packed with feminists in key policy-making positions. Foremost among them were Deputy Assistant Secretary of Defense for Equal Opportunity Kathleen Carpenter, Deputy Assistant Secretary of the Navy for Manpower Mary M. Snavely-Dixon, Department of Defense General Counsel Deanne Siemer, Deputy General Counsel of the Navy Patricia A. Szervo, Under Secretary of the Air Force for Manpower Antonia Handler Chayes, General Counsel of the Army Sara Elisabeth Lister, and Deputy Under Secretary of the Navy Mitzi M. Werthheim.

None of these female Pentagon officials had any experience with the military. All were dedicated to greatly expanding "equal opportunities" for women in the armed forces, including injecting them into combat units, even if it meant drafting females.

Perhaps the most influential woman in the Carter Pentagon was thirty-four-year-old Kathleen Carpenter, who had been special counsel for equal employment practices at Norton Simon, Inc. Soon after taking over her Pentagon post, she began articulating her theories on how the armed forces should operate, unabashed about her absence of any military background.

Carpenter went on record as believing that the physicological and psychological differences between men and women in the armed forces were of no more consequence than the differences between the races. Women being assigned to combat units was a simple matter of civil rights, and outweighed any consideration of military readiness, she declared.[4]

Carpenter refused to concede that physical strength and dexterity were often the difference between life and death on the battlefield. "Tests show that while men have greater upper body strength, women have greater midsection strength," she explained. Therefore, she wanted the military to change its unit structures to "make better use of female midsection strength."

Commanders had no inkling about how they were supposed to reorganize their outfits in ways that could take advantage of what Carpenter had said was greater female midsection strength. These experienced male officers knew that the armed forces are not a "corporation," that a soldier is not holding a "job," and that social experimentation in the military can lead to excessive deaths and disaster—and defeat—in war.

In the Carter Pentagon, the sizable bloc of feminist officials had a staunch supporter at the helm. Within a week after taking over as secretary of defense, Harold Brown ordered a total reappraisal of the role of women in the armed forces.

Brown was an intellectual from the academic community. He received a Ph.D. in physics from Columbia University, taught in a number of prestigious seats of higher learning, and became president of the California Institute of Technology in 1969. He served in that capacity until going to the Pentagon.

Directing the study of military women would be Navy Commander Richard W. Hunter, who, it had been known, was greatly impressed with the potential for females in the armed forces. During his team's research, Hunter consulted often with Martin Binkin, who was a fellow in the Brookings Institution, a "think tank" with which Hunter had been associated a few years earlier while on loan from the Navy.

For several months, Binkin had been working with Air Force Lieutenant Colonel Shirley Bach, who was on loan to Brookings, on a similar study. Although unfinished, the Binkin and Bach work had gained the attention of the civilian brass in the Pentagon, because it was an open secret that the study would recommend a far wider use of women in the armed forces.

Despite his modest rank, Commander Hunter was emerging as one of the Pentagon's leading experts on personnel matters, partly because his views were consistent with those of President Carter and his inner circle in the White House. When Hunter's study titled *The Use of Women in the Military* was finished, it cited two reasons for the "growing urgency" of introducing women into battle forces:

> First is the movement within the society to provide equal opportunity for American women. Second, and more important, use of more women can be a significant factor in making the All-Volunteer Force continue to work in the face of a declining youth population.[5]

Hunter's study admitted that actual combat is the only valid yardstick for measuring the quality of a soldier, aviator, sailor, or Marine, but it held that possession of a high school diploma was the best available predicator for success in combat. Ninety percent of female recruits had high school diplomas.

Alluding to Hunter's report, an Army officer who had been badly wounded in Vietnam when his company was overrun by a far larger enemy force, quipped privately: "I guess what we should have done when the Vietcong charged us was to have waved our high school diplomas. That would have scared the hell out of them!"[6]

Combat officers in the Army officer corps were astonished by Hunter's diploma conclusion. Nearly all of them could cite instances of men with modest formal education who had commanded companies and even battalions in the crucible of combat. They pointed to Audie Murphy, who had dropped out of school after the fifth grade to support his poverty-stricken family. He had entered the Army in World War II as a private, was awarded a battlefield commission as a lieutenant, and became one of American history's most highly decorated warriors.[7]

The leading advocate in Carter's Pentagon for greatly expanding roles for military women was Clifford L. Alexander, Jr., the first black man to serve as a civilian head of a branch of the armed forces. He had been sworn in as secretary of the Army on February 14, 1977.

Born in Harlem on September 21, 1933, Alexander, aided by scholarships, attended two prestigious private institutions in New York City, the Ethical Culture School and the Fieldston School. From there, he went to Harvard and then obtained a degree at Yale Law School. In 1963, he came to Washington at the urging of Louis Martin, deputy chairman of the Democratic National Committee, who was recruiting the "brightest and best of black America" for President John Kennedy's new administration. Alexander was assigned to the National Security Council and reported directly to the White House.

After Kennedy's assassination in 1963, President Lyndon Johnson appointed Alexander to his White House staff as deputy special assistant for personnel and administration, and in the summer of 1967, Johnson named him his personal consultant on civil rights. Later, the president appointed him chairman of the Equal Employment Opportunities Commission (EEOC), where he began aggressively ferreting out what Alexander said was rampant racial discrimination in the nation's economy.

One of Alexander's first acts after taking over his job in the Pentagon was to order a review of all Army military occupational specialties (MOS), many of which were considered combat-related and, therefore, barred to women. He said that he wanted the "narrowest definition of combat that was practicable." As a result, the Army came up with a distinction: Units that aim weapons by line of site on the enemy were combat units.[8]

It meant that women could not fight in the infantry, but could serve in a large number of support roles that have combat missions in time of war. The move left only 24 of 305 military occupational specialties closed to women and reversed the previous combat policy, which had barred units containing women from operating forward of rear brigade areas.

Privately, many uniformed officers were appalled by the definition of combat. If taken literally, it would mean that women could be soldiers in mortar and combat engineering units, both of which suffer heavy casualties on the battlefield.

The thought of American women being involuntarily thrust into battle was greatly disturbing to many active-duty and retired male officers and soldiers who had known firsthand the bloody carnage of battlefields. "No man with gumption wants a woman to fight his battles," declared retired General William Westmoreland, former commander of U.S. forces in Vietnam.[9]

Uniformed officers in the Pentagon were convinced that Secretary Alexander was hell-bent on creating drastic new policies aimed at the eventual inclusion of women in combat units. He appeared to be focusing on means for changing the Army's traditional attitude toward women soldiers and in making certain that they had the same career opportunities as men. "That's what I take pride in," he told reporters.[10]

A woman official in the Pentagon backed up the outlook of the Carter Pentagon when she said, "Women have a right to die for their country." Left unsaid was that they might take to their deaths with them a large number of male comrades because most women were not physically or psychologically constituted to cope with the horrors of the battlefield.

17 ❖ "General, You Are a Male Chauvinist!"

A short time after Secretary of the Army Clifford Alexander had taken charge in early 1977, the brass in the Pentagon decided that MAX WAC, the field exercises held the previous year to test the effectiveness of sexually integrated combat-support units, had been inadequate. MAX WAC had lasted only three days and been held in favorable weather. Consequently, a second field test of longer duration was laid on.

Code named Braveshield, the exercises were held in the Mojave, in southeastern California, a vast desert wasteland where many small, isolated mountain ranges and extinct volcanoes break up the great stretches of sandy soil. Launched in the oppressive heat of July, Braveshield, as had been the case with MAX WAC, resulted in an atmosphere of unreality among the women soldiers, who continued to wear makeup, washed and put up their hair, and carped about the lack of privacy and having to use slit-trench latrines.

After the conclusion of the Mojave field tests and the observers turned in their evaluations, the official Braveshield report stated, in part:

> Many of the troops, particularly the women, had not thought it through to the realization that had it been a war, both male and female soldiers could have been killed or wounded . . . was known that sexual intercourse was occurring, but not more than occurs in garrison.[1]

It did not mention that sexual activity in garrison is harmless from a military point of view, whereas such relations during a battle situation could conceivably result in a disaster for the unit involved.

In September, the Army staged a third exercise, code named REF WAC 77, involving coed units. It was held in the midst of a large NATO (North Atlantic Treaty Organization) war game in the mountainous, heavily wooded region south of Stuttgart, Germany, and lasted for ten days.

REF WAC 77 was far from a success. Twenty-nine percent of the women, as opposed to 14 percent of the men, were excused from going into the field for "personal reasons." Many of the females who did take part were not required to participate in heavy labor, resulting in much griping from the men who had to carry their burdens.

"Leadership and management problems were widespread in the units," the official report stated. On two occasions, women in charge of serving generators that supported communications equipment refused to perform their duties because they were afraid to go out in the field at night. Nehama Babin, a woman psychologist, said that their fear was caused by the prospect of being raped by men in combat units passing through the region where the female soldiers were supposed to be on duty.[2]

In one incident, the report stated, a company commander had to send out a squad of men to "rescue" women soldiers posted on guard duty when "friendly" infantry units were marching through the area. "The infantry thought it was great fun to stalk the female guards of support units because everybody knew the women didn't have live ammunition," the written evaluation added.[3]

Although the best possible face was put on the REF WAC 77 report in keeping with the Carter Pentagon's policy of greatly expanding the jobs available to females, numerous officers in the Army Research Institute claimed privately that the field test raised more serious questions than it answered.

Pentagon feminists were undaunted by the pessimistic evaluation of REF WAC 77. Testifying before the House Armed Services Committee, Air Force Under Secretary Antonia Chayes declared, "We are creating the model for putting women [in combat-related] jobs."[4]

Charles Moskos, the renowned expert on military manpower, told the media: "The secretary of the Army [Alexander] is so hot on getting women into all kinds of tasks that it is very hard to find anything suggesting that there may be some things that women aren't suited for."[5]

Moskos would prove to be perspicacious. "This situation [women in combat] will give politicians and military leaders a great deal of difficulty in the years ahead," he predicted.[6]

In the Pentagon, Alexander remained firm in his goals. "Women have acquitted themselves well in wars," he declared. "They will acquit themselves well in the future."[7]

In the meantime, thirty women soldiers began field tests at Aberdeen Proving Grounds, a facility extending along the shore of Chesapeake Bay for thirty-four miles. There, away from prying hostile eyes, the Ordnance Corps conducts exhaustive tests on weapons, tanks, shells, bombs, supplies, and equipment.

This pioneer platoon of females was trying out the new Army "unisex" uniform and gear. They wore the new unisex helmet, made from Keviar, a tough plasticlike substance designed by computers to fit female heads as well as men's. They put on the new unisex combat boot, sized to fit women's higher instep, and the new Army body armor, which has a roomier bosom.

On the backs of the women was the new Army field pack, an ingenious device with straps that curve out and do not cross over the breast, such as the ones used by men for decades. They carried the unisex gas masks, designed by computers to make a tight fit with women's narrower faces.

There was a great amount of Pentagon heat aimed at Aberdeen officials to move ever faster in the mad rush to create a truly unisex Army. "We've been ricocheting like a bullet in a steel room on this," complained Bernie Corona, an engineer in the Army Human Engineering Laboratory, whose unit was charged with designing the new combat uniforms.[8]

Corona pointed out that the Army brass earlier had concluded that women soldiers could wear the smaller men's uniforms and boots, and now there was an enormous flap to create new designs. "Anatomically, females are quite different than males," he added in a master stroke of analytical genius.

Standard combat boots, even in smaller sizes, proved to be inadequate for women. Reports from training camps disclosed that the boots were hurting women's feet and causing blisters on marches. These complaints reached the desk of Army Secretary Clifford Alexander who got involved in the Aberdeen tests.

"I have been jogging the system," Alexander admitted. "They [Army brass] wanted to wait until they moved out the existing inventory," he explained. "I said, the hell with that. Let's get those [women's] boots out there!"[9]

Clearly, the Pentagon generals had been seeking to save many millions of dollars, while Alexander was more interested in rushing ahead with the new unisex Army.

Alexander was also pushing hard for completion of a pet project: the design of the Army maternity uniform. "We're slower than we ought to be on that," he told reporters.

Many, perhaps most, of the Army women were far from happy over being assigned to unisex units. One of them, nineteen-year-old Private Katherine Flood, a crew member in a Hawk fire-control team near Baumholder, Germany, complained that she had been "defeminized" to the point where "it is depressing." Flood explained: "When I pull guard, if we get to sleep, I sleep in the same room as the men do. If we're in the field, I sleep with the men, married and single, in a tent. There is no separate latrine. I'm tired of being surprised when I walk outside and a guy is using the 'tube' [urinating]."[10]

Private Flood said she wished she had been warned about what she was getting into. "I didn't even know it was a combat job when I enlisted," she complained. "I'll serve out my three-year hitch, and that's that!"[11]

After an exhaustive study, the Army came up with a conclusion that hardly startled anyone: Women are not as physically strong as men. Therefore, it was concluded, females are not able to perform some tasks as well as males. Field tests showed that women have only 55 percent of the muscle strength and 67 percent of the endurance of men of equal size. On average, the study found, women are shorter, weigh less, and walk slower. Many can't maintain the regulation thirty-inch stride on marches. As a result of these findings, the Army changed the physical standards for women. They were given lighter rifles to shoulder. They had to do only eighteen push-ups, as opposed to thirty-five for men, in two minutes. Because the average female recruit had no appetite for firing weapons, she was excused from qualifying on the rifle range.

These factors resulted in problems at Fort Jackson, South Carolina, the Army's coed basic training camp. "If we let a platoon march to the average female speed, then we can't meet the [test] requirements," explained drill Sergeant Donnie Feltman. "If we make the women keep up with the men, we'd have a whole platoon of women on crutches."[12]

Despite the sour notes about female physical limitations flowing out of Fort Jackson, Army Secretary Alexander announced on September 8, 1977, that "unit commanders are authorized to employ women to accomplish unit missions throughout the battlefield."[13]

Army leaders in the Pentagon continued to try to accommodate the female presence at Fort Jackson. Since early in World War II, accidental deaths in training had been accepted as part of the price paid for combat readiness. Now, when a twenty-year-old female recruit fell to her death when her grip gave way during the classic exercise called the "slide-for-life," that toughening technique was abandoned.

Much of this physical activity in training was of no major value, feminist groups and other advocates of women being assigned to combat-related jobs claimed. Because of the changed nature of modern warfare, they were convinced that combat no longer depended on physical strength, toughness, and endurance. No longer will there be dependence on soldiers being burdened with sixty-pound rucksacks while taking thirty-mile marches in scorching heat or bitter cold over rugged terrain, they declared. Nor will the modern soldier be involved in hand-to-hand fighting with trench knives, bayonets, and fists. He will not have to fire machine guns, pitch grenades, and dig foxholes while bullets zip past his head.

Battles of the future, feminists maintained, will consist mainly of tasks for which women are suited: lasers, "smart bombs," guided missiles, microprocessors, and other sophisticated devices. War of the future will be an antiseptic endeavor. No muss. No fuss. "Fighting" will be conducted from a long distance. Much like playing Nintendo games.

In January 1978 Major General John Singlaub, a combat leader in three wars, was ordered to travel to the Pentagon and participate in a conference on the future role of women in the Army. Knowing that President Carter and Army Secretary Alexander were advocating greatly expanded roles for females, including assignments in combat units, he went to Fort Jackson to see for himself how women recruits were hacking it. Although basic training was intended to be tough, it was not nearly as rugged as Ranger, airborne, and Special Forces (Green Berets) training. It came as no surprise to Singlaub to learn from the male sergeants and lieutenants at Fort Jackson that they had been directed to greatly lower physical performance standards to fill the designated quota of qualified women recruits.

Singlaub knew that compromises would have to be made in the All-Volunteer Army, and he was aware that there were hundreds of jobs not requiring physical strength that women could fill as well, or better, than men. But having been involved in battle on many occasions, Singlaub was adamantly opposed to placing women soldiers in combat-support or combat units.

Armed with the firsthand knowledge he had obtained at Fort Jackson, Singlaub left for Washington. At the Pentagon conference, he was confronted by a group of feminist officials led by an officious woman lawyer from the Department of the Army. It was fertile grounds for fireworks—which were not long in coming.

Singlaub articulated his case against sending women into combat-support or combat units, based on his personal war experiences. While he ticked off numerous reasons why females should not be assigned to frontline jobs, he felt the icy glare of the Pentagon women. "General," the Army lawyer snapped, "you are nothing but a male chauvinist!" She stopped short of adding the word "pig."[14]

Ignoring the remark, Singlaub declared that there was a need for and he was in favor of opening many more jobs to female soldiers. "But putting women into combat-support or combat [units] is insane!"[15]

One of the feminists launched a counterattack. "General, the Soviet army used women in combat to great advantage in World War II combat," she said. "You should read your history more closely."

Singlaub kept his composure. "I served in combat in two theaters in that war, ma'am," he said evenly. "I believe I am adequately familiar with its history."

After the confab adjourned for the day, Singlaub contacted a friend who had authored a history of the Soviet army in World War II. "It was a disaster, Jack," the man replied. "Men soldiers' loyalties were badly divided between their duty and the paramours they were serving with. The Red Army learned its lesson, however. Today, there are absolutely no Soviet women in combat assignments. They even have a smaller percentage of women soldiers than we do."

When the Pentagon conference resumed the next morning, Singlaub elaborated on the role of women in the Soviet army. Few of the conferees, however, paid attention. His remarks were brushed off as of no consequence.[16]

Meanwhile, the Navy leadership was edging that service toward breaking a 200-year tradition and integrating women as crew members of seagoing ships. Secretary of the Navy W. Graham Claytor told Congress that the existing exclusion of women on certain "noncombat" vessels, such as tenders and repair, rescue, and research craft, was "incredibly archaic."[17]

In July 1978, Claytor and other advocates of females being sent to sea received an enormous boost for their cause when Judge John J. Sirica, who had gained wide fame as a jurist in the Watergate scandals that had driven President Richard Nixon from office, ruled in the Yona Owens class-action suit. Months earlier, Owens, a Navy interior communications specialist, and two other Navy women filed the litigation against the Department of Defense, claiming that the Navy was guilty of sex discrimination for barring them from assignment to seagoing ships.

Instigating the legal action and providing the funds and lawyers was the American Civil Liberties Union, which had involved itself in countless libertarian causes since 1920, when its founder, Roger Baldwin, and his colleagues defended World War I's conscientious objectors, the pariahs of the era.

Judge Sirica ruled in the Yona Owens class-action suit that prohibiting women from serving on ships at sea "unconstitutionally denies plaintiffs their right to the equal protection of the laws as guaranteed by the fifth amendment of the Constitution."

Sirica added: "Whatever problems might arise from integrating shipboard crews are matters that can be dealt with through appropriate training and planning." He noted, however, that "there remains many unanswered questions about the effects of full sexual integration that may well convince military authorities that women members should be excluded from shipboard combat assignments. Those are essentially military decisions."

The ACLU had scored half a victory. Sirica's ruling had nudged the Navy closer to assigning women to auxiliary ships, but it had stopped short of placing them on combat vessels.

A few weeks after Judge Sirica handed down his ruling, Admiral James L. Holloway, chief of naval operations, sent out a call for women volunteers for seagoing duty. On November 1, 1978, Ensign Mary Carrol walked up the gangplank of the *Vulcan*, a repair ship, at Norfolk, Virginia. Reaching the deck, she gave the traditional salute to the bridge and said, "Permission to come aboard, sir."

Carrol was among the first contingent of 55 officers and 375 enlisted women to be permanently assigned to various seagoing Navy ships.[18]

A few months later in May 1979, Secretary of Defense Harold Brown proposed to Congress that the law barring women from combat be amended to grant the Navy and Air Force secretaries authority to set policy for the assignment of women within their own departments. The Army secretary had always had that control.

Proponents of expanded roles for military women regarded Brown's request as a quantum leap forward. Opponents feared that approval would lead toward females eventually being sent into battle. By the time the personnel subcommittee of the House Armed Services Committee opened hearings on Brown's proposal in November, both sides on the controversial issue had mobilized their heavy hitters.

Under Secretary of the Air Force Antonia Chayes testified, "There must be policy changes to assure women that they can satisfy personal career goals and ambitions by moving up the ladder to senior management." She added: "What we achieve by barring women from combat roles is an obstacle to their career advancement."[19]

Chayes also said, "I do not see that there is any sex or gender differences in the degree of pacifism or willingness to go to war. I think that women throughout history have taken up arms, and very effectively. Look at the Amazons."[20]

Advocates of assigning women to combat units had been researching diligently in the hope of finding clues that Amazons actually had existed. Such a discovery would reinforce the viewpoint that females could perform well in battle if only given the opportunity. According to legend, Amazons had been warlike women who made slaves of men they captured. They were depicted in Grade B Hollywood movies as sturdily built, strong, athletic, skilled with the sword, and absolutely fearless. Men, it was said, had been petrified by the mere mention of the Amazon warriors.

The legend came crashing down, however, when Abby Weltan Klein-baum, a professor at the City University of New York, disclosed that Amazons had been figments of the imagination of ancient Latin and Greek authors. In ten years of research, Kleinbaum said, not a single clue had turned up to give authenticity to the ancient tale.

"One woman told me that when she learned that Amazons had never existed, she felt like crying." Professor Kleinbaum stated.[21]

Among the civilian groups testifying at the House subcommittee hearings on Harold Brown's proposal was the American Civil Liberties Union, represented by attorney Diana A. Steele. "The exclusion of women from combat causes severe injustice to women who are qualified and eager to serve in the military," she declared. Echoing that sentiment, Carol Parr, director of the feminist Women's Equity Action League, testified "there is absolutely no reason why women can't make a full contribution to the nation's defense."[22]

Vice Admiral Robert B. Baldwin, chief of naval personnel, articulated the Navy's official view in favor of amending the law, but he said that he personally was opposed to women serving on combat ships. Off the House floor, Baldwin allegedly told reporters that the idea of amending the law was not the Navy's idea, rather it was the Defense Department's.

Another high-ranking witness, Lieutenant General Edward J. Bonars, the Marine Corps deputy chief of staff for manpower, put his career on the line when he told the subcommittee that the Corps did not support the amendment. He said he had "a feeling that the nation is not ready to see their women participate actively in combat roles."

Also speaking out strongly against Secretary Brown's proposal was a lineup that included Admiral Jeremiah A. Denton, Jr., who had suffered for seven years as a prisoner of war of the Vietcong; retired General William Westmoreland, the former Army chief of staff; Dr. Harold M. Voth, a psychiatrist and rear admiral in the Naval Reserve; and Phyllis Schlafly, president of Eagle Forum, a conservative, family-oriented organization.

General Westmoreland charged that the Carter administration "is trying to use the military as a vehicle to further social change in our society." He said he had no objections to women flying aircraft or firing intercontinental ballistic missiles "where the environment is not hazardous," but he was staunchly against utilizing women in ground combat units, in submarines, and on aircraft carriers in wartime.

Retired Brigadier General Elizabeth Hoisington, a former director of the Women's Army Corps (WAC), was blunt in her assessment of the proposal. "I want my name to go on record as having stood up to oppose women being trained or assigned to combat units," she testified. "My male colleagues tell me—and I believe it—that war is hell. Heads are blown off; arms and legs are maimed; suffering is so intolerable it affects a man for years. It is bad enough that our young men have to endure this, but do we want our women to suffer it too?"[23]

Admiral Denton, in emotional phrasing, told of the horrors of war and the brutalities suffered during his years as a POW of the Vietnamese Communists. Denton, whose book *When Hell Was in Session* became a television movie, said that he and other prisoners had been tortured for days at a time and at one point he was "reduced to a crawling animal," with his face covered with boils after being left bound in a filthy cell for ten days.

"It is inconceivable to think about American women being subjected to that ordeal," he emphasized.

Phyllis Schlafly, an articulate woman, pulled no punches, charging that politics was behind the Defense Department's amendment proposal. "What a way to run the armed forces!" she stated. "We must be the laughing stock of the world!"[24]

After four days of often acrimonious verbal exchanges between members of the subcommittee and witnesses, the hearings adjourned with nothing having been decided.

While the debate was raging in Washington, women in all the services were on duty around the world. Some of them were still not being accepted by male officers. Karen A. Clougherty, a master sergeant in the Air Force, recalled events when she reported for duty at Templehoff Central Airport in West Berlin in the late 1970s:

> Being the first United States Air Force Security Police woman assigned to the unit, I was confronted with a male superior who demanded my immediate transfer. His logic was that a woman "by law" could not protect areas of national security, therefore, I should be transferred. Luckily, the Air Force didn't agree.

18 ❖ A Plan to Register Women

Speeding along Washington's wide Constitution Avenue behind a convoy of motorcycle policemen, a long black Cadillac carried President Jimmy Carter, who sat on the rear seat and scribbled notes. He was bound for Capitol Hill to perform the traditional ritual known as the State of the Union address before a joint session of Congress. It was January 23, 1980.

Only a tiny coterie close to Carter was aware that he was about to drop a bombshell: a request to Congress for permission to register women for the draft for the first time in the nation's history. Five years earlier, Gerald Ford had discontinued registration. So Congress would have to pass an amendment to the Selective Service Act if women were to be included in a renewal of registration.[1]

Carter's dramatic request seemed to many to be an acknowledgement that the U.S. armed forces had been permitted to deteriorate during his tenure in the face of threats to American security from the Soviet Union, which had built a powerful war machine, and from other global locales. One of those dangers resulted from a situation in Iran, a rugged land of snow-capped mountains and barren deserts about 2½ times the size of Texas.

Iran's ruler had been the Shah, a staunch ally of the United States, who had been forced into exile. Power was seized on November 4, 1979, by the aging Ayatollah Ruhollah Khomeini, a Muslim extremist with a deep hatred for the United States. A short time later, angry mobs of Ayatollah's followers stormed the American embassy in Teheran and took hostage fifty-four members of the staff. Ambassador William Sullivan happened to be gone at the time.

It was one of the most embarrassing episodes in the history of the United States. Perhaps encouraged by the image of Uncle Sam's impotence, two days after Christmas the tank-tipped Soviet army invaded neighboring Afghanistan, a primitive country of lofty mountain ranges that had been fought over by warlords since Alexander the Great conquered the region in about 330 B.C.

Moscow announced to the world that the Soviet army had been "invited to intervene" by Afghanistan President Hafizullah Amin. One of the first actions after the invaders seized the capital of Kabul, however, was to capture Amin and turn him over to pro-Russian Afghanistan officers, who murdered him.

President Carter was shocked. Until that brutal aggression, he had always believed, naively, that the "chronic United States–Soviet Union confrontation mentality had been shortsighted and counterproductive."[2]

Now, in his State of the Union address, Carter told Congress he would like to reinstate registration for the draft, and that he was considering requesting authority to include women. Within two weeks, he said, details of his plan would be announced.

There was little, if any, doubt about what the president's decision would be. As a stalwart booster of the equal rights amendment being debated for ratification in state legislatures and an advocate of expanding roles for women in the military, he could hardly exclude females from draft registration.

Carter's proposal astonished many members of Congress, one of whom pointed out that the nation had survived for 204 years without "dragooning our young women into combat by way of registration for the draft." Leaders in the Pentagon were caught off-guard, not having been advised in advance about Carter's plan. A barrage of questions from the media had to be deflected until the Pentagon learned more details.

On February 8, the White House press secretary released a statement in which Carter said he planned to ask Congress for authority to register both women and men. "My decision is a recognition of the reality that both women and men are working members of our society." he added. "It confirms what is already obvious throughout our society—that women are now providing all types of skills in every profession. The military should be no exception."[3]

Carter added that there were 150,000 women serving in the armed forces and "performing well," and he said "there is no distinction possible that would allow me to exclude women from an obligation to register."[4]

Carter's statement stirred up a hornets' nest. The Pentagon was bombarded by angry mail, much of it from mothers who mistakenly blamed the generals for the plan to register their daughters. Phyllis Schlafly, head of the Eagle Forum, rapidly established the Coalition Against Drafting Women. Its board consisted of prominent civic, religious, and military leaders, including Lieutenant General Daniel O. Graham, Marine Corps General Lewis W. Walt, Major General Henry Mohr, and Major General John Singlaub, all retired. Among the clergymen were the Reverend Jerry Falwell and Rabbi Herman N. Neuberger.

"President Carter has stabbed American womanhood in the back in a cowardly surrender to women's lib!" the outspoken Schlafly told the media. "We are not going to send our daughters to do a man's job!"[5]

In the weeks ahead, the Coalition collected more than 200,000 signatures on "Don't Draft Women" petitions and presented them to Congress. Capitol switchboards lit up as mothers inundated their senators and representatives with outcries of protest.

Meanwhile, supporters of Carter's plan also rallied their troops. The Women's Equity Action League viewed the registration as an opportunity for women to take on more responsibility in the public sector. And the National Organization for Women stated: "War is senseless. Neither the lives of young men or young women should be wasted. But, if we cannot stop the killing, we know we cannot choose between our sons and daughters."[6]

Hearings on the controversial topic began in Congress. In the House, female lawmakers were divided. Marjorie Holt, ranking Republican on the military personnel subcommittee, said that as long as women were not going to be put into combat, as President Carter had implied, there was no need to register them.

Democrat Barbara Mikulski, known to her critics as the "Baltimore Bulldozer," predicted a backlash from her Maryland constituency should Congress exclude women from registration. "I come from a working-class neighborhood," she said. "We've told the guys in the unions and on the construction sites to move over and make room for the sisterhood. If the women aren't registered, these guys will say, 'Jesus, you want to be equal on the assembly line but not in the draft.' "[7]

In the Senate, there was heavy opposition. John Stennis, the chairman of the Armed Services Committee, broke with fellow Democrat Jimmy Carter and announced that he was staunchly against female registration. Sam Nunn, also a Democrat and chairman of the manpower and personnel subcommittee, likewise let it be known that he was opposed to registering women.

However, President Carter found a steadfast supporter in the Republican ranks of the Senate—Nancy Kassebaum. She is the daughter of Alfred M. Landon, former two-term governor of Kansas and the Republican nominee for president in 1936 when he was devastated at the polls by incumbent Franklin Roosevelt. Coming to Washington in 1978 from a small working farm in rock-ribbed conservative Kansas, Kassebaum seemed to many a strange figure to climb into a political bed with the National Organization for Women and the ACLU, both of which were going all-out to get women registered.

On April 17, 1980, the Senate's manpower and personnel subcommittee rejected by a vote of 5 to 2 the proposal to register women, but it approved funds for registering men. In its report, the panel stated: "Women should not be intentionally or routinely placed in combat positions in our military services" so there was "no need to include women in a Selective Service System."[8]

A short time before the measure was to be voted on by the full Senate, Nancy Kassebaum introduced an amendment that would prohibit funds for registration unless women were included. Her last-ditch effort went down to defeat by a vote of 51 to 40. Several Democratic liberals, who customarily could be counted on to support feminist causes, ducked out of the controversial issue and did not vote. They included Edward Kennedy, George McGovern, Frank Church, and Joseph Biden.

After the Carter administration received the green light from Congress, it sent out word that all nineteen- and twenty-year-old men would begin registering on Monday, July 21. Then an unexpected turn of events surfaced. On Friday, only three days before the registration date, the U.S. Circuit Court of Appeals in Philadelphia ruled that draft registration that excludes women was unconstitutional and ordered the government not to proceed with the project. Federal attorneys promptly took the matter to the U.S. Supreme Court, and Justice William J. Brennan, Jr., on Saturday, granted a request to allow the registration to begin pending a final ruling by the full court.

This legal threat to registration of men had been dangling for nine years. Back in June 1971, during the height of the Vietnam War, a class-action lawsuit had been filed in the U.S. District Court in Philadelphia by two draft-eligible men who charged that they were being denied their constitutional rights because women were not included in the draft. A month later, the court dismissed the case.

However, attorneys took the case to the Circuit Court of Appeals in Philadelphia, which sent it back to the lower court on the basis that the government had failed to draft females. By the time a three-judge panel was prepared to hear the case in 1973, the draft ended and the All-Volunteer Force was activated. Consequently, the sex discrimination case went into hibernation.

Then, in 1980, the U.S. District Court in Philadelphia resurrected the nine-year-old suit, and the three-judge panel, without hearing additional testimony, ruled in favor of the two male plaintiffs, who no doubt by that time had forgotten about their litigation. The case was then appealed to the U.S. Supreme Court.

The National Organization for Women leaped into the fray and filed an *amicus curiae* (friend of the court) brief, claiming that compulsory military service is central to the concept of citizenship in a democracy. If women were to gain "first-class citizenship," they, too, must have the right to fight, NOW attorneys argued before the Supreme Court.

Laws excluding women from draft registration and combat duty perpetuated "archaic notions" of women's capabilities, NOW declared. "Moreover, devastating long-term psychological and political repercussions are being forced on women," given their exclusion from draft registration.

Captain Kathy Whitworth, a tactical officer at the U.S. Military Academy, articulated the opinion of most women in the armed forces: "I get very upset when people make rules on what I will do. NOW, for instance, is lobbying for women in combat . . . I wish to hell they'd quit lobbying to get into combat. Don't lobby to send *me*; if they want to go, they should lobby for themselves!"[9]

In its *amicus*, the feminist Women's Equity Action League (WEAL) argued that combat exclusion laws for females were discriminatory and therefore unconstitutional. Women, WEAL argued, were not receiving an "equal division of societal obligations and duties."

On the other side of the coin, Eagle Forum, the group headed by Phyllis Schlafly, filed a "family-oriented" *amicus* on behalf of sixteen young women who claimed that they were not being deprived of their constitutional rights because they were not being included in the draft registration.

During the fall of 1980, while the Supreme Court was mulling over the landmark case, Jimmy Carter was locked in a heated campaign for reelection against the Republican challenger, Ronald Reagan, a former governor of California, who, prior to that, was a Hollywood movie actor. It was a classic confrontation: Carter, the staunch liberal, and Reagan, the resolute conservative.

While crisscrossing the nation, Reagan hammered at the alarming decline of America's armed forces during Carter's administration, and he vowed to greatly strengthen the national defense in the face of Communist threats, especially from the Soviet Union. The challenger pointed to what he said was the impotence of the Carter administration in dealing with the "Iranian crisis"—the fifty-four Americans were still being held hostage in Teheran.

Carter, in turn, charged that Reagan, who had served as an Air Force captain in World War II but not in combat, was a trigger-happy extremist who could drag the nation into a global war.

On November 4, Reagan swamped Carter at the polls, taking 51 percent of the vote to the incumbent's 41, and the Electoral College gave him 489 votes to Carter's 49.[10]

In his inaugural address on January 20, 1981, Ronald Reagan announced the beginning of "an era of national renewal." And he warned the "enemies of freedom, those who are potential aggressors," that, "when action is necessary to preserve our national security, we will act" and "we will maintain sufficient strength to prevail if need be."

As the new president concluded his speech at precisely 12:33 P.M., the government in Iran released the fifty-four Americans it had held for 444 days. Reagan sent Jimmy Carter to greet the returning hostages when they landed in Wiesbaden, West Germany.

President Reagan had hardly warmed his chair in the Oval Office than he began to rebuild the armed forces to protect the nation's security in what he described as a volatile and dangerous world.

"It is painfully true that the U.S. armed forces have been neglected to the point that their very ability to defend the nation's interests is in jeopardy," stated *Time* magazine. "The military is undermanned, under equipped, and underpaid."[11]

Time agreed with Reagan's solution to the monumental problem: a lot more money earmarked for national defense.

The new president's choice to put more muscle in the armed forces as secretary of defense was Caspar W. Weinberger, who had been Richard Nixon's director of the Office of Management and Budget. Weinberger, who held a law degree from Harvard University, was no novice to the armed forces. During World War II, he entered the Army as a private, served with the 41st Infantry Division in the Pacific, and was discharged as a captain on General MacArthur's intelligence staff.

Reagan had campaigned against ratification of the equal rights amendment, stating that its passage would cause more harm to women than it would benefit them. Therefore, advocates of expanded roles for females in the armed forces were convinced that women would lose the gains they had achieved after the new administration took over the White House.

Their concerns heightened when the *Air Force Times* reported that the Army and Air Force had covertly given to the Reagan transition team the previous December a report recommending that the Carter administration's plan to greatly increase the number of women in the armed forces be put on hold until its impact on combat readiness could be evaluated.[12]

Credence seemed to be given to that report when William D. Clark, the assistant secretary of the Army for manpower, was called to testify before the manpower subcommittee of the Senate Armed Services Committee in late February, only a month after Reagan took office. Clark said that the Army was reexamining the status of women soldiers, and that the service planned to hold the line with the 65,000 enlisted females then on duty.

Many in Congress were delighted with the decision. They felt that the Carter administration had rushed headlong into greatly increasing the number of women in the armed forces with little or no concern about how this expansion would impact combat readiness. Senator Roger W. Jepsen, the conservative chairman of the manpower subcommittee, declared, "Our armed forces are in being to provide the national security of the country and not to provide the foundation for any social experimentation."[13]

When Jepsen's analysis got big headlines in much of the media, liberal Senator William Proxmire fired back at Clark and the Army. Holding the line on the number of women in the armed forces "is counter to sound military policy as well as an infringement on the rights and obligations of citizenship," Proxmire said.

The senator also charged that the Army was seizing on the advent of the Reagan administration to engage in "a sinister plot to deny women equal pay, promotions, and enlistment rights." He said that "women can compete for just about every job in the military including actual combat."[14]

Five months after Ronald Reagan took the oath of office, the U.S. Supreme Court, in July 1981, ruled that the Constitution permits Congress to limit registration, and presumably the draft itself, to men. By a 6 to 3 margin, the high court thereby reversed the decision of the three-judge Federal District Court in Philadelphia handed down a year earlier.

Writing for the majority, Associate Justice William H. Rehnquist said that the District Court should have deferred to the Congressional judgment that the registration and drafting of women would be "detrimental to the important goal of military flexibility."

By federal law and by military policy, Rehnquist noted, women are not eligible to serve in combat positions. Therefore, he said, women were not as useful as men to the military, and Congress was free to take that difference into account when it refused to extend registration to women.

"This is not a case of Congress arbitrarily choosing to burden one or two similarly situated groups," Rehnquist said, "such as would be the case with an all-black or all-white, or an all-Catholic or an all-Lutheran, or an all-Republican or all-Democratic registration. Men and women, because of the combat restrictions on women, are simply not similarly situated for purposes of a draft or registration for a draft."[15]

In a dissenting opinion, Associate Justice Thurgood Marshall, the first black to sit on the Supreme Court, said that the majority's premise that "every draftee must be available for assignment to combat" was "demonstrably false."[16]

Reaction to the ruling ranged from conservative elation at the reassertion of traditional values to deep disappointment, even consternation, among feminist groups and civil libertarians.

Larry Speakes, the deputy White House press secretary, said President Reagan was "generally pleased."[17]

The Pentagon masked its euphoria by issuing a brief statement saying that the Defense Department was "pleased that there will be no disruptions of the Selective Service System."[18]

"This decision significantly damages the cause of women's rights," a spokesman for the American Civil Liberties Union declared. "It is a tragic decision."[19]

Feminist groups, including the National Organization for Women and the League of Women Voters, complained that women had been relegated to second-class citizens. Eleanor Smeal, president of NOW, said she detected in the decision signs of "a political tide that's essentially putting women back in their traditional place."[20]

Another feminist leader, Bella Abzug, a former member of Congress and now president of Women U.S.A., released a statement that said, in part: "I oppose draft registration and conscription for men and women . . . A conscript army in the service of the [Reagan] administration's militaristic and confrontational foreign policy is a fearful thought."[21]

Translation: Reagan was a warmonger.

On the other side of the political spectrum, Phyllis Schlafly, head of the Eagle Forum, said, "This decision is a tremendous victory for everything we've been fighting for. Thank God the ERA is not in the Constitution, or else the Supreme Court would have been compelled to hold that women must be drafted any time men are drafted, and the women would eventually wind up in combat."[22]

Soon after his inauguration, President Reagan was under pressure to reinstate the drafting of men. He hoped to increase the size of the armed forces by 10 percent, or 200,000 persons, by no later than early 1985. Pentagon brass had advised him that the goal was unreachable, pointing out that in 1979, for the first time since the All-Volunteer Force was established six years earlier, all four services had failed to reach their recruitment goals.

Keeping with his campaign pledge, Reagan refused to abolish the AVF concept. At the president's urging, Congress provided the funds to make military salaries more attractive for men and women (a new enlistee would soon earn $669 per month versus $217 in the Vietnam era). Greatly improved military housing, benefits, and medical care for dependents would permit the armed forces to compete with the private business sector.

A boon to potential female recruits, who generally fare better in academic standings, was that the services set higher admission standards: The ratio of recruits with high school diplomas became more than 96 percent, in contrast to 65 percent in 1973, the final year of the military draft.

The Army revamped and rigidly enforced procedures for evaluating officers and enlisted men and women. Those who did not rapidly adjust to military life or perform well enough to earn promotions within five years were washed out of the service. Said a Pentagon general: "If they don't perform at a certain level, we don't want them!"

U.S. Army nurses in World War I who served in mobile sterilizing units. (U.S. Army)

Yeomanettes at Portsmouth Navy Yard in New Hampshire during World War I. (U.S. Navy Historical Center)

Famed aviatrix Amelia Earhart glances back from the cockpit of her aircraft, being remodeled to hold scientific instruments of an undisclosed nature. This curious fact led to much speculation that she had been on a spying mission for President Franklin Roosevelt. 1937. (Lockheed)

Women Marines attach a depth bomb to the rack of an airplane at the Marine Corps Air Station, Quantico, Virginia. 1943. (National Archives)

Commander Mildred McAfee, World War II WAVE director. (U.S. Navy)

Colonel Oveta Culp Hobby, director of the WAC in World War II. (U.S. Army)

Navy WAVEs lower an airplane engine onto a block at the Naval Training School in Norman, Oklahoma. 1943. (U.S. Navy)

Coast Guard SPARs ensure that a parachute is packed correctly, a task that could save lives. 1943. (U.S. Coast Guard)

General Dwight D. Eisenhower was a booster of women serving in military support roles. With him is the most famous of the World War II WACs and his confidant, Lieutenant Kay Summersby. (U.S. Army)

A contingent of WACs stroll up the gangplank of a troop transport that would take them to Europe. 1943. (U.S. Army)

Air Corps General Ira C. Eaker was the first officer to request that a WAC battalion be sent to Europe. 1943. (U.S. Army)

Several Army nurses and a lady Red Cross worker were among those killed when German bombs hit this evacuation hospital on Anzio Beachhead. Fourteen other nurses were wounded 1944. (U.S. Army)

WASP Elisabeth Gardner in cockpit of B-26 bomber before takeoff. 1943. (U.S. Army)

WASP pilots after flight in B-17 Flying Fortress. Name on bomber nose is Pistol Packing Mama. 1944. (U.S. Air Force)

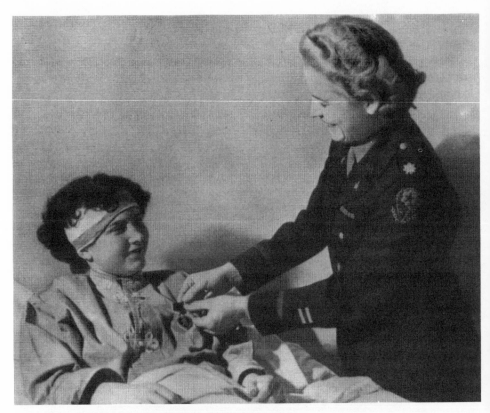

WAC Private First Class Dorothy Whitfield, wounded in service, receives the Purple Heart from Lieutenant Colonel Wilson, WAC director in Europe. 1944. (U.S. Army)

Colonel Jacqueline Cochran, director of Women's Air Service Pilots (WASP), pins coveted wings on recruit Iris Critchell. 1944. (U.S. Army)

Four nurses, among the first to arrive in Normandy after D-Day, take time out from their busy duties for a quick meal. 1944. (U.S. Army)

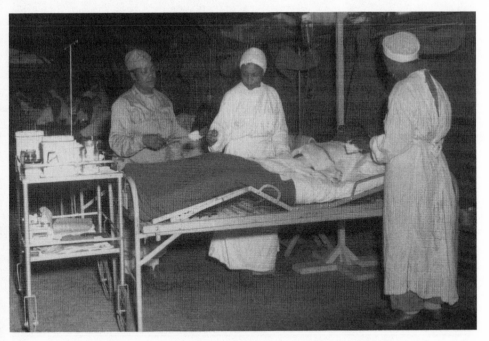

African-American Army nurses provide treatment in the surgical ward of a hospital in New Guinea. 1944. (National Archives)

A World War II Army flight nurse tends to wounded men during an air evacuation flight. 1944. (National Archives)

AGPD-C 200.6 Utinsky, Margaret
(14 Jun 46)

17 October 1946

Mrs. Margaret Utinsky
Apartment 402
1400 Fairmont Street, N. W.,
Washington, D. C.

Dear Mrs. Utinsky:

I have the honor to inform you that, by direction of the President, you have been awarded the Medal of Freedom for meritorious service in a civilian capacity with the United States Army. The citation pertaining to this award is as follows:

MEDAL OF FREEDOM

"Mrs. Margaret Utinsky, United States citizen, serving in a civilian capacity with the United States Army. For meritorious service which has aided the United States in the prosecution of the war against the enemy on Luzon, Philippine Islands, from May 1942 to March 1945. As a leader of the "Miss U" group, Luzon Guerrilla Army Forces, United States Army Forces in the far East, Mrs. Utinsky displayed outstanding heroism and fortitude in organizing missions which alleviated the bitter suffering of American Prisoners of War. Rendering extremely hazardous and valuable services, she resourcefully collected food and medicine from Manila civilians which she surreptitiously smuggled into prison camps, thereby saving hundreds of American lives. She was captured and tortured by the Japanese, but later valiantly returned to continue her merciful work until Manila was retaken by the Americans. Through her inspiring bravery and unfaltering devotion to duty, Mrs. Utinsky made a noteworthy contribution to the effectiveness of guerrilla warfare in the Philippine Islands."

The Medal of Freedom is being forwarded to the Commanding General, Military District of Washington, who will arrange for presentation. The officer selected to make the presentation will communicate with you to learn your wishes in the matter.

Sincerely yours,

Edward F. Witsell

EDWARD F. WITSELL
Major General
The Adjutant General

An American woman spy and guerrilla leader in the Philippines in World War II, Margaret Utinsky (Miss U), was honored by the government for her valor with the Medal of Freedom. (War Department)

WACs sort packages at the 17th Base Post Office in France. 1944. (National Archives)

Anna H. Rosenberg is sworn in as Assistant Secretary of Defense as her mentor, Secretary of Defense George C. Marshall (second from right), looks on. She was the first woman to hold a top position in the Pentagon. 1950. (U.S. Army)

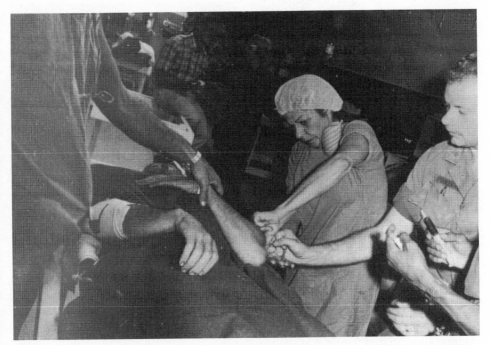

Hollywood star Martha Raye (Colonel Maggie) assisting at a forward aide station of the Green Berets during the Communists' Tet offensive in Vietnam. 1968. (U.S. Army)

In 1982, General H. Norman Schwarzkopf was given the task of attracting more women recruits into the Army. (U.S. Army)

Admiral Frank B. Kelso II, chief of naval operations during the Tailhook episode. (U.S. Navy)

Admiral Stanley R. Arthur retired early after approving washout of female pilot trainee. (U.S. Navy)

Admiral Jeremy M. Boorda replaced Kelso in the Navy hot-seat. He later took his own life. (U.S. Navy)

19 ❖ An Episode in Panama

Major General H. Norman Schwarzkopf III, a hulking man standing six feet three inches and weighing about 240 pounds, arrived in the Pentagon from an assignment in Germany. He would take over the post of director of military personnel and management in the office of the deputy chief of staff for personnel. It was June 1982. Schwarzkopf would gain a reputation among some fellow generals as "the guy carrying the banner for women's causes." It was a flawed analysis, but in his new job, Schwarzkopf would play a major role in advancing the opportunities for Army women, although he remained opposed to assigning them to combat units.

An outgoing, cheerful, yet demanding officer, Schwarzkopf graduated from West Point, where he was a tackle on the football team, in 1956. His first duty station was at Fort Campbell, Kentucky, as a paratroop lieutenant in the 101st "Screaming Eagles" Airborne Division. As a brigade commander in Vietnam, he gained a reputation as a tough, smart battle leader, and was awarded three Silver Stars for gallantry and two Purple Hearts for wounds.

Even as a two-star general, Schwarzkopf was virtually unknown outside the Army. Like many generals in peacetime, he seemed destined to eventually retire on a $50,000 annual pension and fade from public view. His late father, H. Norman, Jr., had been far more widely known. He had gained fame when, as the superintendent of the New Jersey State Police, he had been instrumental in cracking the Lindbergh baby kidnapping, the most notorious crime of the 1930s.

General Schwarzkopf was eager to confront the challenges ahead. It was an exciting time to hold a top personnel post, now that the Army was being strengthened and revitalized under President Reagan.

Schwarzkopf's new boss was Lieutenant General Maxwell Thurman, a thin, dynamic artilleryman who had earned his Army commission through ROTC at North Carolina State University. For more than a year as the Army's top personnel officer, Thurman had been busily overhauling the procedures that governed enlistment, reenlistment, pay, testing, bonuses, promotion, and retirement for everyone from private to four-star general.[1]

One of Thurman's principal actions was to open more jobs to women and make the Army more accessible to them. In 1982, women accounted for only 8 percent of recruits, and Thurman wanted to hike that number by expanding the hundreds of military occupational specialties that were mostly reserved for men. His first step was to create a study called "Women in the Army" to reassess policies on female soldiers.

When the report was finished, it recommended that the Army continue to exclude women from direct combat but immediately ease gender restrictions in noncombat specialties. The report created a stir, inside and outside the Army. But Thurman felt that the recommendations were sound and for the overall benefit of the Army, and he was determined to implement them. To make certain that the policy was carried out with the utmost speed, he put Norman Schwarzkopf in charge of the review process. Each branch of the service was ordered to send a general to the Pentagon to explain how the new gender rules would be applied by that branch.

Schwarzkopf would be a sort of traffic cop to ascertain if each branch would be driving along the guidelines that Thurman wanted. Most of the branches didn't want expanded roles for women, and the general in command of each would present convoluted arguments as to how various jobs would expose women soldiers to direct combat.

Many of the generals became upset with Schwarzkopf when he turned thumbs down on their arguments for keeping women out of their branches. One branch, the military police, said that its wartime mission would be to guard airports, docks, and shipping terminals. Therefore, it was argued, these security outfits might be engaged in direct combat because they might have to fight saboteurs and spies. Schwarzkopf, however, saw to it that the no-women policy applied only to those branches where there was routinely a high probability of direct combat.[2]

While the Pentagon was devising means to get larger numbers of females into uniform, the Defense Advisory Committee on Women in the Services was upset by General Thurman's "Women in the Army" study that had recommended continuing the exclusion of females from direct-combat units. Even though the conservative Reagan administration had taken over the White House, the all-female DACOWITS maintained its liberal ideological bent, mainly because members served three-year terms and new ones were appointed on the recommendation of the outgoing members.

In April 1983, DACOWITS demanded that the Army create what it called "an objective panel" of "mostly women" to examine the plan for utilizing females and report its findings to the Army secretary. This group should be headed by a retired woman general and fully staffed with active-duty and former female officers. DACOWITS also decided to have its board send a letter to Secretary of Defense Caspar Weinberger explaining how the probability-based combat exclusion for women "deprives our Army of many skilled soldiers."[3]

DACOWITS Chairwoman Mary E. Huey, president of Texas Women's University, signed the letter and sent it to Weinberger on June 6. The document stressed that combat exclusion had an adverse effect on promotion opportunities and morale for females. It charged that the Army's definition of combat was obsolete. Modern combat, said DACOWITS, was "of a fluid—and frequently remote—character."

In his carefully worded reply, Weinberger assured DACOWITS that the Department of Defense was committed to ensuring that "women will be provided maximum opportunities to realize their individual potential." He stated that the Army's desire to exclude women from positions with a high risk of being involved in combat was consistent with the view of most Americans.[4]

During the eight years Ronald Reagan served in the White House, his loyal vice president was George W. Bush. Although the two men differed on a few major issues—the equal rights amendment, which failed to gain ratification, for one—they quickly established a warm working relationship. In 1988, it was Bush's turn: He became the Republican nominee for president, and in November, he scored a lopsided victory over Massachusetts Governor Michael S. Dukakis, receiving 426 of the 538 electoral votes.

No U.S. president had ever been sworn into office with such relevant credentials as were those of George Bush. During World War II, as a twenty-year-old Navy pilot, he had been shot down, landed in the ocean, and nearly drowned before being rescued. After the war, he obtained a law degree from Yale, and later served as a congressman, ambassador to the United Nations, envoy to Communist China, director of the Central Intelligence Agency, and vice president.

In the months after George Bush's inauguration in January 1989, tension between the United States and Panama thickened. Since the previous May, the two countries had been on a collision course. At that time, Panama held a free election and a moderate civilian leader, Guillermo Endara, became president.

General Manuel Antonio Noriega, backed by a military junta, announced that the election was nullified and proclaimed himself Panama's maximum leader. Then, in early December, he declared that a "state of war" existed with the United States. "We, the Panamanian people, will sit along the banks of the [Panama] Canal to watch the dead bodies of our enemies pass by," Noriega trumpeted.[5]

Twenty-four hours later, on the night of December 16, four off-duty U.S. officers got lost while driving to a restaurant in Panama City. The car was stopped at a checkpoint of Noriega's 12,000–member Panama Defense Forces (PDF). A Panamanian soldier opened the door and tried to drag out one of the Americans, as an angry crowd of hooting civilians surrounded the vehicle. The car sped away and the PDF men opened fire, killing Marine Lieutenant Robert Paz.

A U.S. Navy lieutenant and his wife witnessed the shooting. Moments later, the couple was grabbed by the PDF, blindfolded, and hauled off to headquarters. There a senior PDF officer walked into the room and, without a word, slugged the American in the mouth and kicked him in the crotch. Then, in the words of a President Bush aide, they "beat the hell out of him."[6]

In an adjoining room, the Navy officer's wife was brutalized. The PDF men said they were going to gang-rape her, and they forced her to stand up against a wall for a half-hour until she collapsed. Then they slammed her head against the floor.

At a White House meeting, President Bush was horrified by the story. Finally, he said in a calm voice, "Enough is enough."[7]

General Colin Powell, chairman of the Joint Chiefs of Staff, dusted off Operation Blue Spoon, a plan drawn up during the Reagan administration for a military takeover of Panama. Bush bought the plan. Secretary of Defense Dick Cheney renamed it Operation Just Cause.

Shortly before midnight on Tuesday, December 19, 1989, guests in Panama City's ornate Marriott Caesar Park Hotel were awakened by sporadic gunfire. A team of elite U.S. Navy SEALs were storming the nearby private Paitilla Airport, where Manuel Noriega kept a getaway Learjet. Four SEALs were killed.

The invasion of Panama by a combined force of 24,000 American Rangers, Marines, paratroopers, SEALs, and soldiers had been launched. Because speed and surprise were crucial to success of the mission and to save American lives, President Bush had approved a Pentagon request not to inform the media until the operation was well underway.

Hours before the invasion hit, a Pentagon-sanctioned pool of reporters was hastily summoned to Andrews Air Force Base outside Washington, D.C. Only then were the newsies and cameramen told about Just Cause. Briefing officers stressed that there was a critical need for the strictest secrecy.

Just Cause was the largest and the smoothest United States airborne operation since World War II, a tribute to Pentagon planners and the courage and skills of the combat leaders and their men. In one lightning stroke, Manuel Noriega was removed from power, a new democratic government was given a chance to take root, some 12,000 American citizens living in Panama were protected from potential harm, and the crucial Panama Canal was safeguarded.

In addition, the invaders also seized 48,000 weapons that might one day have been turned against United States soldiers and civilians in Panama or sent to El Salvador as part of Noriega's gunrunning to left-wing rebels there.

In the wake of the Panama invasion, a headline in the *Atlanta Constitution* stated:

FOR FIRST TIME, A WOMAN
LEADS G.I.'S IN COMBAT

A day earlier, Marlin Fitzwater, President Bush's press secretary, had told White House correspondents that Army Captain Linda L. Bray, the commander of a military police unit already stationed in Panama at the time of the invasion, had been ordered to take a group of her male soldiers to capture a dog kennel that was heavily defended by Panamanian troops.

"It was an important military operation," Fitzwater explained. "A woman led it, and she did an outstanding job."[8]

Fitzwater did not say what had been so "important" about capturing several "enemy" dogs.

A flood of stories that portrayed Linda Bray as a present-day Amazon warrior appeared in scores of newspapers in the United States. Scripps Howard News Service, which first broke the story, described in riveting detail how a three-hour firefight erupted when she and her men attacked the dog kennel, and how she had crashed through a fence in her jeep to come to grips with the enemy force.

When the fierce shootout ceased and the kennel had been captured, media reports stated, there were many dead Panamanian soldiers strewn about. A post-battle interview with Captain Bray quoted her as saying, "I joined the Army for the excitement, the challenge, and loyalty to my country."[9]

Advocates of placing women in combat units were elated over the Linda Bray story. Columnist Anna Quindlen no doubt sought to reinforce the feminist contention that body strength is of no significance in fighting by pointing out that Bray was five feet, one inch tall and weighed a little more than one hundred pounds.

"Captain Bray gave women in the Army a chance to [do the job]", Quindlen stated. "She came, she saw, she conquered."[10]

Patricia Schroeder, chairperson of the House Armed Services subcommittee on personnel, rushed before the television cameras to say that the attack led by Captain Bray demonstrated that women should be allowed to carry out direct-combat roles. Schroeder disclosed she planned to introduce legislation enabling Army women to assume all military roles, including direct combat.

Only hours after Marlin Fitzwater told White House reporters of Captain Bray's exploit, the *Los Angeles Times* splashed cold water on the episode. There had been no fierce, three-hour shootout, there had been no dead Panamanian soldiers around the dog kennel, and Captain Bray had been at her command post half a mile away when a few random shots erupted. She had not crashed the kennel gate at the head of her men, nor had she led a charge by her men.

In the wake of the *Times'* disclosure, U.S. Army commanders in Panama promptly gagged military women from speaking to the media. A Defense Department spokeswoman in the Pentagon, Major Kathy Wood, said she did not know why females in Panama were not being allowed to talk to the press.

Brigadier General Charles W. McClain, the Army's deputy chief of public affairs, said that he had spoken to Captain Bray, who told him she did not know where the reports about the firefight and the dead Panamanians had come from. "She told me that when she and her troops left some time after daylight, there were no bodies," he said.[11]

Meanwhile, the Panama episode left egg on faces in the White House, the Army, and in newsrooms across the nation. In the White House, an embarrassed Marlin Fitzwater admitted to correspondents that his riveting recitation of how the female captain had led her men on the charge against a heavily-defended dog kennel had been taken from newspaper accounts.

20 ❖ Scud Missiles, Culture Problems, and POWs

Four-star General H. Norman Schwarzkopf was climbing onto an exercise bike in his quarters at Tampa's MacDill Air Force Base when the telephone jangled impatiently. On the line was General Colin Powell, chairman of the Joint Chiefs of Staff, who was calling from the Pentagon. Powell said evenly, "They've crossed the border."

Schwarzkopf knew who "they" were—the Iraqi army of dictator Saddam Hussein. The "border" was Kuwait's. It was the last week of July 1990.

For weeks, Saddam had been rattling his saber and accusing the tiny kingdom of Kuwait of "robbing" him of $2.5 billion from oil fields the two nations had been operating jointly. Hussein told the world that Kuwait had shoved a "poisoned dagger" into his back. Kuwait's "greed," Saddam claimed, had prompted its rulers "to conspire with the United States and Israeli imperialists to sabotage Iraq."

Still wearing his warm-up suit, Schwarzkopf rushed to the communications center of his Central Command, the headquarters responsible for much of the Middle East in the event trouble erupted there that might require U.S. action. Grim-faced, the general searched for news from the Persian Gulf powder keg. For hours, there was no news. Then, about 9:00 P.M. (4:00 A.M. in the Middle East), Major John F. Feeley, a member of a U.S. security-assistance team, called from a satellite radio that linked the U.S. embassy in Kuwait directly with Tampa. Feeley said matter of factly: "The Iraqis are in downtown Kuwait City."

Major Feeley then climbed to the roof of the embassy and gave Schwarzkopf and his staff a running, blow-by-blow account of the battle unfolding below him.

Colin Powell directed Schwarzkopf to come to Washington immediately to join with the National Security Council in briefing President Bush. Schwarzkopf bore responsibility for U.S. military operations in the part of the Middle East where war had erupted. His Central Command was largely an administrative and planning headquarters, but in the event of armed conflict, a potent array of Army, Air Force, and Marine units were earmarked for it.

A seemingly endless series of conferences involving Bush took place in the days ahead. The president stressed that Iraqi aggression could not be allowed to go unchallenged by the United States and the rest of the world. There also was another haunting specter confronting Bush. As soon as Saddam had conquered Kuwait, he no doubt would send his army plunging into neighboring Saudi Arabia, whose plethora of oil fields stoked the industry of the United States and many other countries.

Saddam had a powerful force at his disposal. Among the world's armies, his ranked in size behind only those of China, the Soviet Union, and Vietnam—the United States ranked seventh. Saddam's weapons, including hundreds of Soviet T-72 tanks, were some of the best the international arms dealers had to sell. Holding off Saddam from overrunning Saudi Arabia, it seemed clear, would be a bloody affair.

On the night of August 8 (U.S. time), President Bush appeared on television and told the American people that the United States was drawing "a line in the sand" against Iraqi aggression. Twenty-four hours earlier, he had set in motion the largest U.S. armed forces deployment since Vietnam, an action that could lead to a bitter war in the vastness of the Arabian wasteland. The defensive operation had been given the code name Desert Shield.

In the aftermath of Bush's disclosure, the customary "Pentagon sources" were telling the media that U.S. forces in Saudi Arabia would be "impregnable" by that weekend. The upbeat pronouncement was a hoax intended to cause Saddam to hesitate in the event he planned to make a dash for the rich Saudi oil fields, only 200 miles from Kuwait City. Actually, only several hundred paratroopers of the 82nd Airborne Division would be flown into Saudi Arabia by the weekend. These men called themselves the "speed bumps"—meaning that their job was to slow the Iraqi forces if they plunged into Saudi.

Women have participated in virtually every American military crisis since the Revolutionary War, but never had females served in such a wide spectrum of tasks as they would in the Persian Gulf. As the massive deployment continued, women mechanics of the 24th Mechanized Infantry Division were maintaining tanks and others were coordinating the water supply and handling fuel. Female pilots of the 101st Airborne Division were ferrying supplies and troops in Huey helicopters. Women were involved as truck drivers, intelligence specialists, communications experts, flight controllers, cargo handlers, and other tasks.

In the meantime, the Pentagon announced that 50,000 reservists were being called to active duty within the next few weeks. Air Force Captain Sue Barry, a trauma nurse at a Chicago hospital, predicted that she would be one of the large number of reserve medical specialists to augment the nurses in the regular services already in the Gulf or on their way there. Barry graphically described her specialty handling of severe casualties in time of armed conflict as "plug 'em up, plug 'em in, and keep 'em alive is as best we can." She held no illusions about her role in the war zone: The wounds she and her medical unit would see "will be our worst nightmare."[1]

Never had so many American "moms" gone off to war. In her tiny office in a medical evacuation unit in Saudi Arabia, Major Kathy Higgins pinned up a crayon drawing by her son, age five. Some military women tore up photos of their children—it was just too difficult to look at them.

Lieutenant Colonel Carolyn Roaf, a medical officer, had the most emotional experience of her life when she said goodbye to her six-year-old daughter—especially after the child told her, "Mom, if you die over there, I'm coming to rescue you."

Desert Shield also brought in many military women who were married to servicemen. After arriving in Saudi, Army ordnance specialist Karen Norrington learned that her husband also was being shipped over, but in a different unit. She spent much of her off-duty hours scanning the ranks of arriving soldiers at a receiving point.

Kim and Robert Williams considered themselves fortunate: They were stationed together. Said Kim: "The worst part is not knowing how long we'll be away from our kids. Maybe they won't remember us when we get home."[2]

As the weeks passed, for the male grunts at outposts in the northern desert, the "war" was a tale of deep pride, lost mail, long waits, and dark fear of the unknown. They knew that the shortest road home from Saudi Arabia cuts through Iraq-occupied Kuwait. But the prospect of traveling along it filled the grunts with dread.

It was a nuisance to lug around gas masks and protective gear, but no one complained. For the troops on the ground, the greatest fear was of a poisoned-gas attack, a strike by the enemy they couldn't see. Near the gas-monitoring machines and scattered around the bases were live chickens. If the birds were seen keeled over, gas masks went on.

Military women in the rear shared these worries. "I'm scared as hell most of my waking hours," one female Army corporal said. Saddam's vaunted Scud missiles with their presumed poisoned-gas warheads could easily reach far into the rear area. "Anyone who says she isn't scared is lying to herself," said Lieutenant Stephanie Shaw, who helped control missions for a tactical air wing.

A constant reminder of the threat of chemical attack was the protective gear the women wore at all times, just like the men. Most of the females also toted weapons and were trained to use them if need be.

In Saudi Arabia, U.S. military women were confronted by a problem not related to their military duties—the clash of cultures with their Muslim hosts, who practiced the religion of Islam, founded by Mohammed in the

A.D. 600s. Mohammed preached the punishment of unbelievers and evil-doers. In a country where a woman is forbidden to drive an automobile, reveal her face in public, or venture out alone, soldiers in the Saudi army didn't know what to make of female GIs clad in fatigues and sometimes issuing orders to *men*.

Female GIs unloading medical cartons in a hot warehouse took off their jackets and labored in their T-shirts. Angry letters and telephone calls from civilians poured into U.S. military headquarters, complaining about shameless American women disrobing in public view. Saudi women were never allowed to show even their arms in the presence of other people.

Early on, General Schwarzkopf had assured Lieutenant General Prince Khalid Bin Sultan al-Saud, a tall, heavy-set man Saudi King Fahd had appointed as the U.S. commander's counterpart, that female entertainers were not going to be brought into the country. A few weeks later, Schwarzkopf received a frantic call from Prince Khalid: "I must see you right away!"

Thinking that the Iraqis must have launched an assault somewhere in Saudi Arabia, Schwarzkopf rushed to see the prince, with whom he had struck a friendly relationship. "You've got dancing girls entertaining your troops in Dhahran!" Khalid exclaimed.

"We don't have any dancing girls," the general replied.

Khalid was almost apoplectic. "It's on CNN," he replied. "Those pictures are being shown, and you must order them taken off the TV!"[3]

Puzzled, Schwarzkopf returned to his headquarters and told an aide to "find out what in the hell this is all about. And get me a videotape of whatever's being shown."

A few hours later, the general was viewing the tape. The focus was only on the women dancers' bare legs. In the front row, clearly visible to the camera eye, were paratroopers of the 82nd Airborne Division, clapping furiously, shouting encouragement, and waving their arms.

Schwarzkopf ordered his aides to look into the situation. They returned and said the dancing females were not professional entertainers or military women, but were American employees of the Arabian-American Oil Company (Aramco), a Saudi-owned corporation in Dhahran. Some Aramco employees had put together an amateur show for the GIs to make them feel at home.[4]

Two more shows were scheduled for succeeding nights. Schwarzkopf ordered them cancelled before they triggered a total disruption of U.S.-Saudi relations.

Despite the flap over the "dancing girls," the Saudis made some concessions from their ancient culture. U.S. military women eventually were permitted to drive vehicles while on duty; and at one air base they could use a gymnasium during limited hours, but they had to enter through the back door. However, they were not permitted to wear bathing suits or even shorts, jog, or shop unless accompanied by a man.

Many U.S. military women didn't have it too bad, all things considered. Some were quartered in air-conditioned buildings and Saudi schools, as well as in mobile homes. However, boredom quickly took root: There were no movies, no television, no recreational facilities. So females, as with males out in the northern desert, rediscovered that they could read books and engage in conversations during off-duty hours.[5]

By New Year's Day 1991, U.S. intelligence, mainly through satellites and other sophisticated means, estimated that Saddam had a powerful force of 545,000 men, 4,300 tanks, 3,100 artillery pieces, and about 35 mobile Scud launchers in the Kuwaiti theater. (Later some U.S. intelligence sources would state that the actual Iraqi troop strength was nearer 250,000.)

Iraqi defensive positions, called the Saddam Line by Schwarzkopf's headquarters, extended along the entire southern border of Kuwait and forty miles farther west along the border of Iraq—a total of 175 miles. Saddam and his generals apparently were unconcerned over their right (western) flank dangling in the desert, no doubt expecting Schwarzkopf to smash directly against the Saddam Line. When the assault came, Saddam boasted over Radio Baghdad, it would result in the "mother of all battles."

Meanwhile in New York City, the United Nations Security Council authorized the United States and other members of the Desert Shield coalition to "use all necessary means" to expel Iraqi forces from Kuwait if they did not withdraw by January 15, 1991. Saddam ignored the deadline. As a result, Operation Desert Storm was launched on January 17, when U.S. air forces were joined by coalition planes in heavily pounding hundreds of Iraqi targets in Kuwait and Iraq.

For many days and nights, millions of Americans sat comfortably in their homes and were mesmerized by the dominant television image of the Gulf air war that showed grainy clips, cross-hairs bouncing slightly as a tiny bomb headed for a tiny building, and (slight pause) a tiny puff of smoke exploding across the screen. The graphic pictures made the war seem remote and bloodless—even entertaining.

All eyes—including Saddam's, no doubt—were focused on the air pyrotechnics. At the same time, Schwarzkopf was secretly launching his ground battle plan, the key ingredient of which he later would call "my Hail Mary play"—a left hook far to the west around the open flank of the Saddam Line. In a near-miracle of logistics, 200,000 troops (mostly Americans), their vehicles, supplies, ammunition, guns, tanks, and helicopters were shifted 300 miles to the west along a single road, without tipping Saddam to the maneuver.

By early February, there were more than 37,000 military women in the Kuwaiti Theater of Operations (KTO), making up approximately 6.8 percent of the total U.S. troop strength. Roughly, 26,000 Army, 3,700 Navy, 2,200 Marine Corps, and 5,300 Air Force women were deployed. For the first time in American history, the majority of these women were not nurses.

One of the female Army soldiers, Specialist Melissa Rathbun-Nealy, was driving a heavy-equipment transport across the trackless desert when she apparently missed a turn on the narrow Tapline Road, over which Schwarzkopf was secretly shuttling his forces, bumper to bumper, far to the west. She drove northward and failed to return to her unit. General Schwarzkopf only knew that she was missing and ordered a search for her. It was in vain; Melissa Rathbun-Nealy was already at an Iraqi command post—the first American female soldier to be taken prisoner in Desert Storm.

It was dark and a cold rain was pelting nervous Marines as they crouched at their line of departure on the far right of the UN line. Suddenly, the silence was shattered. Scores of big howitzers began to roar and fiery orange muzzle blasts pierced the blackness. With M-60 tanks and Cobra helicopters in the lead, thousands of Marines, many in armored personnel carriers and other vehicles, charged through Iraqi defenses and poured across the Saudi border into Kuwait. It was 4:00 A.M. on February 24—G-Day.

While the Marines were heading north along the Persian Gulf coast road in the east, Schwarzkopf's "Hail Mary play," the assault around the western open flank of the Saddam Line, had been launched. Although delayed for a short time by rain and fog, Major General Binford Peay's 101st Airborne Division was engaged in the largest helicopter attack in history. More than 300 Cobra, Black Hawk, Apache, Chinook, and Huey choppers piloted mostly by men and some women, were transporting an entire brigade (4,000 men) with its humvees, howitzers, and mountains of fuel and ammunition fifty miles northward into Iraq. There the brigade set up a base from which attack helicopters could easily strike the Euphrates Valley, behind the Saddam Line.

On February 27, the fourth day of the ground war, a Black Hawk helicopter with a crew of seven took off on a search-and-rescue mission across the trackless Iraqi desert. An Air Force F-16 jet fighter pilot, Captain Bill Andrews, had been shot down in Iraq and was in radio contact with a U.S. command post. Andrews said he had a broken leg and possible other injuries. It was clear that if the Black Hawk team did not reach him soon, he would be captured.

A passenger in the low-flying chopper was thirty-six-year-old Rhonda L. Cornum, an Army doctor assigned to the 2–229th Attack Helicopter Battalion, which was attached to the 101st Airborne Division. Her services would be needed for the injured Captain Andrews when he was located.

There was an element of danger in the mission because of the fluid situation—a description used, so said the grunts, when the generals weren't certain where enemy forces were located.

Growing up, Rhonda Cornum had been a high school cheerleader in East Aurora, New York, a suburb of Buffalo. She loved animals and dreamed of becoming a veterinarian. But after receiving her bachelor's and master's degrees in biochemistry, she joined the military. The Army financed her studies for a doctorate at Cornell University, and she became a specialist in urology.

An adventurous type, Cornum qualified as a paratrooper and a pilot, and in 1987 she was among the 100 finalists in the National Aeronautics and Space Administration's search for future astronauts. Her husband, Air Force Captain Kory Cornum, was also a doctor in the Persian Gulf, stationed 700 miles from his wife's location.

Now, a short time after the Black Hawk had taken off to find and rescue Captain Bill Andrews, the desert landscape erupted with white flashes of light and streams of bullets hissed past the chopper. Fired from a complex of bunkers, the Iraqi antiaircraft guns followed the Black Hawk as its pilot cut sharply to the left to take evasive action.

Then something struck the Black Hawk. It shook and shimmied. Suddenly, 20,000 pounds of helicopter hit the sand. Five of the men, including the pilot, were dead. Two other crewmen miraculously escaped without serious injuries. Major Cornum received two broken arms and blacked out.[6]

Moments later, the doctor regained consciousness and tried to wriggle out from under the wreckage. She became aware that four or five Iraqi soldiers, armed with AK-47 assault rifles, were standing over her. They began speaking in Arabic, apparently trying to decide what to do with her. Like all the American military women, Cornum had heard stories about what the Iraqis would do if they captured the "infidels." They'd heard about the sexual abuse inflicted on the women of Kuwait by Iraqi soldiers, raping and torturing them and foreign females living there.

In the meantime, under the powerful, trip-hammer blows of the coalition forces, Saddam's vaunted army began to crumble. Iraqi soldiers were surrendering in wholesale lots—some 80,000 of them. Amazingly, only one American had been killed in the assault. By Wednesday, the fourth day of the gound war, the Iraqis were in complete disarray and badly beaten.

Back in Washington, President Bush assembled his war council. General Colin Powell told him, "By tonight, there really won't be an enemy there. If you go on another day, you're basically just fighting stragglers." Another adviser suggested that Bush announce a cease-fire on Thursday, G-Day plus 5. "I'd like to do it tonight," the president replied. "Check this out with Norm."

Powell picked up the White House direct line that connected the president to the commander in the Gulf. Schwarzkopf quickly agreed. One of Bush's men noticed that a cease-fire set for midnight would mark exactly 100 hours of ground fighting. Bush liked the idea.

At midnight, the guns fell silent in the Persian Gulf. True to form, Saddam Hussein immediately took to Radio Baghdad and claimed victory.

On the day before the ground assault began, Major Marie T. Rossi, an Army helicopter pilot, had been interviewed on Cable News Network (CNN), which flashed her image to millions of homes across the United States. "When I saw her on television it made the war seem personal to me," said Marie Smith, a resident of Rossi's hometown of Oradell, New Jersey. "Prior to that, I didn't know anybody over there. Now I felt I knew her."[7]

Just over a week later, on a Sunday night, Oradell residents were shocked. Again Marie Rossi's picture was on television screens, but this time, it was reported that she had been killed in a helicopter crash the day after the cease-fire. All along the streets of the small community about twelve miles from Manhattan, residents quickly festooned trees with yellow ribbons and hundreds of American flags were displayed, many of them at half-staff.[8]

A few days after General Schwarzkopf signed an official cease-fire document with Iraqi commanders at Safwan, north of Kuwait City, on March 3, Baghdad released the thirty-five prisoners of war it had been holding, including seventeen Americans, and they were flown to Saudia Arabia. Among those on board were Captain Bill Andrews, the F-16 pilot the search-and-rescue team had set out to find; two surviving crewmen on the crashed Black Hawk, Sergeant Troy Dunlap and Staff Sergeant Daniel Stamaris, and Major Rhonda Cornum. On hand to greet the former POWs at the Riyadh airport was General Norman Schwarzkopf.

As Cornum emerged from the airliner, Schwarzkopf was standing there. She instinctively tried to salute, but both of her arms were in casts. "I'm sorry, sir," she said. "I normally salute four-star generals."

After her capture, Major Cornum later said, Iraqi soldiers transported her in a pickup truck to a small prison. While in the truck, she was sexually molested by one of her captors. A male prisoner had to watch helplessly. "You don't expect to be raped when you walk down the streets of your hometown," Cornum added, "but it is an occupational hazard of going to war, and you make the decision whether or not you are going to take that risk when you join the military."[9]

On March 10, seventeen days after she had been taken prisoner, Rhonda Cornum, along with her husband Kory and the other American POWs, lifted off in an airplane for Andrews Air Force Base outside Washington, D.C. When the craft landed, the freed captives were greeted by a throng of thousands. Among them were Secretary of Defense Dick Cheney, Joint Chiefs of Staff Chairman Colin Powell, and a galaxy of other generals. Powell remembered: "I will never forget that day. Rhonda came off the plane with her arms crossed in front of her where she had been injured. Secretary Cheney and I couldn't have been more proud."

Desert Storm had been one of the most astonishing battle victories in history, not only for the brief period of time it had taken one huge army to conquer another large army, but for the minimum number of U.S. casualties. Three hundred and five Americans died from accidents, disease, and combat during Operations Shield/Storm. Eleven of the dead were women, five due to enemy action.

21 ❖ "We're Talking About the Battlefront"

From Bangor, Maine, to San Diego, California, the victorious troops of Desert Storm were welcomed by Americans with tumultuous homecoming celebrations of a kind not seen since World War II. Although it would be months before all 540,000 American servicemen and -women in the Gulf came home, the arrival of the first few thousand touched off widespread displays of pride and patriotism.

Long before all of the 37,000 women were brought back, a clamor erupted from feminist groups and their supporters in Congress to remove all restrictions barring women from combat. There would be no waiting for the Pentagon to conduct studies on the tangible contributions that women had achieved in the Gulf or on the multitude of problems involved during their deployment. Rather, the combat-now activists felt that it was time to strike, while most Americans held television-spawned images of women soldiers garbed in camouflage uniforms and steel helmets, and thought that they actually had been engaged in frontline fighting.

Consequently, during the last week of April 1991—a bare two months since the end of the brief conflict in the desert—DACOWITS convened in suburban Washington. Its members were highly confident that the current political climate was ideal for demanding that Congress repeal the forty-three-year-old law that excluded women from combat. Five American women had been killed by hostile action and two had been captured briefly in the Gulf, so females already had shared the risks, most of the DACOWITS' members pointed out. So let the women fight equally alongside the men. Let women be warriors, too.

Four women on the advisory committee did not hold that belief. They argued against daughters, wives, and mothers being hurled into the caldron of armed conflict. One of the dissenting panelists, Eunice Ray, declared that the theory of equality is admirable in nearly all facets of American life, but it has no place on the battlefield, in hostile skies, or on perilous oceans, where the issue could be living or dying, winning or losing a war.

Calling a vote at this time was "ill advised and premature," Ray argued. She urged postponing any recommendation to repeal the exclusion law until DACOWITS received more detailed information from Pentagon studies.

Ray said she feared a repeal would have a bad effect on American families. "Women may have to [eventually] register for the draft," she said. "And if they do, we're not just talking about the homefront anymore; we're talking about the battlefront."[1]

The few voices calling for restraint were soon stifled. By a vote of 29 to 4, DACOWITS recommended the removal of the combat exclusion law that would lead to assignments "based on ability rather than gender, greater opportunities for women to compete for promotions, and acceptance of women as full partners in the armed forces."

When the result of the secret balloting was announced by DACOWITS President Becky Constantino, the 300 largely feminist activists in the audience erupted with whoops of triumph. When the raucous cheering dwindled, Constantino said in a shaky voice: "I worked very hard during this conference not to let my emotions get to me—and you just blew it!"[2]

Again the room was filled with hurrahs of approval.

"The combat exclusion is the final barrier," Jeanne Holm, a retired Air Force major general and long an ardent advocate of women being in the cockpit of combat aircraft, declared. "It's the linchpin for everything else."[3]

Before adjourning, DACOWITS agreed to take direct action to get women in the forefront of fighting in future wars or lesser armed conflicts. Although the role assigned to the committee in 1951 had been to advise the secretary of defense on women's issues in the armed forces, members now planned to lobby their home-state senators and representatives, and President Constantino arranged to testify before a subcommittee of the Senate Armed Services Committee in July.

So eager was the feminist majority of DACOWITS to charge ahead with its women-in-combat offensive that they failed to find out how those most directly concerned felt about the issue—the servicewomen who would bear the burden. "Congress should not repeal the exclusion law until each soldier is home [from the Gulf], off leave, and able to give her side of the story," Captain Gloria Nickerson told a reporter. A qualified paratrooper based at Fort Bragg, Lieutenant Sandra Nieland, who spent six months in the Gulf, agreed: "The smart thing is to research all the problems before Congress acts."[4]

Few of the women who served in the Gulf recommended the experience, retired Colonel David Hackworth, the Army's most highly-decorated soldier in Vietnam who covered the Gulf conflict for *Newsweek* discovered. Soon after they returned, some 500 women of the airborne service at Fort Bragg were interviewed by Hackworth.

"All knew they had not been in real combat like World War II, Korea, or Vietnam," Hackworth said. "And none wanted anything to do with living in the trenches. All knew from being near the front that war is not a push-button, romantic game that ends at 5:00 P.M., when everyone goes home for a shower and a change into something pretty."[5]

Hackworth, who, years earlier, had been left for dead on a Korean battlefield, added:

> Most of these dedicated female grunts said all the talk about women having the same opportunity as guys on the battlefield was from Patricia Schroeder types and senior Army officers who would never have to live in the muddy, high-risk killing fields. These women soldiers said their becoming cannon fodder was a bad move for them, but a good thing for those female military officers who need to climb the ladder to stardom and glory at their expense.[6]

Hackworth added that hundreds of other women soldiers he had interviewed while covering Desert Shield and Desert Storm were "committed to serving America, but in jobs according to their ability."

Army Major Richard A. Kidd found an identical reaction when he asked a group of 200 women soldiers if they had the option, would they choose a combat MOS [military occupational specialty]. Only three raised their hands.

Although Desert Storm brought its stories of valiant women soldiers, most females who had to live through the difficult conditions didn't appreciate the homefront feminists' candy-coated versions of their experiences, said Trudy Hutchens, assistant editor of *Family Voice* magazine. Hutchens singled out Sergeant Wendy Thornton as typical. In October 1990, during Desert Shield, Thornton drove five-ton tractor-trailers through the scorching sands, hauling water.

"Those feminists who say we women have a right to fight were not sitting out there in the heat, carrying an M-16 rifle and a gas mask, spending sixteen hours on the road every day, and sleeping in fear you're going to be gassed," Sergeant Thornton declared.[7]

After returning to Fort Bragg from the Gulf, paratrooper Master Sergeant Penny Sweeny pointed out that "only a tiny minority [of military women] want combat units. Women don't grow up playing with GI Joe dolls."[8]

Another Desert Storm veteran, Major Kathleen Shields, a seventeen-year reservist, was angry about legislation introduced by Representative Patricia Schroeder that would wipe out the combat exclusion for women. Shields snapped to reporters: "Tell Schroeder to get out of my boots! She's never been in the service and doesn't know what she's talking about!"[9]

On April 23, at the same time DACOWITS was meeting elsewhere in Washington, another conference was being held in the Russell Senate Office Building to discuss what was learned from the Gulf war. Sponsored by the Center for Defense Journalism at Boston University and the Rockford Institute, a so-called think tank, the debate was heated and focused on the topic of women being assigned to combat duties.

The active-duty and retired women officers participating in the discussions said the combat-exclusion statute should be eliminated. Captain Terry VandenHolder, who flew C-141 Starlifters loaded with troops and cargo between the United States and Saudi Arabia, declared, "Women serving in combat is a moot point. We were there."[10]

Captain Carol Barkalow, a thirty-two-year-old West Pointer who had been in a support unit attached to the 24th Infantry Division (Mechanized) in the Gulf, likewise argued that women should be allowed to serve in any combat capacity, including the Rangers, Special Forces (Green Berets), paratroopers, Navy SEALS, and other rugged outfits that are so physically demanding that a large percentage of male recruits are soon washed out.[11]

Another topic focused on mothers in the military. Television images of women bidding tearful farewells to children they are leaving behind as they departed for the Persian Gulf were still fresh in the minds of American citizens. Captain Barkalow was not impressed by the "mother issue." Those who use children as an argument for excluding women from combat are "looking for another way to keep women out," she declared. "My fear is that those who don't understand what women do in the military are going to make policies for those of us who serve."[12]

Wilma Vaught, a retired Air Force brigadier general and a staunch advocate for putting women in combat cockpits, asked, "Why is it just a mother who is concerned about children? I think the decision of who remains with the children belongs to those responsible for the children, and not the law."[13]

Suzanne Fields, a columnist for the *Washington Times*, took exception to General Vaught's view. "The importance of an infant's relationship with its mother during the first years of life has been well established by child experts," Fields said. "How these children will be affected by their mothers' absences during the [Gulf] war won't be learned for many years to come."[14]

Reflecting the opinion of most professional male officers, four-star General Frederick "Fritz" Kroesen stressed that "motherhood and [combat] soldiering are not compatible." Kroesen, who had seen heavy fighting in three wars and had retired after commanding the U.S. Army in Europe, said, "In my opinion, one or the other must suffer. And in my experience, the military responsibilities normally suffer first—and rightly so."[15]

At the Capitol, Patricia Schroeder was waxing enthusiastic over what she perceived to be a drastic change in the mood of Congress in the wake of the Gulf crisis. "We [feminists in the House] are very pleased that DACOWITS held their ground and came out strong," the congresswoman told the media.

Schroeder, who failed a year earlier to win congressional approval for a four-year test of women in Army combat jobs, said she believed the Gulf conflict had convinced more policymakers that it was time to drop the last remaining barriers to women serving in combat.

"The Air Force leaders seem to be the most willing to say, 'We're ready!'" she said. "Now the pressure is on the [Bush] administration."[16]

At the same time, eleven experienced fighter pilots—lieutenants and captains—stationed at Luke Air Force Base, Arizona, put their careers on the line by the public release of a joint statement that took issue with those who had "fallen into the new 'politically correct' way of thinking" with regard to women in combat. "Never mind any valid reasons as to why women should not be [in combat], because, valid or not, any mention of it would be considered sexist," the officers stated.[17]

"When dealing with life and death matters, equal-opportunity employment is of no importance," the pilots declared. "That is why the exclusionary law came into existence. It seems that Congress has forgotten that fact, and certain individuals, like Representative Patricia Schroeder, jump in and try to exploit our quick victory over a paper tiger [Iraq]."

Schroeder's claims that the performance of women flying tankers and transports in the Gulf area merits positions in combat cockpits is like comparing apples and oranges, the pilots explained. "Advocates for women flying fighter planes in combat grasp for solid ground by referring to the excellent job women did," the pilots stated. "That in no way represents a valid test of their capabilities in combat. Tankers and transports do not fly through direct hostilities."

The fighter pilots' statement added:

> Another argument is the physical strength difference that so many try to dismiss because it is politically correct to believe that gender differences no longer exist. Why in such an educated society do we find it necessary to close our eyes to the facts of life? There is no question that a woman can fly a fighter plane during takeoff and landing. Now let's put that fighter in its fourth engagement of a sortie, at nine G's with a MiG on the tail, an air-to-air missile on the way, chaff and flares, and we find ourselves in a completely different scenario.
>
> At nine G's all the muscle mass in the body is being called upon to squeeze blood back into the brain, the neck, which is used to support a thirty-pound head-helmet combination, is now maneuvering two hundred and seventy pounds, and the lungs are still trying to catch up with the previous three assignments. This is just the physical side. The mental side is trying to communicate with [the leader] and come up with a split-second plan that will mean the difference between life and death.
>
> Are there women who can possibly deal with these physical demands? No question about it. The question is will those unique few be identified among the many who would *apply*.[18]

Only three weeks after DACOWITS had begun to put the heat on Congress, the House voted 268 to 161 to approve a military budget bill that included an amendment repealing restrictions on women flying combat aircraft.

"There were a lot of cowardly lions roaring in the cloakroom earlier, but they wouldn't go out on the floor and vote against it," Patricia Schroeder, who had sponsored the provision, told the media.[19]

"The Persian Gulf [conflict] helped collapse the whole chivalrous notion that women could be kept out of danger in war," Schroeder said. "We saw that the theater of operations had no strict combat zone, that Scud missiles were not gender-specific—they could hit both sexes."[20]

22 ❖ A Spirited Debate

Captain Terry VandenHolder sat in the rear of a packed room as the manpower and personnel subcommittee of the Senate Armed Services Committee was holding hearings about allowing women in combat. She fumed, not liking what the witnesses were saying. She perceived that the "ol' boys" in the Washington power seats were balking at permitting her to achieve the job to which she aspired—a fighter pilot. It was mid-June 1991.[1]

VandenHolder was a cargo plane pilot in the Air Force reserves. She had been called up during Desert Shield, and had been shuttling supplies, weapons, and bodies to the Gulf and back, but this was her day off. She grew increasingly angry as the chiefs of the Army, Navy, Marines, and Air Force testified. "I'm not enthusiastic about increasing the exposure of women to combat," said General Merrill McPeak, the Air Force boss.

"Old fashioned!" VandenHolder scribbled on a pad. Minutes passed. More scribbling. "Last bastion of male domination of the military!"

"For women, there's no longer a protective barrier, some easy-to-see frontline," she told a reporter. "A woman can get hit by a Scud missile. There's no more hiding behind rocks—or social mores."[2]

However, she was encouraged by a reassuring statement by Christopher Jehn, the Pentagon's top personnel official, who testified that the military planned to allow more roles for women. But, he added, restrictions would be lifted only if there were "no adverse impact on readiness or combat effectiveness."

The high-profile activities of military women in the Gulf—televised into millions of American homes almost every night—had been "too anecdotal from which to make judgments," Jehn declared.

General Alfred M. Gray, Jr., the Marine Corps commandant, heartily agreed. "[Desert Storm] was not the ultimate test of sustained combat," he told the subcommittee. "It was a short war."[3]

It was not just "ol' boys" making their views known to another group of "ol' boys": some military women came out in staunch opposition to repealing the combat exclusion law. One of them, Captain Cheryl R. Finch, who was assigned to the hospital at Minot Air Force Base, North Dakota, wrote the panel a letter that stated, in part:

> As a military officer, physician, a woman, I think it would be a mistake to [remove the law against females in combat] . . . I am appalled that now some women are arguing for "combat" as though it is a right. This perspective is not shared by the majority of service men and women. Yet there seems to be the one unspoken prohibition against voicing those concerns—fear of a discrimination suit. As I have experienced it, the prejudice is in favor of women. Criticism of women by men [in the military] is discouraged even if warranted.[4]

Navy Lieutenant Brenda Holdener, a helicopter pilot stationed at Norfolk Air Station, disagreed with Captain Finch's viewpoint: "I am very selfish . . . I would like to see [the law] changed just because that would afford me more opportunities [for promotion]."[5]

General Robert H. Barrow, a highly decorated warrior in three wars who retired in 1983 as commandant of the Marine Corps, told the subcommittee: "I know the female Marines; they're terrific. They serve with great skill, they have a spirit about them; they're *creme de la creme* and most of them do not—I never met one—want to be an infantryman. Who wants them to be an infantryman? The hard line feminists do. They have an agenda, and it doesn't have anything to do with national security.

"The feminists want to put our daughters at risk, and the other attendant problems that result from such a situation—sexual harassment, fraternization, favoritism, resentment, male backlash, all of these things would be an insurmountable problem to deal with," Barrow continued. "Who deals with that? Not some faceless bureaucrat or political appointee over at the Pentagon, but the corporals and the sergeants, the lieutenants and the captains who have to maintain good order and discipline—and also fight the war."[6]

Civilian pressure to open the combat ranks to women was virtually nonexistent, Secretary of the Army Michael B. Stone testified. "I get a letter a day from clergymen saying we ought to change our policy on homosexuals," he added. "I don't get a letter a month saying we ought to change [combat exclusion policy] for women."[7]

Late in July, the full Senate was engaged in a spirited, often contentious debate over a $291 million defense-budget bill. In an effort to kill an amendment allowing women to fly combat aircraft, Senators John Warner, John Glenn, Sam Nunn, and John McCain offered a competing measure that would create a fifteen-member commission to study the issue of military women and make recommendations by November 1992.

The four sponsors warned that the Senate would be rushing pell-mell into a momentous decision with scant evidence to back it up if the women-in-combat-cockpits amendment were to become law. "If we're going to make such a radical change, a year or so of careful deliberation would be invaluable," said

Senator McCain, a Navy pilot in the Vietnam War who had been shot down and spent several years in a brutal Vietnamese POW enclosure.

"Substantially more study is required before we can act conclusively on the future role of women in combat," agreed Senator Glenn, a Marine pilot in World War II and Korea and later an astronaut.

On the other hand, supporters of the amendment to lift the ban described the existing law as an "archaic, antiquated, Neanderthal" statute that discriminated against women. "That law is bad for women because it denies them an equal opportunity for service and advancement in the military," Senator Edward "Ted" Kennedy declared.

"This restriction is as old and outdated in today's military as a World War II propeller," said Senator William V. Roth, Jr.

By a lopsided vote of 90 to 3, the Senate passed the competing amendment to establish a study group to be called the Presidential Commission on the Assignment of Women in the Armed Forces. It looked as though the strategy to kill the measure to permit women to fly in combat planes had paid off. However, twenty-nine Republicans and forty Democrats then voted for the "permitting women to fly combat aircraft" amendment as well.

"This is a victory for the women pilots who demonstrated in the Gulf their capabilities, their heroism, and their competency," said Senator Ted Kennedy, whose older brother, Joseph, had been killed while on a flight mission over France in 1944, shortly after D-Day in Normandy.[8]

Later in the day, the Senate approved the entire budget bill by a voice vote.

Patricia Schroeder was elated, but she felt that the Senate action was only another step toward her ultimate goal. "If the services want to, [they] can open up every single slot for women," she told the media.[9]

Congress did not order the Air Force, Navy, and Marine Corps to assign women as pilots, navigators, and weapons systems officers on combat aircraft; rather it gave the various services the authority to further expand the assignment choices for women. There had been no law restricting women from serving in any role in the Army, although by policy, females had not been assigned to attack helicopters or the infantry, armor, combat engineers, artillery, mortars, or other ground units with a high probability of direct confrontation with an enemy.

In passing the measure, Congress had neatly laid a trap for the leadership in the various services: The decision on actually assigning women to combat had been transferred from the legislators' shoulders to those of the civilian and uniformed chiefs in the Pentagon.

Many female military officers were happy over the victory. "I'm very pleased with Congress' action," said Lieutenant Colonel Kelly S. Hamilton, who had flown KC-135 Stratotankers during the Gulf operations and was later posted to Camp Smith, Hawaii. "This is something I've been looking for since the day I walked in [to the Air Force]."[10]

Captain Peggy Carnahan, a T-37B Tweet instructor pilot at Randolph Air Force Base, Texas, echoed Hamilton's sentiment. "It's something that's been a long time coming," she said.[11]

In Washington, Captain Carol Barkalow, who had served in the Gulf and then was assigned to the Pentagon, told the media, "Until Desert Storm the American people didn't understand the modern battlefield."[12]

Barkalow didn't seem to understand the modern battlefield either, Martin Binkin, a senior fellow in defense manpower at the Brookings Institution in Washington, felt. He held no illusions that a future war will be fought by people pushing electronic buttons while far removed from the blood and gore of face-to-face combat. Technology had played a major role in defeating the poorly led Iraqi army, but frontline soldiers and Marines still had to engage the enemy eyeball-to-eyeball. In that setting, women would have been at an enormous disadvantage.

"U.S. forces need to be ready to fight the difficult war where the opposing forces are more evenly matched than they were in the Gulf," Binkin declared. "The champions of women in the military ignore that possibility altogether."[13]

In the wake of the Persian Gulf conflict and the crumbling of the Communist bloc in Europe, Captain Carol Barkalow envisioned great changes in the armed forces. "As the military downsizes in the coming years," she told a reporter for *Newsweek*, "there will be a need to keep the best and the brightest. And women will need to be convinced they have the chance for future advancement. That means combat arms can't be closed to them."

Should women be allowed to serve in the infantry? "Most certainly," Barkalow replied. "If they're qualified."

In an interview with *The New York Times*, Barkalow blasted the leaders in the Pentagon, a surefire way to get a career killed if the blaster were a male officer. She said the generals have archaic attitudes toward females being assigned to combat units.[14]

"Some [generals] twenty years my senior still see women as mother, wife, girlfriend, or daughter," she said. "They know how to deal with guys of [my generation] but may not know what to do with women. It makes them uncomfortable."[15]

Charles Moskos, a professor of sociology at Northwestern University and chairman of the Inter-University Seminar on Armed Forces and Society, had a different viewpoint than that of Barkalow. His writings on military sociology have been translated into eleven languages. When asked about the possibility of Congress further expanding the role of women into combat units, he replied:

A lot of agitation for changing the exclusion law comes from some women [officers] who can't reach the top unless they have combat experience. I don't know if everyone will rush to expose enlisted women to combat so female officers can advance their careers. Enlisted women are certainly not clamoring to fight.[16]

23 ❖ Fallout from a Tailhook Convention

The Las Vegas Hilton, a plush, thirty-story structure with 3,000 guest rooms and suites, several restaurants, and a large gambling casino, was jumping with 4,000 guests attending the 35th annual Tailhook Association convention, the largest to date. Named after the device that catches an aircraft after it lands on a flight deck, Tailhook had 15,479 members, including active duty, reserve, and retired Navy and Marine Corps pilots. It was the first week in September 1991.

Tailhook 91 had as its main thrust an evaluation of Navy and Marine aviation in Desert Shield/Desert Storm through a series of symposiums conducted by naval aviation experts and concerning new developments in tactics and weapons systems. These briefings have led to more effective and safer performances in the cockpit by providing professional "cross talk" between aviators and top commanders.

For many of the Navy "top guns," Tailhook also was a celebration of victory over the Iraq armed forces, similar to the boisterous revelries held by their predecessors on Victory in Europe and Victory in Japan Days in World War II. In essence, most of the younger pilots rightfully regarded themselves as returning war heroes, knowing that the U.S. Navy had suffered six casualties in the Gulf conflict, all of whom were aviation officers.

Although Tailhook is an independent organization, it always had been customary for the Pentagon to provide high ranking officers and civilian leaders to participate in forums and speak at two banquets. The major symposium was the Flag Panel, a unique aspect of Tailhook conventions, where Navy admirals and Marine generals, in an informal atmosphere, reply to tough questions from members of the audience.

The Flag Panel sessions were free of the stifling aspects of military protocol. Those in the audience wore civilian clothes (usually shorts and T-shirts), so his or her identity or rank would be unknown to the panel of brass, thereby encouraging candor from the questioners. For their part, the participating admirals and generals benefited by learning firsthand the reactions of those in the ranks to high-level decisions that sound great in the stultifying climate of Washington, but often have unexpected or adverse impact upon those in the fleet.

New and worthwhile ideas sometimes emerged from junior officers at the Flag Panels. In the past, the Navy had implemented several practical suggestions heard at these sessions. Mutual respect between the audience and the brass was the hallmark of these frank cross-talk sessions. On Friday afternoon, 1,500 attendees crowded into the ornate main ballroom of the Hilton to hear from and discuss issues with the Flag Panel of seven admirals and one general.[1]

That night, Pentagon correspondent David Martin did a piece focusing on the Flag Panel on the CBS-TV *Evening News*. In a videotape, a feminine voice off-camera was heard asking when Navy women might be given combat assignments. Vice Admiral Richard M. Dunleavy, the assistant chief of naval operations for air warfare, knowing that he had been put on the hotseat, gave a "hoo-boy" reaction that was caught on the film. His gesture ignited soft laughter in the room. At that point, the CBS-TV report concluded.[2]

Had the television piece not been chopped off, *Evening News* viewers would have heard Dunleavy tell the audience, "If Congress directs SecNav [secretary of the Navy] to allow qualified women to fly combat aircraft, we will comply." He also pointed out that female pilots already were flying helicopters in the fleet.

Perhaps the CBS-TV report had halted abruptly because of strict time constraints in a thirty-minute broadcast. Because Dunleavy's response was not broadcast, however, it no doubt appeared to viewers that the admiral had brushed off the woman's question with only a ridiculing remark.[3]

Much of Tailhook's leisure time activities centered around the pool patio and in the third floor corridor. Along this hallway were twenty-two bi-level hospitality suites—the upper sections contained a bathroom and sleeping area, and the lower parts a living room. Nineteen of the suites were registered to Navy and Marine squadrons, and three were occupied by Navy aviation training commands, schools, or centers.

Most suites were used for pilots and their guests to meet, talk, drink, and relax. Some of the suites were set up to provide entertainment, including disc jockeys playing music for dancing and performances by female strippers imported from the Las Vegas night spots. There was no shortage of alcoholic beverages. During the three-day convention, the squadrons in the twenty-two hospitality suites spent $33,500 on booze. In addition, a local beer distributor delivered 271 kegs of beer, or 4,200 gallons, to the suites.[4]

For years, it had been known throughout the Navy that Tailhook conventions were boisterous affairs during night hours. Perhaps the aviators' freewheeling antics at Tailhook 91 emerged from a combination of booze and a "live today, for tomorrow you may die" mindset, a subtle reminder that carrier aviation is a perilous endeavor, even in peacetime.

One Navy commander, a veteran of the Gulf conflict, compared the atmosphere in the Hilton to that of a "cruise party." After a carrier has been at sea for a long time and the pilots go ashore in a port for the first time, they set up an administrative suite in a hotel. "This is normally a common suite where guys can meet," he explained. "It's kind of our living room ashore for a brief period of time. It's a place of some pretty good parties, although Tailhook is a lot rowdier."[5]

Admiral Frank B. Kelso II, the chief of naval operations, a President George Bush appointee, was the featured speaker at Friday night's dinner hosted by Captain F. G. Ludwig, the current Tailhook Association president. At the banquet on Saturday night, Secretary of the Navy H. Lawrence Garrett, III, also a Bush appointee, told the audience that reduced budgets and force levels meant difficult times ahead for the Navy. However, he stressed that naval aviation had survived such challenges before, and he was confident it would do so again.[6]

After the Saturday night banquet, most of the audience returned to their rooms to change into casual clothing, and much of the activity shifted to the third floor of the Hilton where the hospitality suites were located. Female Navy officers, who years earlier had been barred from attending the conventions, were present at the convention in record numbers. Some male officers brought their wives. Young civilian women flocked to the conclave, presumably to meet and consort with dashing pilots. In all, there were an estimated 470 women at Tailhook 91.

As time passed that night and the booze flowed freely, the partying grew steadily more rowdy. Outside the hospitality suites in the corridor, a milling, inebriated group of junior officers backed against the wall to either side to form a "gauntlet," said to have been a Tailhook tradition for many years.[7]

A large number of young women, alone and in pairs, traversed the gauntlet, giggling and seeming to enjoy being fondled, grabbed, and pinched. A few of them were seen going through the gauntlet two or three times.[8]

Other women were upset about being pawed and mauled, however, and they resisted fiercely. One pulled out a Tazer, a device similar to a small cattle prod and designed to ward off attackers. She waved the Tazer menacingly and escaped without being molested. A man tried to grab one woman, she pulled out a zapper (a sort of stun gun), and the offender executed a strategic retreat.

At about 11:30 P.M., Navy Lieutenant Paula A. Coughlin, a twenty-nine-year-old helicopter pilot and aide to Rear Admiral Jack W. Snyder, Jr., wandered into the third floor corridor. Someone grabbed her by the buttocks from behind, and other men pulled at her clothing. One man tried to reach inside her tank top, and Coughlin sank her teeth into his forearm and hand. She broke away and took refuge in an empty hospitality suite for a short period of time, then left the third floor.[9]

The story of the Tailhook 91 debauchery broke in October when a letter from the president of the association berating some pilots for activities "far over the line of responsible behavior" was leaked to the *San Diego Union-Tribune*. The disclosure ignited an uproar. Feminist groups complained loudly. Empurpled speeches erupted on the floors of Congress. Angry editorials condemned the male participants and the Navy in general.

Within hours, leaders in the Pentagon ordered the Navy Investigative Service (NIS) to conduct an exhaustive probe. One of those extensively interviewed was Lieutenant Paula Coughlin. From photos shown by NIS investigators, she picked out a Marine as one of her principal assailants. When it was found that the man she had identified had not been at the convention, an unknown party allegedly tipped her off to the error. Then she called NIS and said, "I hear I picked the wrong guy!"[10]

Coughlin added, "If it's not him, it's his brother."[11]

About a month later, NIS showed Coughlin six more photos. From these she identified Marine Captain Gregory Bonham. Later, she was informed in advance that he would be included in a lineup. After picking him from the lineup, she told NIS agents, "What is bothering me is I am afraid I have this minor shadow of a doubt. I think that is him. I recall him being larger."[12]

Captain Bonham denied even being on the third floor of the Hilton that night. A fellow Marine officer backed his account, saying that they had been together elsewhere in the hotel throughout the evening. Nevertheless, based on Paula Coughlin's identification of Bonham, charges would be drawn up against him.

On April 28, 1992, NIS had compiled a 2,000–page report based on 2,200 interviews. Someone leaked portions of the confidential document to the media. When it became public that the report listed forty-four incidents of coarse behavior justifying possible disciplinary action against Navy and Marine officers, the number of cases cited fell far below the expectations gained from earlier leaks and media speculation. There were loud charges of "cover-up."

Congresswoman Patricia Schroeder spoke for most feminists and their supporters: "The Joint Chiefs simply are not getting it."

During the time the NIS investigation had been in progress, Assistant Secretary of Defense for Manpower and Reserve Affairs, Barbara S. Pope, attended nineteen progress meetings and apparently had been satisfied with the scope of the investigation. Now, however, she joined with those demanding a much larger "body count."

She threatened to resign unless the commanders of all the squadrons that had hospitality suites at Tailhook were disciplined, even if they had not been personally involved in misconduct or unruly behavior.

Pope also demanded that the ongoing NIS investigation structure be altered to include the interrogation of senior Navy officers by admirals and a civilian appointee of President Bush.

Admiral John Gordon, the Navy judge advocate general, who was responsible for the integrity of Navy probes and the protection of constitutional rights of persons being investigated, objected to Pope's demand. Having admirals probing the conduct of those serving under them and inserting a civilian appointee into the process would inject politics and unfair command interference into what was supposed to be an impartial investigation, Admiral Gordon said. The "interference" of high Navy officials and a political appointee would create a legal problem "so severe that [there will not be] one successful conviction come out of this process," he added.

Eventually, Barbara Pope's demand to politicize the Tailhook investigation was rejected.

While the intramural skirmishing was taking place in the Pentagon, on the night of June 24, 1992, the lead story on the ABC-TV *World News Tonight* with Peter Jennings focused on Tailhook 91. Lieutenant Paula Coughlin was the star of the show, and she told of her experience. She complained that the Navy had been dragging its feet in its investigation.

Two days later, President George Bush summoned Defense Secretary Dick Cheney to the White House and expressed his deep displeasure over the Tailhook affair. After the Oval Office session, a top aide of the president spoke by telephone to Navy Secretary Lawrence Garrett and said Bush requested his "resignation."[13]

A few hours later, Bush called Lieutenant Paula Coughlin to the White House, and he and wife Barbara met with her in a private room. After Coughlin related her experience at Tailhook 91, the president allegedly started to weep, saying that he had a thirty-one-year-old daughter himself.[14]

Bush told Coughlin that Secretary Garrett would soon "resign" and he assured her that there would be a fair and full investigation. In a prepared statement released to the media by White House aide Paul Clarke, Bush stressed "my complete intolerance of such [Tailhook] behavior."[15]

Presumably as a result of the intervention of President Bush, the Tailhook probe was transferred to Derek J. Vander Schaaf, the Department of Defense deputy inspector general. Identifying the pilots involved proved to be a difficult task because of "closed ranks and obfuscation," the new investigator complained.

Many of the officers interviewed disputed the existence of a gauntlet, a term that had appeared in countless headlines. One Navy lieutenant said the gauntlet was a "figment of someone's imagination." Some said they understood the milling about of pilots that was described as a gauntlet was a Tailhook tradition in which women willingly walked through groups of drunken aviators knowing they were going to be fondled, pinched, or touched.[16]

In an initial report, Vander Schaaf was highly critical of the original Naval Investigative Service probe. Admiral John Gordon, the judge advocate general who had opposed politicizing the investigation, was rebuked for "failure to abandon his traditional neutral role." Duvall M. Williams, head of the NIS, and NIS Inspector George Davis were blasted by Vander Schaaf for "failure to have broadened the investigation to include cultural problems."

Then Acting Navy Secretary Sean O'Keefe called a news conference and announced that Admiral Gordon and Duvall Williams were retiring "as a matter of conscience." O'Keefe, and presumably other Pentagon bigwigs, knew that statement was a lie: Gordon's retirement date had been set months earlier. The two men were being sacrificed to appease vocal critics of the Tailhook investigation, many in the Navy felt.

Four weeks later, O'Keefe issued a memorandum absolving Gordon, Williams, and George Davis of any wrongdoing or biased actions during the NIS investigation. Although officially vindicated, heavy damage had been inflicted upon their reputations. Most of the major media, which had played up their "conscience" retirements, had lost interest in that part of the ongoing Tailhook story.

Congress reacted to the Tailhook exposé as though it had declared war on the Navy and was trying to sink that time-honored institution. From June 4 to July 2, 1992, Congress delayed the promotions of some 4,500 Navy and Marine officers above the rank of lieutenant commander and major until it had been determined if any had been involved in unseemly Tailhook incidents. Morale plummeted throughout the Navy.

Many changes of major commands were postponed, including those of forces responsible for the waters off the Balkans, where a bloody civil war was in progress. John P. Murtha, chairman of the House Appropriations Committee, explained "this is directly connected to the obstruction and arrogance of the Navy" when his panel voted to double its original cut of 5,000 positions from Navy headquarters.

In a June 26 interview on Cable News Network (CNN), Patricia Schroeder lambasted the Navy hierarchy for its handling of the Tailhook investigation. Inferring that the underlying problem in the Navy was its unequal treatment of women, she said, "If you're the best for the job and you want the job, you [should] get it."[17]

That same day in another television interview, Senator Barbara Boxer said, "The thing about the military is, it has always been a place for opportunity, first for people of color, and then for women. We have much more work to do here, but we've got to make sure we move forward"[18]— into combat for women, she implied.

Not since the days of World War II, when Admiral Ernest J. "Big Bear" King had to constantly grapple with momentous problems, has a chief of naval operations been burdened with such a complex set of circumstances as was Admiral Frank Kelso. In the wake of Tailhook 91, Kelso was being bombarded from all sides. He was damned if he did, and damned if he didn't.

Kelso, who had directed naval and air strikes against Mu'ammar El Quaddafi in Libya and orchestrated the capture of the terrorists who had hijacked the cruise ship *Achille Lauro* in which an American citizen was murdered, was the target of loaded questions by the media. "How do you ever expect to change attitudes toward women in the Navy if they are treated like second-class citizens?" a female reporter asked Kelso in early 1992.

Long before Tailhook 91 and its aftermath burst like a fiery rocket onto the nation, Admiral Kelso had been highly active in protecting the rights of Navy women and seeing that they received fair play. In July 1990, he had ordered an immediate investigation into the Naval Academy's honor code and conduct in the wake of an incident in which a woman midshipman was chained to a urinal and taunted by males. Three months later, Kelso ordered a new study on the progress of women in the Navy, including steps to curb sexual harassment.

Soon after the high jinks at Tailhook 91 went public, Kelso sent a sharply worded message to all commanders reiterating the policy, set before his tenure, of zero tolerance for sexual harassment. Then he directed the Navy chief of personnel to create a plan to enforce zero tolerance, including provisions for mandatory discharge for offenders.

On July 1, 1992, Kelso relieved two commanding officers at Miramar Naval Air Station, a fighter-weapons school in California, in the wake of a skit in the "Tomcat Follies," a production for the entertainment of Air Force officers, some of whom played stage parts. In this particular skit, derogatory, off-color comments were made about Patricia Schroeder. Then Kelso apologized personally to the congresswoman.

Throughout the summer of 1992, Derek Vander Schaaf and his contingent of investigators pounced on hundreds of Navy officers. Persistent rumors of heavy-handed techniques filtered back to Washington and throughout the fleet worldwide. It was alleged by some in the Navy that, in their zeal to extract damning evidence from the Tailhook 91 affair, the investigators tried to coerce Navy pilots into "confessing" their guilt by falsely telling them their comrades had implicated them.

In one instance, three junior officers were promised immunity if they would testify at a court-martial against the commander of the Navy's elite Blue Angels flying demonstration team. He was thought to have been present in a Las Vegas Hilton hospitality suite while a couple engaged in a public sex act. A hero of the Persian Gulf air war, the Blue Angels' leader was removed from his squadron and subjected to months of humiliation and worry. When the time would come for their testimony, none of the immunized "witnesses" could actually place him in the hospitality suite.

There also were unconfirmed stories that the investigators had humili-ated other pilots by hooking them up to polygraphs (so-called lie detectors) and asking them detailed questions about their past sexual practices and preferences.

"This witch-hunt does so much to destroy the morale, cohesion, and the effectiveness of combat units, it makes my blood boil!" a highly decorated Marine colonel told the *Washington Times*.[19]

In September 1992, chief investigator Derek Vander Schaaf issued a report entitled "Events of the 35th Annual Tailhook Symposium." The 247-page document focused on sexual conduct and bawdy behavior allegedly per-petrated by drunken pilots against eighty-three females. All of the woman were listed in the report as "victims," even though many had told investi-gators that they had been willing participants.

24 ❖ "Today's Battlefield Is More Horrific"

Tinges of spring were in the air and the Japanese cherry trees in their fragile beauty were straining to burst forth in blossoms in Washington, D.C., where fifteen members of the Presidential Commission on the Assignment of Women in the Armed Forces gathered in the Hubert H. Humphrey Building. There they were sworn in by United States Solicitor General Kenneth W. Starr. It was March 25, 1992.

When Congress established the Commission three months earlier, it directed that the President appoint members after consulting with the Democratic chairmen and ranking Republicans of the Armed Services Committees of the House and Senate. Congress specified that Commission members were to be diverse with respect to race, ethnicity, gender and age, and they were to have credible track records in the public or private sectors in matters pertaining to national defense.

President Bush named retired Air Force General Robert T. Herres to be chairman of the Commission. A former vice chairman of the Joint Chiefs of Staff, Herres, during his thirty-six years of military service, had assignments in fighter interceptor aircraft, technical intelligence, military space activity, and strategic offensive operations.

Although Bush had given the newly minted commission no specific instructions or course to pursue, only a week after the panel had been sworn in, Secretary of Defense Dick Cheney restated the focus of the U.S. armed forces in a speech to a Pentagon gathering:

> It's important for us to remember that what we are asked to do in the Department of Defense is to defend the nation. The only reason we exist is to be prepared to fight and win wars. We're not a social welfare agency. We're not an agency that's operated on the bais of what makes sense for some members of Congress' concerns back home in their districts. This is a military organization. Decisions we make have to be taken based upon those kinds of considerations, and only those kinds of considerations.[1]

In the months ahead, members of the commission, in groups and individually, crisscrossed the nation, holding hearings in major cities, interviewing members of the armed forces, and visiting defense installations. Theirs would be a hands-on approach. On the carrier *John F. Kennedy*, members watched a catapult launch and dozens of takeoffs and landings. Men aboard the *Kennedy* were encouraged to speak their minds. Their average age was nineteen. Most expressed opposition to the assignment of women to any combat ship, citing such reasons as physical strength, lost time due to pregnancy, concern about inevitable romantic involvements, and the risk of false charges of sexual harassment.[2]

A number of sailors and junior officers on the carrier *Kitty Hawk* expressed a feeling of betrayal, disappointed that Navy leaders had allowed the Tailhook sexual molestation scandal to tarnish the entire service. They felt that the Navy brass should be more forceful in telling the American people that Tailhook involved only a relative handful of pilots and was not representative of the hundreds of thousands of members of the Navy.[3]

A trip to the Coronado Naval Amphibious Base, where the elite SEALs train, convinced most commission members that the enormous physical strength and endurance involved in the behind-the-lines missions of these commando units would make it impossible for women—and most men—to be assigned. The success of SEAL operations largely depends on backpacking heavy survival gear, weapons, ammunition, and explosives for great distances in rugged terrain.

Rear Admiral Raymond Smith, head of the Naval Special Warfare Command, told commission members: "We make no compromises in SEAL training. This, I believe, is the crux of the issue. Would the integration of females in a SEAL platoon improve our combat effectiveness? My belief is that such an integration would reduce it."[4]

Four-star General Carl Stiner, who had played a leading role in the 1989 parachute assault in Panama and now was in charge of the Special Operations Command, echoed Admiral Smith's views. When interviewed by commission member Samuel G. Cockerham, a retired Army brigadier general and combat veteran of the Korean and Vietnam wars, Stiner said, "There is no question that introducing women in special operations combat units, including aviation, will most definitely downgrade combat readiness . . . The physical demands and mental endurance of combat are limiting factors in the integration of women further into the military."[5]

During a three-day visit to the Survival, Resistance, and Escape (SERE) training center at Fairchild Air Force Base near Spokane, Washington, commission member Elaine Donnelly witnessed a few of the techniques that prepare men and women aircrew members for existence as a POW at the hands of brutal enemy captors. She saw military women being locked into small wooden boxes for extended periods of time, and other women verbally browbeaten by men acting as enemy interrogators. It was merely a mild simulation of the real thing.

"If a policy change is made and women are allowed into combat positions," one SERE officer said, "there must be a concerted effort to educate the American people on the likelihood that [our] women will be raped and will come home in bodybags."[6]

"The SERE program makes sense," Elaine Donnelly said later. "But I am deeply disturbed over the grim possibility that the American people might have to be 'desensitized' [meaning become accustomed to] the specter of women POWs being brutalized by an enemy on an equal basis with men."[7]

Two pilots who were POWs in Vietnam told the commission that the presence of women captives would increase men's vulnerability should the enemy torture these females to coerce males into giving valuable military information. Air Force Colonel Fred Cherry, who was held by the North Vietnamese for over seven years, said: "I am certain had the cries and screams and being next door to my fellow prisoners being tortured by the rope treatment and the bamboo beatings—I'm sure it would have affected [me] more severely had that been a woman, rather than a man."[8]

Air Force Colonel Norman McDaniel told the commission: "There is no doubt in my mind that it would make a difference . . . I would certainly lean toward giving the enemy something if I knew they were raising hell with a fellow female prisoner."[9]

Commission members also made fact-finding trips to Nellis Air Force Base, Miramar Naval Air Station, and the Marine Corps Air-Ground Combat Center where they interviewed women who flew a variety of noncombat aircraft and served on noncombatant ships. Commissioners witnessed women engaging in damage control exercises aboard the *Cape Cod*, a destroyer tender with a crew of some 800 males and 400 females.

Observations of amphibious operations were made by commissioners at Camp Pendleton and Hawaii with elements of the 3rd Marines. Carrying full combat gear, the Marines had to climb over the side of a cargo ship and into a landing craft bouncing on fifteen- to twenty-foot waves. "One mistake under those conditions would result in a catastrophic injury," an officer pointed out.

Training exercises were witnessed at the Army's Jungle Training Center in Fort Sherman, Panama. Specific tasks requiring great strength and endurance that were unique to jungle fighting included long-distance swimming while towing heavy equipment and repelling down bluffs.

Some commissioners viewed men of the 7th Marines engaged in high altitude, cold weather combat at the Mountain Warfare Center, Pickel Meadows, California. During sustained marches on snow shoes, the men had to lug loads exceeding 100 pounds up and down steep inclines, often in the dark, for periods of several hours.

At Fort Bragg, North Carolina, home of the 82nd Airborne Division, a field exercise, using live ammunition, was laid on for commission members. In an assault on a bunker, foot soldiers were seen carrying comrades with "wounds" away from the action. It was one-on-one: an infantryman laboriously lugging a comrade.

Later, some witnesses testifying before the commission claimed that evacuating a 200-pound man while under heavy fire would be no problem for *two* men. However, paratroop officers at Bragg pointed out that the burden must be borne by a lone soldier: Others are needed to continue the assault or to provide covering fire.

During the hundreds of hours of hearings, the commission often was told by those with no military background that technology had transformed modern warfare into button-pushing exercises. Most of these witnesses' knowledge had been derived from watching television pictures of the Gulf conflict. However, Major General Binford Peay, who had led the 101st Airborne Division in Desert Storm, told the commission that despite sophisticated technological advances, combat today is no more refined, no less barbaric, and no less physically demanding than it has been throughout history. "In fact, technology has made today's battlefield a more lethal, violent, shocking, and horrific place than it has ever been," Peay stressed.[10]

Marine Sergeant Major Harold Overstreet, who had seen heavy fighting in Vietnam where his unit had taken heavy casualties, echoed General Peay's contentions:

> We hear that combat is combat is combat. I'm here to tell you, it is not. First of all, it's one thing to be in a combat *area*, it's different when you know that you are the guy that is going to have to seek out, close with, and do whatever it takes to wipe out the enemy. You. You're going to go out there and confront him—one on one. You realize this is no game. There is no second place. And if you are in second place, you don't come back. It's quite different from those who [think] they've been in combat because they were working or refueling or resupplying in a combat area. They don't have to go and seek out the enemy face to face.[11]

In hearings in Los Angeles, much of the focus was on physical requirements for ground fighting. Marine Corps Staff Sergeant Barry Bell, who served as a combat engineer during Desert Storm, told the commission:

> My rucksack when I went in weighed seventy-five pounds. And I walked twelve miles from the border to the mine field . . . If you're not in peak physical condition during this type of environment, you're not going to be able to perform. And, unfortunately, we weren't in peak physical condition. During the six months prior to going in, we did PT, we did try to get in some semblance of shape, but we did not get to the point where we are at now, and it kicked our butts . . . we were bent over, our backs were killing us. The weight was just way too heavy for us, let alone a female Marine or female soldier . . . Physically, women are just unable to do it. If we were almost unable to do it, I know we would have a hard time pulling the female Marines up to where we were at. Physically, they are just not capable of performing everything we are able to do, and I think that's one of our major concerns.[12]

Army Lieutenant Colonel Douglas Tysand, a tank commander in Desert Storm, agreed with Bell's observations:

Strength requirements [in combat] are extreme. The stress over time, stamina is required. In my experience, I've met very few women that I believed could handle the stress, coupled with the physical requirements we have . . . A crew is a primary group, as the psychologists call it, and we believe that in combat motivation you fight for the primary group, which is only as good as its weakest member.[13]

Army Lieutenant Colonel Stephen S. Smith, a mechanized infantry commander, described the intense physical demands of Desert Storm's brief, but often violent, land campaign: "Even if certain women have the physical capability to lift the rucksacks, walk the distance, raise the [tank] hatches, load the TOW missiles, break the tank track and put it back together again, assigning them to combat units would still introduce complicating factors that would make the task harder."[14]

"This is not Olympic diving," Colonel Smith concluded. "We do not get extra credit for adding an extra degree of difficulty."[15]

Another relevant topic discussed by expert witnesses in commission hearings around the United States was whether existing policies restricting the assignment of women to combat aircraft units should be retained, modified, or rescinded. Experienced fighter pilots explained there was a vast difference between *flying* and *fighting* an aircraft.

Air Force Lieutenant General Buster Glosson, who had been responsible for much of the air campaign strategy and its daily execution in the Gulf conflict, told the commission that "those who say technology has removed the personal demands and horrors of combat are misinformed. The air combat arena comes down to stamina and cohesion."

Glosson continued: "The common perception of a combat air mission— to plan the mission to the target, brief with a wingman, fly an hour or two, fifteen minutes of intense being fired at and avoidance of enemy ordnance—avoidance of the threat—deliver your ordnance and return and have the rest of the day off is simply a misconception.

"The physical demands encompassed in this area are tremendous," Glosson explained. "The high speeds of the modern aircraft, as a result of technology, the high rates of turn that require the high instantaneous G loads that literally makes your body shake or may put you in G lock, as we call it, when you lose consciousness, that we have to deal with all the time—the current requirement for sustaining consciousness is strength and endurance, and to us that is overall stamina."[16]

Navy Lieutenant John Clagett told commission members that he was not just presenting his views but those of twenty-three fellow Navy lieutenants and Marine captains who were Top Gun instructors:

Yes, we do have women flying F-18s [jet fighters] today, and that is a fact. They are certainly not flying the F-18s that any of us have flown in the fleet or out in the combat missions. To compare the missions that they are doing today to what we are doing is like comparing driving on the L.A. Freeway to driving in the Indianapolis 500. It's just not the same.

We are out there max performing the greatest airplane in the world every day, or attempting to. The women are not asked to do that. That is not their job. They have not been trained in the missions that we have been trained in. They have not performed the missions we have been performing.

And I just really object to the television news or whatever coming out and saying, "Oh, they're already doing that job." That's not true. Yes, they are flying F-18s. They're not flying combat mission F-18s, you know, and to put them in the same role is just ludicrous.[17]

Although most pilots who appeared before the commission were strongly opposed to women in combat planes, there were exceptions. Navy Commander Robert McLane testified: "I don't have any heartburn at all with putting a woman on my wing and flying up to Iraq or anywhere else we happen to go and blowing somebody away."[18]

Retired Navy Captain Rick Hauck, who flew 114 missions in Vietnam and later participated in three space shuttle missions as an astronaut, told the commission: "I would have no problem going into combat with a highly trained, highly motivated woman as my bombardier-navigator, or my pilot, or as my wing person, or as my flight leader."[19]

At Northwestern University in suburban Chicago, five men who flew B-1 bombers told the commission that although they saluted the performance of women in Desert Storm, the flight deck should remain an all-male domain in times of combat. Air Force Captain Ronald Gaulton, a B-1 commander stationed at Ellsworth Air Force Base in South Dakota, said, "I think women are just as courageous as men." But, he added, "It's real important to have [male] bonding in our business. If there's just the slightest bit of uncertainty, that could cost you your life."[20]

Gaulton, who flew A-10 combat missions in the Persian Gulf, said "a female coming into a fighter squadron would be an 'outsider' and cause a lot of apprehension."

Captain Randel Averett, who, unlike Gaulton, was trained by a woman instructor on another type of aircraft early in his career, said his teacher was "top flight." But he said he had "strong reservations" about being part of a mixed-gender crew in a B-1.

"How would I feel about a female crew member in a situation where we were shot down, captured, and faced possible torture?" Averett stated. "Would I put my life at risk to help her? The answer is yes. That's the way I was raised."[21]

25 ❖ Charges and Countercharges

While the hearings were being held at Northwestern in early July 1992, a rash of stories in the national media told of charges by feminist critics that President George Bush had stacked the commission with members who opposed putting women in combat. These detractors claimed that the hearings "amount to a traveling dog-and-pony show."

When a reporter for the *Chicago Tribune* contacted Congresswoman Patricia Schroeder at the Democratic National Convention in New York, she fired a broadside at President Bush. "It is suspicious to me, on an issue that has been studied to death [women in combat], that he said, 'We'll get this commission to study it some more.'"

Schroeder chose to skirt the fact that the Commission had been established by Congress, not by Bush.

Schroeder charged that the Commission was ignoring the recommendations of witnesses "who are a little more objective." She was especially critical of the Commission chairman, General Robert Herres. "When I talked to him, he was very combative," she said. "It seems like all this is a sideshow to divert people's attention."[1]

Herres responded: "How does Pat Schroeder know how I'm going to vote on the issues?"[2]

Tanya Domi, a retired Army captain who billed herself as a defense analyst, agreed with Schroeder. "It's really clear that [President Bush] weighed the majority of the commission heavily with conservative, if not right-wing, elements," she declared. She attacked commission member Elaine Donnelly, claiming that her "roots come from Eagle Forum," the family-oriented organization that had spearheaded the defeat of the equal rights amendment ten years earlier.

Domi also lashed out at three other commissioners. Sarah White, a master sergeant in the Air Force reserve, was biased because she had once been a legislative analyst for Concerned Women for America, Domi charged. That group is a conservative organization with a membership total double that of the feminist National Organization for Women.

Another panel member with a "biased viewpoint," Domi claimed, was retired Army General Maxwell Thurman, who had commanded the U.S.

invasion of Panama three years earlier. Domi charged that Thurman had authored a 1982 Army policy that "put the glass ceiling on women. He is no friend of women."[3]

Thurman, to the contrary, had opened hundreds of Army jobs for women and created new techniques for recruiting more females when he had been personnel chief in the Pentagon in 1982.

A fourth "biased" commissioner singled out by Tanya Domi and other feminist activists was Kate W. O'Bierne, a Washington attorney, who was married to a career infantry officer. He had seen heavy fighting in Vietnam. O'Bierne apparently had become a target when she told the Commission: "The purpose of the armed forces is to fight and win wars. It doesn't make any difference whether it's a big war, a little war, a war of limited duration, or a war that goes on for years. The military has but one purpose—to secure victory."[4]

O'Bierne had stressed that everyone should favor increased opportunities for women, but service in the armed forces is different than law, medicine, politics, the assembly line, or the executive boardroom of General Motors. "Most Americans have had good laughs watching the popular television series of a field medical unit in the Korean War, *MASH*, and have gained the notion that America's soldiers, sailors, airmen, and Marines are merely civilians in uniforms, each day preparing for tomorrow's high jinks," O'Bierne said. "There's nothing funny about being killed or maimed in combat."[5]

O'Bierne had emphasized the crucial significance of "bonding" to a military unit. "When the chips are down and life or death is at stake, the male warrior must know that his comrade will be alongside him," she said. "Most feminists, however, equate bonding with sedentary young men in fraternity rites or those wearing funny hats at men's clubs. But among warriors facing a common lethal crisis—a platoon under heavy enemy fire, a pilot and his wingman over hostile territory, or sailors under attack on warships from enemy aircraft, gunfire, or torpedoes—bonding is essential for achieving a military objective—or even surviving."

Commission member Mary E. Clarke, a retired Army major general with thirty-six years of service, strongly disagreed with the contention that unit cohesion would deteriorate if "someone different" were to be injected into it. "There is no evidence that cohesion would be affected by placing women in squadrons that have an offensive combat aviation mission," she declared.[6]

Clarke was one of three commissioners that some observers had labeled as feminists and presumably biased to their liberal points of view. General Clarke, at one time, had been assigned to the Pentagon as principal adviser on women's issues, and she had been instrumental in a policy change that resulted in females being sent on overseas assignments where women had not been previously. After retiring, Clarke became vice chairman of DA-

COWITS when that group was energetically lobbying Congress to permit women to serve in combat.

The other Commission members regarded as feminists were Army Captain Mary M. Finch, a West Point graduate on active duty, and Meredith A. Neizer, a 1978 graduate of the Merchant Marine Academy. Finch, a helicopter pilot, had been commander of a separate aviation detachment that was mostly male while stationed in Germany. Neizer had been chairman of DACOWITS after leaving the Merchant Marine.

With the bright glare of unfavorable media reports about the Navy's Tailhook 91 episode shining fiercely on the Pentagon, Les Aspin, chairman of the House Armed Services Committee, summoned the uniformed heads of the four services to Capitol Hill to be grilled about alleged widespread sexual harassment of military women. Aspin was known to be a staunch supporter of expanded roles for females in the armed forces. His two main confederates on the committee were Patricia Schroeder and Beverly Byron.

It appeared to many observers that Aspin's hearings were designed to gain wide public exposure, mainly through the battery of television cameras that would capture each moment of the Joint Chiefs' testimony. The hearings were even given a slanted title: "Gender Discrimination in the Military," as though that was an established fact.

Testifying at the hearings on July 30, 1992, were General Carl Mundy of the Marine Corps, General Merrill McPeak of the Air Force, Admiral Frank Kelso of the Navy, and General Gordon Sullivan of the Army. During their many hours of testimony, the nation's highest military officers recited a litany of *mea culpas* over abuses of females and ticked off the male officers they had punished for these offenses, rules they were enforcing, studies they had initiated, and surveys they had launched to identify gender-related problems.

Despite their recitals, the four highly decorated service chiefs had to sit like contrite schoolboys while being scolded by Patricia Schroeder and Beverly Byron for their alleged lack of vigilance on sexual harassment complaints and a reluctance to put women in combat assignments.[7]

General McPeak, the Air Force chief, told the committee: "I believe the combat exclusion law is discrimination against women. Of course, the mission of the armed forces is not to provide excellent career opportunities. Our mission is national security. Combat is killing people. And I'm afraid that . . . I have a very traditional attitude about wives and mothers and daughters being ordered to kill people."[8]

Marine General Mundy echoed McPeak's sentiment. "I have to come down . . . on the fact that our ultimate business is to win in combat . . . combat in the sense that we usually associate with the direct role of looking another human being in the eye and killing him. And it's not a pleasant job.

"And often it's not done with a precision munition," Mundy elaborated. "It sometimes is done with your hands, it's done with a shovel, and it's done at close range. And it's something that I would not want to see women get involved in, and, for which, I do believe—and I'm grateful that this is my perception—that women are not suited to do."[9]

The Army head, General Sullivan, cited the combat-support achievements of women in his service in the Panama invasion and in the Gulf but opposed extending females further into the line of fire. "We do have the combat exclusion policy which relates to infantry battalions, tank battalions, direct-support artillery battalions, and [armored] cavalry squadrons, and we're comfortable with that and I think it's the right policy at this time," he stressed.[10]

When Patricia Schroeder and Beverly Byron declared that extending full combat duty to women would end or alleviate sexual harassment, Sullivan replied, "I think it's too complex a problem . . . to just say, OK, open up everything and it won't occur again. I just don't think it would happen that way."[11]

Admiral Kelso, who had borne the brunt of a cascade of bitter criticism and condemnation from the feminist lobby and elements of the mass media, was alone among the service chiefs in saying the combat exclusion policy for women may have fueled some instances of sexual harassment. "A lot of people in the Navy, particularly the younger ones, feel that in order to void yourself of the cause of sexual harassment you've got to have general equality," he said.[12]

At one point, Patricia Schroeder demanded to know why there were no senior female military officers seated in the second row behind the four-star generals and admiral. Apparently her question was intended to make the point that women had been denied higher posts in the military because of their exclusion from combat roles.

General Mundy responded by asking two of his Marine aides, a female major and a female captain, to stand up, although he acknowledged they were not in the second row. His gesture set off a chain of requests for female aides to stand up behind more senior Navy, Army, and Air Force officers. Admiral Kelso said that he had female aides in the audience, and General Sullivan asked a female lieutenant colonel to stand, noting that she would soon be promoted to full colonel.

"I've got a [female] tech sergeant back there," quipped General McPeak as the audience laughed heartily.[13]

At the conclusion of the sometimes contentious hearings, most observers felt the television spectacular had been a flop with regard to persuading the service chiefs to agree that women should be thrust into combat roles to eliminate sexual harassment. Only Admiral Kelso had implied that the issue should be considered.[14] By the fall of 1992, the Presidential Commission on the Assignment of Women in the Armed Forces had heard testimony from a wide spectrum of people, including authorities on culture and religious issues, scientific and medical experts, and retired and active-duty members of the armed forces, from junior enlisted men and women to generals, admirals, and Pentagon officials.

Commissioners had logged hundreds of thousands of miles to conduct hearings and visit defense installations. Members studied a mountain of Department of Defense documents, reports from a wide variety of organizations, books, articles, graphs, and charts. Hundreds of historical and current writings and analyses were reviewed. More than 11,000 letters were received after interested Americans had been invited to express their opinions.

A Roper poll taken for the Commission reported that 74 percent of the active-duty military personnel sampled said No to women in the infantry, 72 percent said No to women in Marine infantry, 66 percent were against women in Special Operations Forces (Green Berets, SEALs, Airborne, Rangers), and 59 percent were opposed to women in tank crews.

When Roper asked the same question of military personnel who actually served in the combat arms, the figures jumped upward to 83 percent against women in the Army and Marine infantry, 82 percent opposed females serving in special operations, and 71 percent were against women being in tanks.[15]

Also studied by Commission members was an earlier poll taken by Charles Moskos, the expert on military personnel. His survey raised doubts about who would serve in the ground direct-combat forces if the bar against women were to be lifted. In his poll of 800 Army servicewomen, only 12 percent of the enlisted females said they would even consider duty in combat units. Moskos concluded that the only way ground combat units could have large numbers of women in their ranks would be by Congress passing a law to draft them.[16]

The Commission also sought views on women in combat by sending questionnaires to 6,109 retired generals and admirals, 64 percent of whom responded. Ninety percent said No to women in the infantry; 76 percent were opposed to females on combat vessels; and 71 percent were against women in combat aircraft.[17]

General Joseph J. Went, a former assistant commandant of the Marine Corps, expressed the written sentiment of nearly all of the respondents when he replied:

> My own experience with servicewomen in peacetime is that well qualified, motivated women perform just as well as well qualified, motivated men, and on occasion, better. Simply said, my experience with women in uniform has been very positive. But combat is another matter.

During the first week of November 1992, the Commission convened at the Holiday Inn Crown Plaza in downtown Washington for the final two days of hearings before drafting a report to the President. One witness, retired Army Brigadier General Theo C. Mataxis, who had been wounded twice while commanding infantry outfits in World War II, Korea, and Vietnam, focused on body strength, not just of one individual, but its effect on the infantry squad, the "team upon which an army depends to achieve victory on the battlefield." Mataxis said: "Imagine the Washington Redskins forced to play Monday night football with women on their team, up against the Chicago Bears with all male players. Which side would you bet on?"[18]

Balancing Mataxis' appearance were three active-duty female officers: a recent West Point graduate; a captain who had served in intelligence in Desert Storm; and a major, a physically fit long-distance runner. All claimed they could command combat troops, although none had been in actual combat. They shrugged off questions about strength as "not significant."[19]

Brigadier General Thomas V. Draude, a commission member who was on active duty as the director of public affairs at Marine Corps headquarters in Washington, made an emotional appeal for letting women fly combat missions. He had served three stints in Vietnam and had been the assistant commander of the 1st Marine Division in Desert Storm. His daughter, Navy Lieutenant Loree Draude, was training to be a jet pilot, and her boyfriend, also a Navy pilot, was on the staff of the commission.

"When I talk about women aviators, the face that I see is of my daughter Loree," General Draude told the panel. "I am proud beyond words of her achievements and the fact that she has chosen a profession to serve her country and make use of her talents the way she has."[20]

Draude added: "I'm asked, would you let your daughter fly combat with the possibility of her becoming a POW? My answer is Yes, because we have to send in our best to support our best."[21]

Sarah White, a master sergeant in the Air Force Reserve, who had introduced a measure to bar women from flying combat missions, told the panel that there "are women willing to kill or be killed to promote equal opportunity" in the armed forces.[22]

Following hours of bitter wrangling, conservative members of the Commission walked out of one session, complaining that they were not being given sufficient chance to voice their opposition to women in combat. General Draude asserted that they were "engaging in blackmail to get their way."[23]

Finally, the talk concluded: It was time to vote on the nonbinding recommendations to the President. A hush fell over the audience of mostly Pentagon officers and civilian officials sent to monitor the proceedings. By a vote of 8 to 2, women serving in direct-combat units was rejected, and the tally was 8 to 7 against females flying combat aircraft. At the last moment, a swing vote by General Maxwell Thurman tipped the scales in favor of continuing to bar women from combat cockpits.

"The prisoner-of-war issue was the deciding factor for my vote," Thurman said later. "The idea that we would position women in the arena of being subjected to violence, death, and depravity as prisoners of war was something I won't sign up to."[24]

The Commission voted to ban women from combat ships as well. But the panel amended its decision after the chairman, General Herres, appealed to the members to take some steps to open more jobs to women, arguing that a complete endorsement of the status quo would undermine the credibility of the Commission. Consequently, the panel approved, 8 to 6, to recommend that women be permitted to serve on combat ships, except for submarines and amphibious-assault vessels.

Not unexpectedly, the Commission's decisions triggered strong reactions, pro and con. Lieutenant Paula Coughlin, who had been molested by a few drunken Navy and Marine pilots at the Tailhook 91 convention in Las Vegas, had been in the audience during the hearings. She denounced the recommendations barring females from combat aircraft as a blow to all women in the military. "I think the composition of the Commission was predetermined and selected for just this outcome," she told reporters eager to get her views.[25]

Captain Mary Finch, a Commission member, attacked the majority findings of the panel as "an insult to all servicewomen." She was quoted as saying: "If I were the President, I would throw a lot of those recommendations out."[26]

Commissioner Kate O'Bierne, on the other hand, was relieved over the outcome. "During my eight months on the panel, I heard just about every conceivable reason why men and women in the armed forces should fight side by side to protect their country," she said. "In the end, I decided—as did a majority of my colleagues—that coed combat is a bad idea whose time hasn't come."[27]

On November 3, at the time the Commission was meeting in Washington, Americans across the nation were going to the polls. In a timeframe of less than eighteen months, President Bush's popularity rating of an incredible 91 percent after Desert Storm had plunged dramatically as the country's long-standing economic recession persisted. So when the ballots were counted, Bush received only 38 percent of the votes and was defeated by Bill Clinton, the governor of Arkansas, who garnered 43 percent. An independent candidate with deep pockets, H. Ross Perot, was favored by 19 percent of the electorate.

When the Commission submitted its voluminous report to George Bush twelve days later, he was a lame-duck president. It would be up to Bill Clinton to accept or reject the panel's recommendations.

26 ❖ Trials and Tribulations

On the night of October 4, 1993, the Kennedy Center in Washington was packed with Navy brass and their exquisitely gowned wives for a concert honoring the sea service's 218th birthday.[1] Seated in the box of honor were the new secretary of the Navy, John H. Dalton, and the chief of naval operations, Admiral Frank Kelso. Although all seemed serene in the box, undercurrents of electricity wafted through the air. Only days earlier, Dalton had recommended that Kelso be fired for his alleged failure to halt excesses at the 1991 Tailhook convention in Las Vegas.

Kelso, a submariner by trade, was to complete his four-year tour in July after more than thirty years of exemplary service.

Dalton, a Clinton appointee, was known throughout the Navy as the "Quota-meister" after his plan to commission new officers "in a percentage approximately equal to the racial makeup of the American populace" became known. "That translates to about twelve percent African-Americans, twelve percent Hispanics, and five percent Asian Americans," Dalton had pointed out.

A graduate of the Naval Academy in 1964, Dalton resigned from active duty after five years and went into private business. Like his friend Bill Clinton, he had been a finalist in the Rhodes Scholar competition.

Dalton's plan to scuttle sixty-year-old Frank Kelso was botched from the beginning. The Navy secretary had made his decision known privately after reviewing the cases of thirty-four admirals and one Marine Corps general who had attended the 1991 Tailhook convention. But someone in the Pentagon leaked the proposed move to the media over the weekend before the affair at the Kennedy Center. So Admiral Kelso learned of his fate in the press.

Service secretaries are generally seen but not heard in the Pentagon's major policy debates. Each serves as a budget custodian, promoter, and master of ceremonies for his respective military branch. Firing a member of the Joint Chiefs is the prerogative of the secretary of defense and the President, not the service secretary. Two years earlier, Defense Secretary Dick Cheney decided that Admiral Kelso should not be dropped over the side as a Tailhook casualty.

Dalton's request to dump Kelso was contained in a report to Defense Secretary Les Aspin, the former chairman of the House Armed Services Committee, spelling out disciplinary action for twelve of the admirals who attended the Tailhook convention. Aspin found himself in an awkward position. If he disagreed with his subordinate, Dalton, he would have to publicly rebuke the Navy secretary he would be working with for more than three years.

As Aspin weighed Admiral Kelso's fate over the weekend and talked with President Clinton, the low-key chief of naval operations let it be known he wanted to keep his job. Colleagues and veterans groups rallied around him. Kelso had always denied strongly that he had seen the debauchery that had taken place on the third floor of the Las Vegas Hilton.

Both Dalton and Aspin condemned the media leaks that had brought the behind-the-scenes maneuvering into the public eye. "I want to emphasize that I reached my recommendation only after much soul-searching and agonizing consideration," Dalton told reporters. "I believe that the damage done to the Navy's reputation by the incidents at Tailhook could have been prevented or minimized by aggressive leadership and foresight by senior Navy officers."[2]

Les Aspin moved rapidly to exert a degree of damage control, but there was no graceful way to overrule his Navy secretary. So Aspin released to the media copies of a memo he had sent to Dalton in which he said Dalton had failed to offer proper justification for his recommendation to fire Admiral Kelso. Kelso's job was safe—for the time being. Aspin said if superiors were to impose the Navy rule that a captain of a ship is responsible for whatever happens, then "the time for applying such a standard to [Kelso's] behavior has passed."[3]

When President Clinton announced that he had chosen Les Aspin, the fifty-five-year-old Wisconsin legislator was widely hailed by liberals in Washington as a thoroughly qualified military intellectual, which meant he took office with one strike against him as far as the realistic generals and admirals in the Pentagon were concerned.

After studying at Yale, Oxford, and the Massachusetts Institute of Technology, where he earned his Ph.D. in 1965, and after teaching economics for a while, Aspin had worked in the Pentagon as one of Defense Secretary Robert McNamara's trumpeted "Whiz Kids" during the Vietnam War. That was a second strike against him among top uniformed officers: They, like most in the professional military, blamed McNamara and his reliance on his young intellectuals as a root cause for the American disaster in Southeast Asia.

One group that was euphoric over Aspin's ascension to power in the Pentagon was the feminist lobby. While serving in the House of Representatives for twenty-two years, he had earned a reputation for being a staunch advocate of expanded roles for women in the armed forces.

Despite the embarrassing public dressing down he had received from Secretary Aspin, Dalton continued trying to isolate the "culprits" responsible for the Tailhook convention debauchery. On October 15, 1993, Rear Admiral Riley Mixon, chief of the Navy's Air Warfare Division and a highly decorated warrior, received a letter of censure from Dalton.

Mixon had attended the Las Vegas affair (his first Tailhook convention in thirteen years), and he was shocked to see how gross its nightlife had become. Almost immediately, he sent a report to his superiors in which he warned that the antics that had taken place must never be allowed to happen again.

Despite Mixon's action, Dalton charged him with being responsible for the arrangements at Tailhook 91. Rather than to meekly accept the severe reprimand, Mixon vigorously defended his reputation. In a written reply to the Navy secretary, Mixon refuted Dalton's charge. During much of the time plans were being drawn up for Tailhook 91, Mixon wrote, he was on the other side of the world directing air combat operations against Iraq.

"I can assure you, my thoughts in the [Persian Gulf] were not on Tailhook 91," he stated pointedly in his letter.[4]

Dalton was unimpressed at this convincing evidence that Mixon could not have been involved in making arrangements for Tailhook 91. Mixon remained officially censored. Consequently, the admiral missed out on a third star and the opportunity to become commander of Navy air forces in the Pacific fleet. A short time later, he retired from the Navy he had served with such great distinction.

By the fall of 1993—two years since the Tailhook 91 probe had been launched by the Naval Investigative Service—120 Navy and 20 Marine cases were considered for possible disciplinary action. About half of these accusations were dropped for lack of evidence.

Even when the charges did stand up, most of the male officers "went to the mast"—an internal, nonjudicial disciplinary procedure. Forty-one pilots found guilty of lying or unbecoming conduct were fined, reprimanded, or disciplined in some form. Ten other pilots had their careers put on hold for months before being cleared. Three admirals were censored for their alleged roles; two more were reassigned; and twenty-one, including Admiral Kelso, received nonpunitive letters of caution.

Navy and Marine officers had careers torpedoed for being at the wrong party at the wrong time, but Navy female officers walked away from unseemly behavior and lying to investigators with only mild reprimands or no disciplinary punishment. A woman ensign had accused a Navy lieutenant, along with two other men, of trying to "gang rape" her at the convention. Under oath, however, she confessed to concocting the entire scenario, allegedly to keep her fiancé from learning she had engaged in consentual sex with the lieutenant, who spent agonizing months before his name was cleared.[5]

Navy Lieutenant Rolando Diaz was tried for conduct unbecoming an officer. He had been charged with operating a "leg-shaving booth" in one of the Hilton hospitality suites, and his "customers" included a large number of women who raised their skirts for the ritual while others watched. Diaz received a career-threatening reprimand. Three female Navy officers, who allegedly had their legs shaved, one while wearing her dress whites, were not disciplined on such a severe basis.

When Marine Captain Gregory Bonham, the man Paula Coughlin had hesitantly picked out from photographs and a lineup as one of her assailants, came to trial in a Navy court, she testified her attacker wore an orange T-shirt. A photo taken the night of the incident and introduced as evidence showed Bonham wearing a distinctive green-striped shirt.

Coughlin testified she bit her attacker "as hard as I have ever bitten anyone" on the hand and forearm. "I think it drew blood," she added. Bonham showed his hands and arms to the court. There were no scars from heavy bites. Several witnesses who saw Bonham later on the night of the incident and the next day said they had seen no bloody teeth marks or other wounds.

As they had done during the NIS investigation, several witnesses said that Bonham attended church regularly, did not drink heavily, did not use profanity, and was respectful toward women. The captain testified that he spent that Saturday night quietly with friends, drinking a few beers. Captain Matthew Long backed Bonham's account, saying that he had been with him nearly all of the time that evening and that they had not been near the third floor corridor where Coughlin was molested.

On the witness stand, Coughlin admitted she drank champagne, wine, and vodka before the third-floor incident, but denied she was drunk. She also admitted she had spent much time during her three days at Las Vegas with a married male Navy officer, who, she testified, slept on the couch of her hotel room. She also acknowledged that after being molested, she went to the Circus Circus Hotel, drank a cocktail, returned to the Hilton, drank a beer, and played the slots.

The star witness in the Tailhook affair admitted that she initially had trouble identifying the man she accused of grabbing her breasts and buttocks.

Charges were dropped against Captain Bonham.

In the meantime, the U.S. Court of Military Appeals in Washington severely criticized the Navy's prosecution of Tailhook 91 cases as an "assembly-line technique that merged and blurred investigative and justice procedures . . . at best, it reflects a most curiously careless and amateurish approach to very high-profile cases. At worst, it raises the possibility of a shadiness in respecting the rights of military members."

During January 1994, Commander Gregory Tritt, Commander Thomas Miller, and Lieutenant David Samples—all Navy pilots—were being tried at Norfolk, Virginia, for dereliction of duty and failure to stop Tailhook misconduct they allegedly had seen. Their attorneys argued that the three defendants' prosecution was fundamentally unfair, that they could not be held accountable for their actions when the senior uniformed Navy officer, Admiral Frank Kelso, was also present at the Las Vegas Hilton, allegedly knew of the bawdy behavior, and took no action to stop it.

Presiding at the case against the three pilots was Navy Captain William T. Vest, Jr., the senior judge in the Tailhook trials. Vest, who began his twenty-eight-year naval career as a swiftboat driver in the brown waters of Vietnam, had been a Navy judge for nine years. For nearly a year, Vest had listened to testimony on alleged molestations, drunkenness, lies, and dereliction of duty as case after case paraded into his courtroom. His friends said he lost a lot of weight during the ordeal and agonized over his decisions, but always remained meticulous and dedicated to the Navy.

A few months earlier, during the fall of 1993, Admiral Kelso and the then-secretary of the Navy, H. Lawrence Garrett III, had been called to testify before Judge Vest about their presence at Tailhook 91. Before the two officials took the stand, Judge Vest warned defense and prosecution attorneys and observers that despite their high rank and stature, the two men were to be treated like any other witness. No undue deference would be paid to them, Vest said, and no one would stand when they entered the courtroom.

On the witness stand, Kelso said that he was not in any of the Tailhook hospitality suites on Friday and Saturday nights at the Tailhook convention and that he had seen no misconduct.

On February 8, 1994, many weeks after Kelso had testified, Judge Vest surprised many courtroom observers by dismissing all charges against Commanders Tritt and Miller and Lieutenant Samples. In delivering his 111-page ruling, Vest stated that Admiral Kelso had "erred in his testimony," meaning the judge felt that the chief of naval operations had lied about what he had seen or not seen at the Las Vegas Hilton.[6]

Vest said that Kelso had used "unlawful command influence" to "manipulate the initial investigative process and the subsequent [discipline] process in a manner designed to shield his personal involvement in Tailhook 91." The judge said that Kelso had been "suspect" in the scandal and thus had acted improperly in appointing Vice Admiral J. Paul Reason to decide whether or how other officers should be tried or punished despite Kelso's order to Reason to use "independent discretion." Vest found Reason's conduct "above reproach."

In dropping charges against the three Navy pilots, Vest said they could not be guilty of dereliction of duty if senior leaders knew of and condoned the misconduct at the Las Vegas Hilton.

When word of Judge Vest's ruling was flashed to the Pentagon, Admiral Kelso was shocked. "I have never seen the admiral so furious," said a staff officer. "He was deeply, personally offended."[7]

After a snow and ice storm had shut down most of the federal government in Washington, Kelso invited reporters to his office. "I've been accused of lying. I've been accused of manipulating the system to protect myself and other [admirals]," Kelso told the correspondents. "I categorically deny that I did either of those things."[8]

The Navy chief would not talk specifically on Judge Vest's ruling. "What I'm commenting on today is my integrity," the admiral said. "I am standing up for where I am and who I am. I am an honest man. I didn't lie and I didn't manipulate any process."[9]

Did Kelso plan to resign? "For the good of the Navy, I will remain," he replied.

Reporters then rushed to get the view of Patricia Schroeder, the outspoken feminist on the House Armed Services Committee. She was all for bouncing Kelso forthwith. "It was the Navy who came up with the idea that the captain goes down with his ship," she said.[10]

Many retired admirals rallied behind Frank Kelso, whom they felt was being unjustly accused. "He had the misfortune to be the CNO [chief of naval operations] at a time the Tailhook affair, which had been simmering for many years, finally exploded," said retired Vice Admiral John D. Bulkeley. Known as the Sea Wolf because of his bold exploits against the Japanese and Germans as a PT-boat squadron skipper during World War II, Bulkeley is one of American history's most highly decorated warriors. A secretary of the Navy once described him as "the greatest Navy legend of them all."[11]

Veterans groups also leaped to Kelso's side. They were convinced that he was being made a scapegoat, although they did not question Judge Vest's integrity.

Meanwhile, Secretary of Defense Les Aspin was involved in a prolonged fight with Congress and the Joint Chiefs over his desire to get women heavily involved in the combat arms and to let homosexuals serve in the military. He also was being blasted for his rejection of an urgent request by field commanders in Somalia, where U.S. forces had been ordered to capture local warlords, for tanks. When American Rangers were pinned down in Mogadishu, suffering eighteen deaths and seventy-five injuries, renewed cries went up for Aspin's scalp.

On December 15, Aspin announced at a press conference that he was resigning effective January 30, 1994.[12] "Aspin's inability to make decisions drove the uniformed guys crazy," said one senior national security official.

President Clinton had difficulty in finding a replacement for Aspin in the prestigious cabinet post. Former Senator Warren B. Rudman, a Republican, and Sam Nunn, chairman of the Senate Armed Services Committee, both turned down the job. A retired admiral and former deputy director of the Central Intelligence Agency, Bobby Ray Inman, accepted the appointment, then called a news conference to try to explain why he had changed his mind.

Clinton set his sights on William J. Perry, assistant secretary of defense, who balked. Vice President Al Gore and White House Chief of Staff Thomas F. McLarty III were sent to twist Perry's arm, a maneuver that proved to be successful. Although expressing strong reservations, the mathematical scientist accepted the assignment.

Shortly after New Year's Day 1994, members of the now defunct Presidential Commission on the Assignment of Women in the Armed Forces began hearing persistent rumblings that President Clinton was going to ignore most of the panel's recommendations on keeping women out of combat. On January 13, these rumors became reality. Les Aspin, the lame-duck defense secretary, notified Congress that the Navy was going to "allow women, both enlisted and officer personnel, to be assigned permanently to surface combat ships, all combat aircraft squadrons, all afloat staff, and units of the Naval Construction Force."[13]

At the same time, Aspin advised the armed services chiefs that "we've made historic progress" and "expanding the roles of women in the military is the right thing to do, and it's also the smart thing to do."

On February 10, six days after Judge William Vest cleared the final three Tailhook defendants, the Navy Department released a statement involving a junior officer:

> Paula Coughlin . . . has requested the Navy permit her to resign from the service. In a letter dated February 7, 1994, to Secretary of the Navy John H. Dalton, [Coughlin said] "I feel continued service would be detrimental to my physical, mental and emotional health."
>
> Coughlin further wrote: "The physical attack on me by Naval aviators at the 1991 Tailhook convention, and the covert and overt attacks on me that followed, have stripped me of my ability to serve. The foundation on which I serve my country remains steadfast, but I am unable to continue serving effectively as a United States Naval officer or as a Naval aviator."[14]

In a separate statement, Lieutenant Coughlin said:

> During the past 2 1/2 years, I have not been able to deal with the personal impact of the attack on me. The time has come for me to spend the time I need to heal. At this point in time, I have no specific plans for the future, except to concentrate on regaining my physical, emotional and mental health. My request to resign should not be viewed as a message to other women to refrain from reporting a physical assault. I have no regrets about the course of action

I chose in reporting the assault on me at the 1991 Tailhook convention. This [is] simply a personal decision forced by my own current needs.[15]

A day later, Derek Vander Schaaf, the chief Tailhook investigator, sent a memorandum to Defense Secretary William Perry supporting Admiral Frank Kelso's contention that he had not seen bawdy behavior at the Las Vegas convention. "During our investigation, we were unable to find any credible evidence that Admiral Kelso had specific knowledge of the improper incidents and events that took place," Vander Schaaf wrote.

"We reached that conclusion based on numerous witness interviews. We found individuals who believed they saw Admiral Kelso on the third floor during the infamous Saturday night," Vander Schaaf continued. "However, based on all the testimony, we believe that he was not present on Saturday and that those who believed they saw him are mistaken."[16]

Vander Schaaf's memorandum was included in a "fact sheet" that also disputed Judge Vest's opinion that Kelso had "manipulated" the Tailhook investigation by appointing Admiral Reason to recommend whether legal action should be taken against those charged with misconduct or other offenses. Sean O'Keefe, the Navy secretary at the time, said in an attached statement that he alone had made the decision to appoint Reason.[17]

27 ❖ Two Admirals Walk the Plank

Early in 1994, four-star Admiral Stanley R. Arthur, a hero of two wars, was nominated by President Bill Clinton to be commander of U.S. forces in the Pacific, one of the most complex and potentially explosive military regions. It includes the Korean peninsula, where the Communist regime in North Korea was making threats to invade U.S.-protected South Korea.

North Korea's greatest threat to peace in the Far East, however, may have been its development of nuclear weapons. The Central Intelligence Agency believed that North Korea already had such devices. Kim Jong Il, the nation's strongman, refused to permit international inspectors to poke around known nuclear sites and visit other locations where weapons-grade plutonium may have been stashed.

Admiral Arthur's credentials were impressive. He was a warrior, not an ivory-tower theorist, and he had earned an extraordinary eleven Distinguished Flying Crosses while on more than 500 combat missions in the Vietnam War. During the Persian Gulf conflict, Arthur had been in command of the Seventh Fleet.

"Stan Arthur is one of the most aggressive admirals I'd ever met," General H. Norman Schwarzkopf said later. "He had run three aircraft carriers up into the shallow and constricted waters of the [Persian] Gulf where the Navy had always refused to allow even one."[1]

Not only had Arthur been a fighting man, but his Pentagon experience was exemplary: Nearly three years as head of the Navy's mammoth, worldwide logistics system and the past two years as the vice chief of naval operations.

Washington observers felt that Arthur's nomination would sail through Senate confirmation with flying colors. However, Senator David Durenberger, who was not a member of the Armed Services Committee, took to the floor to declare that he had serious reservations about Arthur's nomination. He said that a constituent, Navy Lieutenant (j.g.) Rebecca Hansen, had complained to him that she had unfairly failed helicopter flight training after accusing a male instructor of making "sexual remarks" to her.[2]

Earlier, a Navy investigation found that Hansen had been sexually harassed. The instructor was disciplined and later left the Navy. But the probe also revealed that Hansen had failed to qualify because of a poor flight aptitude and performance both before and after the incident involving the instructor. Two other women trainees who had joined with Hansen in filing the harassment complaint against the same man later earned their wings.

Admiral Arthur routinely reviewed Lieutenant Hansen's flight training records and concurred in the findings of the investigators. He wrote to Durenberger:

> From [Hansen's] review I do not have sufficient confidence that she could safely and successfully operate an aircraft in a dangerous and unforgiving operational environment . . . I do not desire to see her or perhaps others die because she could not perform at a level consistent with our standards.

After more investigations, the inspectors general of both the Navy and the Department of Defense could uncover no evidence of reprisal against Lieutenant Hansen. Consequently, Secretary of the Navy John Dalton approved a recommendation that she be discharged from the service.

Senator Durenberger had been indicted by the Justice Department a year before on felony fraud charges accusing him of bilking the taxpayers by hiding his ownership of a Minneapolis condominium to collect thousands of dollars in reimbursement for lodging when he traveled to his home state. If convicted, the Minnesota senator faced a maximum sentence of ten years in prison and a $500,000 fine.

With that fraud charge still pending, Durenberger now disclosed a hitherto hidden lofty ethical standard as champion of Lieutenant Rebecca Hansen. He put a "hold" on Admiral Arthur's confirmation, a maneuver traditionally honored by fellow lawmakers.[3]

Some Capitol Hill observers believed that Durenberger had taken on the role to ingratiate himself with feminist groups and thereby, in some manner, avoid being tried, found guilty of fraud, and sent to prison. The evidence against him was heavy, including documents he had allegedly altered to pull off his bilking scheme.

Key senators privately advised the Pentagon that Admiral Arthur would be confirmed, but because of Durenberger's "hold," hearings might be delayed until fall.

While Stanley Arthur had been placed in Navy purgatory awaiting some action by Congress, Pentagon officials submitted to the Senate a retirement package for Admiral Frank Kelso, who was to depart in July after thirty-eight years of service. Without Senate action, four-star rank automatically reverts to two stars at retirement, with an annual pension of $67,467 instead of $84,340. Rarely, if ever, has the Senate denied retirement at full rank to a chief of a military service.

But now, the Washington climate was different. So when the Kelso retirement came up in the Senate on April 19, 1994, a firestorm of controversy erupted, much to the surprise of Pentagon civilian leaders who had expected the matter to slide through without acrimony.

All seven women senators—five Democrats and two Republicans—joined hands in castigating Kelso and seeking to block his retirement at four-star rank. Amidst a bevy of television and still cameras, eight women in the House, led by Patricia Schroeder, pranced across Capitol Plaza to the Senate chamber. They entered the cavernous room smiling but looking a bit awkward at invading the higher body.

The House outsiders walked behind Senator Barbara Boxer as she talked in the well, a means for getting in range of C-SPAN television cameras. At that time, the cameras did not pan, so the House women had to stand directly behind Boxer to be seen by viewers.

Male senators who supported Admiral Kelso were angered by what they perceived to be a blatant public-relations gimmick by the House women. But none took the floor to protest this violation of Senate custom. They only glared at the House females as they clustered behind Senator Boxer, who was standing on a box to provide better exposure for the cameras. After venturing over to the Republican side of the aisle to shake hands with Senator Kay Bailey Hutchison, the House women left the chamber.

Despite their annoyance over the invasion of the House females, most men in the Senate seemed intent on keeping the firestorm contained. But nerves were taut as the debate over Admiral Kelso grew more heated, erupting in a testy exchange between Senator Ted Stevens, a combat veteran, and Senator Carol Moseley-Braun. When Stevens questioned her understanding of a point in the debate, Moseley-Braun replied testily that it "defines chauvinism to suggest such a thing."[4]

One by one, the female Senators took potshots at Kelso. The Senate should "send a message to the Navy and the world that Tailhook-style behavior will not be condoned," said Kay Bailey Hutchison. "The U.S. military culture must change," declared Senator Barbara Mikulski. "The buck for Tailhook stops with Admiral Kelso," said Carol Moseley-Braun.[5]

In a highly emotional tone, Senator Patty Murray said she often encounters young women who want to be aviators, astronauts, or senators. "What do I tell them about Tailhook if they want a career in the armed forces?" she asked.[6]

"Do I believe [Kelso] was there?" Senator Dianne Feinstein asked. "Yes," she stated. "Do I believe he was protected by some of his flag staff around him? Yes."

Continuing, she said, "I recognize it would have been unpopular for Admiral Kelso to go in from the patio and say, 'Hey, guys, knock it off. This thing is at an end.' But that's what he should have done to end the age-old attitude in the military that 'boys will be boys.'"[7]

Male senators who supported the admiral were furious and believed he was being turned into a signal, as Carol Moseley-Braun put it, "that we are no longer content to stand by and watch women treated as less than equal citizens." Kelso, his Senate boosters felt, was a handy pop-up target for all the complaints females everywhere in society have voiced.

At one point, Senator Bob Smith sarcastically referred to male senators as "those of us who happen to be men by circumstances beyond our control."[8]

Absent from the Senate floor was Nancy Kassebaum, who, years earlier, had spearheaded a drive to have Congress pass a measure that would register women for the draft. Her press secretary said the senator was unable to attend the debate because she was "tied up in conferences and utterly exhausted." However, Kassebaum issued a statement saying that while Kelso had tried to take steps to help women in the Navy, he had "demonstrated a complete failure of leadership in the Tailhook affair."[9]

Male senators came down strongly on both sides of the controversy. Most were speaking from their convictions. A few, including Senator Arlen Specter, chose to play sexual politics to advance their own personal agenda. Back in 1991, Specter had brought the wrath of the feminist lobby down on his head for what it perceived to be his harsh questioning of Anita Hill during Senate confirmation hearings for Clarence Thomas, who had been nominated to the Supreme Court by President Bush. Hill had claimed she had been sexually harassed by Thomas ten years earlier.[10]

Now, future events would disclose, Specter had his eye on being president himself, so he savagely attacked Admiral Kelso on the Senate floor, no doubt seeking to curry favor with the feminist lobby that had sought Specter's scalp four years earlier.

Specter said his staff had tried to "get to the bottom" of the Tailhook matter and asked the Defense Department for the full inspector general's report on Kelso and other flag officers present at Las Vegas. But the Pentagon refused to provide the document, Specter complained.

At one point, Senator John McCain, a former Navy pilot who had been a prisoner of the North Vietnamese for more than six years and was a Kelso supporter, refused to yield the floor to Specter, saying that he had yielded to Specter once and had not gotten the microphone back in a timely fashion. The two men later exchanged sharp words and had to be reprimanded to be silent so that Senator Patty Murray, who was speaking at the time, could be heard.

Supporters of Admiral Kelso mounted a counterattack, led by Senator Sam Nunn, who headed the committee that recommended the full pension and four-star retirement rank. Although ill, Nunn spoke at length. He agreed that Tailhook had been "repugnant." But he said that he knew Frank Kelso personally and believed the admiral's contention that he had not seen any of the bawdy behavior at Tailhook 91 and that he had not tried to impede the subsequent investigation in any way.

Arguing that Kelso should not be made a scapegoat, Nunn asserted that if the Senate took away four-star retirement from every admiral or general who had presided over a branch of the armed services when some disaster or scandal occurred, "no one would have gotten four stars."[11]

Nunn pointed out that Kelso had offered to resign $2^1/_2$ years ago, but that his civilian superiors in the Pentagon had asked him to stay and help stabilize the gender problems in the Navy. "Now some are trying to penalize him for staying," the senator said.[12]

Senator J. James Exon said Defense Secretary William Perry and General John Shalikashvili, chairman of the Joint Chiefs, also vouched for Kelso and concluded that he had not known of any wrongdoing or engaged in a cover-up.

Support for Kelso came from an unexpected source. Navy Secretary John Dalton, who had tried to fire the admiral a few months earlier, telephoned three or four undecided senators to remind them that he had nevertheless always supported retiring Kelso in his current rank.

For six hours, the Senate chamber echoed in contentious, often empurpled speeches of praise and condemnation of Admiral Kelso. One camp wanted him to retire with his full pension and four stars intact; the other camp wanted him to be humiliated as an example to other military leaders. When the final oratorical note faded away, the Kelso forces had carried the day by a vote of 54 to 43, with thirty-six males joining with the seven women in a losing cause.

Among the Republicans voting to penalize Admiral Kelso two stars and, in essence, fine him $16,873 annually for the rest of his life (the difference between two- and four-star pensions) was Senator Bob Packwood. At the time, he was under investigation by the Senate ethics committee for sexual harassment after several women in his home state of Oregon complained that the senator had kissed and fondled them against their will.

Soon after the Kelso matter was settled in Congress, Secretary of the Army Togo D. West, Jr., sent a memorandum to Defense Secretary William Perry, proposing that women should be assigned to combat engineers, air defense artillery, special operations aircraft that carry commandos, and field artillery.[13]

West, a graduate of the Army's Judge Advocate Officer Basic Course in 1969, had been helped in drawing up the proposal by Assistant Secretary of the Army Sara Lister. Both officials were appointees of President Clinton.

In his memorandum, West stated: "America's Army is proud to be in the forefront of providing opportunities for all service members."[14]

West's document used phrases such as "career opportunities" ten times, but any reference to armed forces readiness was absent.

Before sending his proposal to Secretary Perry, West hadn't conferred with Army Chief of Staff Gordon Sullivan, a highly decorated combat veteran. Sullivan was in favor of opening more jobs to women, but he was strongly opposed to placing them in combat units. Sullivan reportedly learned of the memo only after it had been leaked to the media and its contents published. According to one aide, he "hit the roof."

Pentagon generals were staunchly opposed to West's recommendation. Binford Peay, now a three-star general and deputy chief of staff, who had led the 101st Airborne Division in Desert Storm, testified before the Senate Armed Services Committee, "I do not think it is appropriate to open up [to women] the traditional positions of infantry, armor, field artillery, air defense at certain levels on the battlefield, special forces aviation, and a few others."[15]

Retired officers also attacked West's proposal. "Apparently he had never taken the time to read after-action reports from Vietnam where combat engineers moved right into battle with infantry companies," wrote Michael Marks, a retired Army lieutenant colonel and editor of *Military* magazine. "Nor did he understand how hairy it can get breaching minefields and obstacles in front of the infantry and armor when they had attacked in Desert Storm."[16]

Special operations helicopters, a job West wanted opened to women, do not stay in the air at all times, Marks, a Vietnam combat veteran, pointed out. "Typically, they fly Green Berets, Rangers, and other commando-type teams deep behind enemy lines," he added. "If these choppers are shot down or otherwise unable to take off for the return flight, pilots must fight as infantrymen, often while their group is surrounded."

During escape and evasion, the helicopter pilots have to lug heavy packs, equipment, weapons, and also help carry wounded men. "Any American chopper pilot who had to fight his way off a 'hot LZ' [landing zone] through a ring of tough, battle-hardened enemy soldiers in Vietnam knows that few women could hack it," Marks stated.[17]

Frank Kelso quietly retired in July 1994 and was replaced by fifty-five-year-old Admiral Jeremy M. "Mike" Boorda, a "mustang" in military parlance, an officer who came up through the enlisted ranks. A pipe smoker and articulate speaker, Boorda was the first of that breed to become Chief of Naval Operations.

After dropping out of high school, Boorda lied about his age, forged a birth certificate, and joined the Navy when sixteen. In 1962, he graduated from Officer Candidate School and received a degree in political science from the University of Rhode Island in 1971. Before taking over in the Pentagon, he had been commander of the North Atlantic Treaty Organization (NATO) forces in southern Europe.

One of Boorda's first acts was to announce that the Navy would help solve its problems in the wake of the Tailhook affair by a 20 percent increase in the recruitment of women. He also said he was seriously considering assigning females to submarines, thereby triggering much eyebrow lifting among most senior Navy officers.

On submarines, narrow "hot bunks" are assigned to two or more crew members working different shifts. Privacy is absent. Even bodily functions often must be carried out in view of others. Setting aside preferred living accommodations for the exclusive use of females would cause serious dissension in the crew, critics of Boorda's proposal were convinced.

On the same day the media ran stories on the submarine coed crew suggestion, the *Navy Times* published an article about the tender *Puget Sound*. The skipper of the sexually-integrated vessel had disciplined eight men and women for fraternization, adultery, sodomy, sexual harassment, communication of threats, and violations of orders.

Meanwhile, some members of Congress continued their attacks on Admiral Stanley Arthur, whose nomination for the top command in the Pacific had been put on "hold" by David Durenberger, the senator under federal indictment for fraud. In their fervor to bring Arthur down, some critics in the Senate even invented new standards for high command: Admiral Arthur, they said, was not suitable because he was overweight.

Previously, the senate had confirmed Arthur's nomination as Seventh Fleet commander and again as vice chief of naval operations when he had tipped the scales at the same poundage. On the other side, one senator pointed out that the commander in chief of the armed forces, Bill Clinton, was some thirty pounds overweight, according to his physician.

Meanwhile, Lieutenant Rebecca Hansen, the centerpiece in the brouhaha over Admiral Arthur, was given extraordinary treatment for a junior officer. Accompanied by Durenberger's assistant, Anne Crowther, Hansen personally pleaded her case to Navy Secretary John Dalton, Assistant Navy Secretary F. Y. Yang, and Admiral Mike Boorda.

Subsequently, behind-the-scenes maneuvering apparently took place at the highest levels in the Pentagon, resulting in the chairman of the Joint Chiefs, General John Shalikashvili, allegedly encouraging Admiral Boorda to obtain Arthur's consent to having his nomination withdrawn and "retiring."

On June 24, 1994, the Navy Department issued a statement saying Arthur "agrees with the chief of naval operations [Boorda] that the nomination be rescinded." It explained that an "anticipated delay in [Arthur's] Senate confirmation" would not permit a "prompt relief" for Admiral Charles R. Larson, whom Arthur would have succeeded as commander in the Pacific. Larson was scheduled to become superintendent of the Naval Academy.

Arthur, therefore, would retire as soon as his current job, vice chief of naval operation, was filled, the statement said.

Nonsense, declared James Webb, a Marine infantry commander in Vietnam and secretary of the Navy during part of the Reagan administration. "Admiral Larson's new assignment [to the Naval Academy] was not time-sensitive," Webb explained. "In fact, it also awaited Senate action. It had been widely reported that Admiral Boorda was less concerned about a delay in Admiral Arthur's confirmation than about becoming ensnared in another sexual harassment scandal [Tailhook]."[18]

Thus Admiral Stanley Arthur was forced to "walk the plank," the method used by pirates of old to get rid of a crewmen who had fallen into disfavor with the ship's hierarchy.

Angry voices were raised around the country. "Both the Senate Armed Services Committee and the whole Defense Department leadership caved in," said Harry G. Summers, Jr., a retired Army colonel, ground combat veteran, and later a syndicated columnist.[19]

"From the White House to the Pentagon to the Senate, people who should have stood by Admiral Arthur, and the integrity of the system he was trying to defend, all capitulated to the grandstanding of [Senator Durenberger]," said Elaine Donnelly, president of the Center for Military Readiness. "It was an appalling demonstration of sexual politics at its worst."[20]

On June 24, twenty-four hours after the decision had been made to withdraw the Arthur nomination, Admiral Mike Boorda, the new Navy chief, met with Lieutenant Rebecca Hansen at the Great Lakes Naval Training Station near Chicago. Many flag officers and lesser Navy ranks were astonished: Perhaps for the first time the Navy's top uniformed leader engaged in what one admiral called "a hand-holding session with a lowly lieutenant."

Boorda reportedly offered Hansen a job on his staff. To many Navy officers, that action conveyed the impression that Boorda had swapped one of the Navy's most illustrious admirals for a junior lieutenant who couldn't fly straight.

If Boorda's goal had been to appease Rebecca Hansen, as many critics claimed, he failed. She rejected the cushy Pentagon assignment, then presented the Navy chief with a long list of demands that included: a personal apology from Navy Secretary John Dalton; critical comments and performance evaluations in her Navy records be expunged; these records be rewritten in words of her own choosing; her flight-performance ratings be upgraded to "outstanding"; she be promoted on a noncompetitive [guaranteed] basis; she be given time off and government money to complete civilian flight training; she be retained on active-duty status while attending a law school of her own choice at taxpayers' expense; and written assurance that she could eventually join the Navy judge advocate general's staff, handling women's issues.

Admiral Boorda, of course, had no authority to meet those demands, so he flew back to the Pentagon. There he and other top Navy leaders huddled to put the best face possible on what had become known in the fleet as the "Arthur affair." On July 1, only one week after the withdrawal of the Arthur nomination, President Clinton nominated Vice Admiral Richard C. Macke (no doubt on the recommendation of Pentagon leaders) for the Pacific command. Macke, a capable but far less experienced officer, had been earmarked to replace Arthur as vice chief of naval operations. Macke's confirmation breezed through the Senate.

Just over a year after Macke had taken command of 330,000 U.S. soldiers, sailors, airmen, and Marines in one of the world's most strategic regions, he was forced into retirement after nearly thirty-six years of service. His demise began with an alleged rape of a twelve-year-old Okinawa girl for which two enlisted Navy men and an enlisted Marine were tried in a local civilian court. A few days later, Macke told reporters that the rape, though regrettable, could have been avoided if the three accused Americans had hired a prostitute.

Shortly after news reports of his remark became known, Macke issued a written apology. A few hours later, Defense Secretary William Perry announced that the fifty-seven-year-old Admiral Macke would retire. "We decided that his lapse of judgment was so serious that he would be unable to perform effectively his duties," Perry said in a written statement.[21]

For more than 200 years, the United States had refused to have female soldiers too close to the front lines. On October 1, 1994, that tradition was shattered. Women now could be placed on an involuntary basis in air cavalry helicopter units, some engineer outfits, special operations aviation, air defense artillery, and in certain battalion and regimental headquarters.

"It is the right thing to do," said Defense Secretary William Perry, whose profession is mathematical science.

Perry and his civilian staff in the Pentagon had ignored the advice of the generals and the vigorous protests of veterans groups.

"The Clinton administration has taken the unprecedented action of rewriting personnel policy to assign women in or near ground combat units, without regard to the legislative role of Congress in making policy for the armed forces," said Allen F. Kent, national commander of the Veterans of Foreign Wars.[22]

Earlier, the VFW passed a resolution that stated in part: "The VFW questions the wisdom of the decisions that place women in harm's way to be killed, wounded, and captured in large numbers . . . We go on record as opposing the assignment of women to jobs that call for them to aggressively seek out, close with, and kill or capture enemy forces."[23]

28 ❖ The Ike Makes History

Haiti was a trouble spot for the Bill Clinton administration in the summer of 1994. A tiny, poverty-stricken country with a population of some seven million, Haiti is the western third of the Caribbean island of Hispaniola. The Dominican Republic makes up the remainder of the island.

Four years earlier in 1990, Haiti citizens went to the polls and elected Jean-Bertrand Aristide president. He was a controversial figure in the United States. A one-time Catholic priest, Aristide had been defrocked by the Vatican for refusing to tone down pulpit diatribes urging the people to commit violence on more-affluent members of the populace.

Eight months later, Aristide was overthrown in a coup led by General Raoul Cédras and his junta of military officers. They took control of Haiti's government, and Aristide escaped to the United States where the State Department provided him with a luxury apartment in Washington, D.C.

Throughout the first half of 1994, President Clinton had been warning General Cédras to step down and permit the restoration of Jean-Bertrand Aristide to office or the Haitian strongman would be forcefully driven out by the U.S. armed forces. Clinton's threat to invade Haiti triggered a controversy in Congress and elsewhere around the United States.

In the meantime, U.S. military history was being made. Although women had served on Navy support vessels for more than fifteen years, the nuclear powered aircraft carrier *Dwight D. Eisenhower* would be the first combat ship to deploy with females integrated into its crew. On board the *Ike*, as the huge floating platform was popularly called, were 415 women, including nine pilots, and 4,552 men.

Earlier, a few million dollars were spent reconfiguring the *Ike* to accommodate female crew members. Bathrooms (heads to the Navy) and sleeping quarters were renovated. More heads had to be allotted to women so that they wouldn't have to walk far to find a facility on the 1,092–foot-long carrier.

Doctors trained in gynecology were brought aboard. Even the ship's barbers were given special classes in cutting and styling women's hair. Females quickly learned that their lingerie would be ruined in the laundry, which had no "gentle" cycle, so adjustments had to be created. Menus had been geared to hungry young males with few low-fat items, so dieticians were employed to create "unisex menus."

Male sailors were put through a strenuous indoctrination on how to conduct themselves around women aboard ship. They were given color-coded brochures (drawn up under the eagle eye of a top Pentagon officer) that stated that a polite compliment to a female was in the "green zone" and acceptable. Unacceptable behavior fell in the "red zone," and included suggestive remarks and promising promotions to females in return for sexual favors.

The *Ike's* skipper, Captain Alan Mark Gemmill, sternly warned that sexual relations would be prohibited on board. Earlier, Lieutenant Commander Maureen Davidovich, who worked on women's policy issues for the Navy, explained: "Sexual activities on Navy vessels is considered to be detrimental to good order and discipline."[1]

By deluging male sailors with a bewildering array of "do's" and "don'ts," Navy brass apparently hoped to avert the notoriety generated by the support vessels *Arcadia* and *Yellowstone* during the Persian Gulf deployment. Altogether, fifty-six female crew members had returned pregnant to the United States. Other women on the two ships complained that they had to guard against shipboard scuttlebutt about who's sleeping with whom. "Rumors spread like wildfire," said Petty Officer Monique Code of the *Yellowstone*.[2]

In August 1994, while the armed forces were preparing to invade Haiti, thirty-four-year-old Navy Lieutenant Commander Kenneth A. Carkhuff was assigned to lead a helicopter detachment in the operation. His unit included two women pilots. After days of prayer and soul-searching, Carkhuff felt honor-bound to privately inform his immediate superior, Commander Douglas Beeks, that his religious beliefs held that it was morally wrong to thrust women into violent situations where they could be killed, mutilated, or captured by a brutal enemy. At no time did Carkhuff, a devout Episcopalian and father of five children, say that he would not lead his detachment—including the two women pilots—into battle if so ordered.

A graduate of the Naval Academy who had served his country with distinction for thirteen years, Carkhuff was the type of gifted, bright, dedicated young officer that had been the backbone of the Navy since its founding with two wooden gunboats in 1794. Glowing efficiency reports by his superiors had described him as a "Navy superstar" with "unlimited potential" who was "destined for [high] command."

Word about Carkhuff's privately expressed religious beliefs rocketed up the Navy chain of command and landed with a heavy thud on the third floor of the Pentagon's outer ring (the "E" ring), where the highest ranking Defense Department civilians as well as the uniformed top brass reside.

From the windows of their plush suites, Navy Secretary John Dalton and Admiral Mike Boorda, chief of naval operations, could look out across the expanse of the Potomac toward the Capitol.

The arrival of the Kenneth Carkhuff report in the "E" ring executive suites ignited a major flap. It was as though a dangerous enemy saboteur had been apprehended inside the supersecret War Room of the Pentagon. On Friday, September 2, Carkhuff was informed by his immediate commander—no doubt on orders from on high—that if he were to submit a written resignation from the service by Monday, only three days away, the Navy brass would allow him six months to find a civilian job prior to his departure. If he refused to resign, he was told, the Navy would discharge him.

Confused, worried, and concerned about how he would support his wife and five children, Carkhuff submitted his resignation. A few days later, he withdrew the document after a civilian lawyer, Stephen Gallagher, informed him that the Navy could not precipitously bounce him from the service.

"I'm not going out the back door of the Navy!" Carkhuff declared.[3]

Perceptive officers in the fleet understood that they were expected to take a "correct" posture in what was now being called the "Carkhuff affair" or have their careers killed. Consequently, Carkhuff's uniformed superiors submitted letters endorsing his ouster.

Elaine Donnelly, the Center for Military Readiness president, explained: "This is the *new* Navy: An officer's career depends on his having the 'politically correct' view on women in combat, as defined by professional feminists who know how to exploit sexual politics to get their way."

"These Navy officers no doubt were shielding themselves from the shriekings of feminists and their supporters in Congress," Donnelly continued. "The Senate must approve nominations for promotion to flag [admiral] and also an officer's retirement rank. So they were hoping to avoid the ordeals inflicted on three top admirals [Kelso, Arthur, and Mixon], all of whom 'retired' earlier in 1994 after being attacked by a vociferous group of female senators for not being sufficiently supportive of the feminist agenda for the armed forces."[4]

Soon, the Navy leaders initiated legal proceedings against Carkhuff. He was charged with "failure to demonstrate acceptable qualities of leadership required of an officer in his grade, as evidenced by his refusal to support and execute [Navy] policies regarding women in combat."

At this time, Secretary Dalton blocked the promotion to rear admiral of Captain Mark Rogers, an exemplary officer who had a distinguished record as a ship commander before being appointed to serve as deputy director of the White House Military Office in May 1993. Rogers allegedly had made disparaging remarks in private about certain women on President Clinton's staff. Dalton broadly interpreted Rogers' confidential asides as "sexual harassment."[5]

Meanwhile, in a televised speech on September 15, President Bill Clinton pledged to "restore democracy" in Haiti by putting Jean-Bertrand Aristide back in the presidential palace. Clinton called General Raoul Cédras and his clique "murderous thugs," said they would have to go, time was up, and all diplomacy had been exhausted.

Two hours later, Clinton flip-flopped. Rousting former President Jimmy Carter out of bed by telephone at 11:00 P.M., Clinton asked him to head a bargaining team that would leave promptly for Haiti. Carter accepted. Going with him would be retired General Colin Powell, who had gained fame while chairman of the Joint Chiefs of Staff during the Persian Gulf crisis, and Sam Nunn, chairman of the Senate Armed Services Committee.

Negotiations at Port-au-Prince between the Carter team and General Cédras were tension-packed and dragged on for forty-eight hours.

At noon on Sunday, September 18, President Clinton and his top advisers were in the Oval Office of the White House, anxiously awaiting word from the Carter delegation. If the last-ditch negotiations failed to convince Cédras to leave Haiti and permit a peaceful U.S. invasion, paratroopers of the 82nd Airborne Division would bail out at midnight, only twelve hours away, to spearhead an invasion by U.S. troops. At 1:00 P.M., General John Shalikashvili, chairman of the Joint Chiefs, flashed word for the airborne men to start heading for their airplanes at Fort Bragg, North Carolina.[6]

It was 5:30 P.M. in Port-au-Prince when Brigadier General Philippe Biamby, the Haitian army chief of staff, burst into the negotiating session and excitedly told Cédras: "They're laying a trap for us!" Biamby said his spy in North Carolina had just faxed a report that the 82nd Airborne was moving out.[7]

Faced with an imminent assault, Cédras ordered his army not to resist the invasion. But he balked over signing a document agreeing to leave Haiti. However, at Colin Powell's suggestion, Cédras gave his word "as a professional military officer" that he would depart the country in due time after the invaders were ashore. Going into exile with him would be a king's ransom from Uncle Sam's treasury.[8]

"Recall! Recall!" The order blared through the crowded Joint Operating Command Center aboard the USS *Mount Whitney* off the Haitian coast. Sixty-one planes winging toward the island with paratroopers aboard swung back toward Fort Bragg. Within hours, some 15,000 other U.S. troops including sizable numbers of women, debarked from ships, landed in transport planes and helicopters, and deployed in Haiti without a shot being fired.

Soon word leaked back to the United States from Haiti that the Army was putting into practice the unisex policies that had grown more prevalent since the Persian Gulf conflict three years earlier. Some male and female soldiers and officers were being housed together in small tents, with no privacy between the cots. When queried by the media about cohabitation, Major Cindy Sito, a Pentagon spokeswoman, explained that the Army wants its people to be able to "reach out and touch everybody."[9]

"Putting young, healthy men and women together in small tents is an excellent technique to achieve that goal," Elaine Donnelly, president of the Detroit-based Center for Military Readiness, declared. "The last time I checked, however, male-female 'touching' was contrary to the Uniform Code of Military Justice."[10]

"I have been and am a supporter of women in non-combat roles," Donnelly stressed. "In several wars and in peacetime they have served their country exceptionally well. We are all extremely proud of them."[11]

After learning of the Army's coed housing policy in Haiti, Donnelly charged that Defense Secretary William Perry and other top civilians in the Pentagon had deliberately mislead Congress. Perry had informed J. Strom Thurmond, ranking Republican on the Senate Armed Services Committee, that appropriate privacy for military men and women was being provided in Haiti on land as well as at sea.

Donnelly felt that Secretary Perry had a peculiar definition for "appropriate privacy." She feared that if the Pentagon's social engineering experiment with small unisex tents in Haiti could be declared a success, the policy would develop into a prototype for all the armed forces in the future.[12]

While the Haitian mission was being mounted, in July 1994, culpability in the celebrated Tailhook 91 molestation case shifted from the military courts to a civil lawsuit in Nevada. Paula Coughlin, the former helicopter pilot who had resigned from the Navy five months earlier, was suing the Tailhook Association and the Hilton Hotels.

Coughlin accused the Association of failing to supervise the convention properly and the Hilton of negligence in not providing better security. Four days before the case was to begin in Federal District Court in Las Vegas, Coughlin settled with the Tailhook Association for $400,000. That agreement left the Hilton as the remaining defendant.

While preparing for trial, lawyers for the Hilton chain took many hours of depositions (testimony taken down in writing under oath) from Coughlin. She said that on Friday—the first of the two nights—she returned to her hotel room about 5:00 P.M. and went to bed at 9:00 P.M. But a couple who attended the convention would testify they saw Coughlin that Friday night among a crowd of male pilots drinking alcoholic beverages on a third-floor balcony.

"When I got to talking with her, it became clear that she was intoxicated to the point that if I were working as a commercial bartender I would be hesitant, if not outright certain, that I would not serve her," testified Ross Lindholm, who accompanied his wife to the convention. Lindholm, a Washington aide to Senator Connie Mack, said he recognized Coughlin because she had met with the senator earlier that year while lobbying to repeal the bar against women flying combat missions.

Lindholm, who had worked briefly as a bartender in college, added: "I don't think that I'm making a subtle judgment here based on, you know, my arcane knowledge of bartending and psychology of people with alcohol. My wife—my now wife—as we drifted away [that night] from Paula Coughlin, said, 'Boy, she's sure having a good time.'"[13]

His wife, Lori Lindholm, who was then a Navy helicopter pilot and had lobbied along with Coughlin on Capitol Hill, confirmed her husband's account in a separate sworn deposition. She left the Navy in 1993.

The Hilton defense team also produced two witnesses who said they saw Coughlin getting her legs shaved in a squadron hospitality suite. Lieutenant Rolando Diaz, a Hawkeye pilot, already said in a military courtroom that he shaved Coughlin's legs on two occasions in a ritual that included a baby-oil massage. He repeated the assertion in a deposition, saying he shaved her legs once while she wore a dress-white uniform.

Now, the first witness to independently corroborate Lieutenant Diaz's account came forward. Tamela Redford, who in 1991 was a Navy transport pilot, testified she passed through Diaz's suite that Friday and saw a woman in uniform being leg-shaved. She said she realized the woman was Paula Coughlin the following summer when Coughlin went public with her molestation charges and her picture was published in newspapers.

"I just turned around and I noticed in the corner they had a leg-shaving booth set up and there was a girl getting her legs shaved, which would not have really caught my eye except for that she was in her uniform, in her whites, and she had bare legs, you know, no hose on, and she had her skirt, you know, hiked up fairly high," Redford said in a deposition.[14]

"And it just struck me as somewhat offensive, not in that, you know, somebody was getting their legs shaved, because, you know, what goes on between consenting adults is fine. But that it was in uniform, I thought that that was inappropriate and disrespectful."[15]

"Who was the person you saw in the chair?" she was asked.

"Paula Coughlin."

Redford initially told Naval Investigative Service agents about the incident in a November 1991 statement. She said then she could not identify the woman officer. Months later, however, after seeing Coughlin's photograph in the newspapers, Redford attempted to tell inspector general agents about the incident during their separate Tailhook investigation. But she said "the agents were not interested in hearing any negative comments about their star witness."

"They didn't want to hear about it and they certainly were not going to do anything about it," Redford said in her deposition.[16]

Just prior to the opening of the Las Vegas trial, U.S. District Judge Phillip M. Pro ruled that the Defense Department's official Tailhook investigation report could not be used as evidence in a civil trial. Pro said the report was replete with uncorroborated and hearsay testimony attributed to unidentified persons. Therefore, the judge said, admitting the report as evidence would "confuse and mislead the jury."

When the trial got underway, Paula Coughlin testified that she feared that the Navy pilots in the Hilton corridor would rape her. Weeping, she said, "I got attacked by a bunch of men that tried to pull my clothes off." After reaching an empty suite, she told the court, "I was crying. I was really upset."[17]

Under cross-examination by lawyers for the Hilton, Coughlin acknowledged that after the molestation at around 11:30 P.M., she went to the Circus Circus Hotel, drank a cocktail, returned to the Hilton, got a beer, and played the slot machines before going to her room. Earlier, Coughlin testified to having spent much time during her three days in Las Vegas with a married male Navy pilot, who, she said, she let sleep on the couch in her hotel room.[18]

In her second day on the witness stand, Coughlin said she endured great harassment from her colleagues in the Navy after going public with her story on the molestations. "Most of the people in the Navy . . . were afraid to talk to me," she said. "I was shunned."[19]

Coughlin spent most of her three days on the witness stand defending her conduct in the year and a half after the incident. Under cross-examination, she admitted that despite what she said was her fragile mental state and recurring thoughts of suicide, she continued to pilot helicopters. Generally, military pilots are not permitted to fly if they are under stress or unusually distracted by personal problems. A pilot who admits to suicidal thoughts is almost invariably grounded.

Coughlin testified that she had told two superiors about her suicidal thoughts. "I made an agreement with my commanding officer that I would never fly if I was too distracted or incapable," she said.[20]

On October 31, after a seven-week trial, the four-man, four-woman jury awarded Coughlin $5 million in punitive damages and $1.7 million in compensatory damages.

"I think justice was served," Coughlin said, speaking with reporters for the first time since the trial began.[21]

29 ❖ Disaster on an Aircraft Carrier

Navy Lieutenant Kara S. Hultgreen was at the controls of an F-14 Tomcat fighter plane as it circled above the carrier USS *Abraham Lincoln* forty miles southwest of San Diego. With her was Lieutenant Matthew Klemich, the radar intercept officer (RIO). It was mid-afternoon on the clear day of October 25, 1994.

Hultgreen was one of eighteen women who had been qualified to fly carrier-based combat aircraft after Congress removed the ban. An indomitable and courageous woman, she was fully aware that hers was an exacting and demanding profession, that flying the thirty-five-ton F-14 was risky business.

"It's like dancing with an elephant," she had told CBS-TV News a few weeks earlier. "You can ease it over to the right and sort of nudge it over to the left. But when it decides it's going to sit down, there's nothing you can do about it."

Now off San Diego, twenty-nine-year-old Kara Hultgreen headed for a landing on the carrier, possibly the most dangerous task in the peacetime armed forces. The margin between life and death is razor thin. As the Tomcat neared the *Lincoln*, it appeared that she made a series of minor errors and overcorrected each of them. Apparently, she was flying too slowly and applying too much rudder trying to move the plane to the left. The angle of the wings in relation to the flight deck was too steep, a factor that dropped the left wing and turned the Tomcat to the left, depriving the left engine of enough air.[1]

As the plane neared the deck, the engine stalled. Some twenty seconds later Lieutenant Klemich called out that the plane was going five knots too fast. Seven seconds later he said, "We're ten knots slow—let's get some power on the jet!"

Moments before the Tomcat reached the flight deck, the LSO (landing signal officer) on the *Lincoln* waved off the plane, ordering Hultgreen to level its wings, apply power, and climb. Then the LSO ordered: "Eject! Eject!"[2]

In a split second of one another, Klemich and Hultgreen ejected. Klemich splashed into the water and was rescued, shaken but not seriously injured.

Hultgreen, still strapped to her seat, disappeared into the deep. So did the Tomcat.

Within days of the tragedy, a rash of articles and broadcast reports around the nation speculated that engine malfunction had caused the crash. There was not even a hint that pilot error could have been a contributing factor. Then Roger Hedgecock, a talk-show host in San Diego, home port of the *Abraham Lincoln*, received a seven-page fax from an anonymous source, no doubt a Navy pilot on active duty.

The document said that Lieutenant Hultgreen's grades had been below average in flight school, and that "something is terribly wrong with the U.S. Navy today, and it ought to be fixed before it is too late. We owe it to Kara Hultgreen." Hedgecock read part of the fax over the air.

A short time later, the talk-show host received a telephone call from someone who said that Hultgreen's flight instructors had been ordered to pass her "whatever her grades." Hedgecock read that remark over the air, also. Then came another telephone call from a person who said Hultgreen had received special treatment because she was a woman. "We have taken the minimum [qualification requirements] and changed them so that we can allow various people in [the Navy] for social programs, including me," the caller declared.[3]

Columnists, editorial writers, and broadcast commentators reacted vigorously. *The New York Times* alluded to "spurious accusations about [Hultgreen's] flight record . . . apparently from disgruntled male aviators." Georgie Anne Geyer complained in her syndicated column that some pilots from "the old school sent anonymous faxes around impugning her qualifications." Peter Jennings of ABC-TV labeled the anonymous fax "a smear campaign."

A *Newsweek* article said: "Traditionalists are spreading the rumor that she was unqualified [for carrier landings]. The goal, it seems, is to suggest that Hultgreen was unfit for combat aviation and that the Navy had bent its own rules to help her qualify. This posthumous slur, cruel by any standards, enrages feminists and fair-minded men as well."[4]

Bobbie Carlton, a former Navy public relations officer and now a civilian and outspoken activist for women's issues, declared: "It's unheard of to attack the flight record of a dead pilot."[5]

Hultgreen had often said that she didn't want to be the recipient of special treatment or double standards. Rear Admiral Robert Hickey, commander of the Nimitz carrier battle group in San Diego, recalled the lieutenant telling him a year earlier: "Guys like you have to make sure there's only one standard. If people let me slide through on a lower standard, it's my life on the line. I could get killed."[6]

Yet the Navy's own flight records seem to indicate that Hultgreen indeed had been given extraordinary handling during flight training prior to being designated as carrier qualified in August 1989. During the next ten months, she accumulated more than 700 hours in A-6 (Intruder) aircraft. In June of 1993, Hultgreen began F-14 training on the west coast. Her instructors included numerous favorable comments—dedication, enthusiasm—on reports, but these records also disclosed that she had struggled with the F-14, acknowledged by male pilots to be a difficult jet to fly.

While on her third hop (flight) in the familiarization phase of her Tomcat training, Hultgreen had a near mishap while attempting to land at Naval Air Station Fallon in Nevada. Her instructor reported that she had felt the aircraft was not slowing properly during landing roll out, put on the brakes too aggressively, and blew both main tires. She received a grade of unsatisfactory (a "down" in Navy parlance).

Four months later in early April 1994, Hultgreen engaged in a series of field-landing practices in preparation for qualifying for aircraft-carrier operations. She had the lowest landing grades of the nine pilots in her group, receiving a cumulative field grade of 2.82, which is below the accepted minimum.

Since April 1989, no Navy pilot with grades as low as Hultgreen's had been allowed to attempt carrier qualification. Yet she was permitted to continue field-landing practice, and on March 31, she received a second pink sheet ("down") for "making power corrections that were erratic and unpredictable."

Because she failed to receive minimum scores, Hultgreen was given a DQ (disqualification). Her situation had plenty of precedents. Between 1986 and 1994, 305 male pilots had undergone carrier-qualification training, and 40 had been DQ'd on their first attempt.

Hultgreen was given a second shot at carrier qualification and ran into more difficulties. During conventional weapons training, she dropped mock bombs from such a low altitude that her instructor reported, had these been live bombs, fragmentations from the exploding ordnance would have destroyed her and her aircraft. She was given another "down."

In July 1994, Hultgreen finally passed carrier qualification with an overall grade of 3.10 which, the Navy would later point out, was above the 2.99 average for male pilots. What would be left unsaid was that Hultgreen was a "second look" pilot—that is, she was making a repeat effort to qualify, and her 3.10 grade was being compared to the average of male first-time qualifiers.

Moreover, male pilots, on their first tour in the Tomcats, were given twenty passes at a landing to carrier qualify. Hultgreen received thirty-two practice landings, a factor that raised her overall number of successful touchdowns.

If Navy brass had manipulated regulations to qualify Kara Hultgreen for carrier duty as some would charge, why had they done so? Navy Reserve Lieutenant Ellen B. Hamblet expressed the view of many in the seagoing service:

Most senior officers are—in a word—scared. They do not want to take disciplinary actions against women, even when deserved, because they are scared they will get slapped with a sexual harassment suit and have their careers ended.

These are some of the Navy's top decision makers. Thanks to them, women who are unqualified are being advanced. Senior officers who refuse, for whatever reason, to offer honest feedback and criticism and to enforce tough, unpopular decisions [are] perpetuating a terrible disservice to the poorer performers, who are allowed to continue in an atmosphere where they cannot compete safely.[7]

In the wake of the Kara Hultgreen crash, the Navy took the unusual step of launching an effort to recover the F-14. On December 24, two months after the mishap and at a cost of several million dollars, the plane wreckage was retrieved from the ocean floor, 3,600 feet below the surface.

The principal purpose of this costly operation was to assess the working condition of the F-14's engines, the Navy explained. If the left engine, or both engines, had failed, an examination by experts would disclose the nature of this failure. Later, a confidential internal investigation would reveal that "the left engine was found to be fully capable of producing normal power" at the time of the accident, and "there were no performance-related discrepancies found on the right engine."[8]

In the meantime, Navy divers recovered the body of Lieutenant Hultgreen, and she was buried with full military honors in the Arlington National Cemetery across the Potomac River from Washington, D.C. Like countless others in the hallowed ground, she had given her life for her country.

On February 28, 1995, four months after the accident on the *Abraham Lincoln*, the Navy held a news conference at the North Island Naval Air Station in California to release the results of the Navy's official thirty-nine page Judge Advocate General Manual (JAGMAN) investigation. This report is basically a standard legal document prepared primarily by lawyers in the event of possible litigation against the Navy.

At the conference, reporters were handed (or in some cases, sent) a news release from Naval Air Force, U.S. Pacific Fleet, which, in part, stated:

The emergency resulting in the mishap was precipitated by a left engine malfunction at an extremely vulnerable moment as the [Hultgreen] aircraft was approaching the carrier to land. The pilot attempted to continue flying the aircraft to safety but was unable to do so.[9]

The news release also quoted Vice Admiral Robert J. Spane, commander of naval air forces in the Pacific: "This pilot did her best to keep this aircraft flying under conditions that were all but impossible."[10]

A series of endorsement letters from top Navy brass reinforced the JAGMAN report: "Pilot inexperience" was acknowledged, but the impression given was that engine failure had caused the accident.

A reporter asked whether Lieutenant Hultgreen had any "downs" in her flight record. After a brief pause, Rear Admiral Jay B. Yakeley III, commander of Carrier Group Three, responded that she had only one "down." Actually, official flight records show that she had four "downs." When asked if the crash would result in changes in the Navy's training program for women pilots, Yakeley replied: "Absolutely not!"

In an editorial, the *Detroit News* described the news conference as a "masterful job of obfuscation."[11]

Navy public affairs officers also released to the television networks four seconds of a video—taken by the camera mounted on the deck of the *Abraham Lincoln*—that showed Hultgreen's plane on its approach to the carrier. These four seconds were part of a twelve-second video; the Navy kept from the public the remaining eight seconds.

Despite tight security, copies of the longer video found their way into the hands of former Navy pilots. The previously missing eight seconds showed that the landing signal officer on the *Lincoln* had tried repeatedly to wave off Lieutenant Hultgreen as she approached the carrier's fantail (end). Some seven seconds passed between the first wave-off and the time her plane spun out of control, but she had made no visible effort to fly out of her predicament, it appeared to these experienced observers. They pointed out that carrier pilots must react instinctively to such emergencies, with their hands and feet moving automatically without conscious signals from the brain.

In the meantime, on the night of the West Coast "vindication for the Navy" press conference, Admiral Spane appeared on *Nightline*, an ABC-TV talk show hosted by Ted Koppel. Spane said nothing to contradict the rash of media accounts that held that a defective engine was solely to blame for Hultgreen's death.

Navy Captain Rosemary Mariner appeared on *Nightline* with Spane and launched a verbal assault on male pilots, labeling 10 percent of them as "jerks."[12]

"So it was the engine, after all, and not the pilot," exulted syndicated columnist Ellen Goodman. "Lieutenant Kara Hultgreen did not die on the altar of political correctness or reverse discrimination."

Syndicated columnist Linda Chavez held an opposite view. She claimed that Navy brass, by blaming the mishap solely on engine failure, "left gullible journalists to conclude that pilot error could not have been the cause or contributing factor in the crash including misleading information about Hultgreen's training record."[13]

Fourteen days after the Navy released the JAGMAN report and the four-second video, a second document relating to the *Lincoln* crash, a

Mishap Investigation Report (MIR), was distributed to key figures within the service. Unlike the JAGMAN report, the MIRs are highly confidential and never released to the public. The focus of an MIR is to find the true facts in an airplane accident, thereby permitting any needed corrective procedures to be implemented and improving the safety of future flight operations. Those persons interviewed—from four-star admirals to apprentice seaman—are protected from prosecution and legal liability to assure that the true facts are uncovered.

Type on the front cover of an MIR warns active-duty and retired Navy personnel that any unauthorized disclosure of the contents is a criminal action and could result in a prison term for the offender. Despite these dire consequences, an unknown Navy officer leaked the document to several major media outlets on about March 25, 1995—six days after the internal distribution of the secret MIR.

In contrast to the JAGMAN report that focused on engine failure, the MIR stated that when Lieutenant Hultgreen overcorrected on a bad approach to the carrier, she stalled one of her two engines. A clogged engine, a stall-warning light failure, and patchy training were partly to blame, but the MIR faulted Hultgreen for failing to deal properly with the emergency. An experienced pilot might have coped, the MIR said.

Efforts by a few media reporters to get the Navy brass' reaction to the MIR resulted in official no comment.[14]

On March 22, the office of Rear Admiral Kendell Pease, Chief of Naval Information, fired off an advisory to major media about "what is being called the Mishap Investigation Report." Reporters were urged to check with Navy public affairs officers before writing about the topic.

Joining in the high-level damage control project, Rear Admiral J. S. Mobley, commander of the Naval Safety Center at Norfolk, released an emotional memorandum. He charged that the person responsible for leaking the secret MIR had undermined a trusted institution that had been "paid for in blood," just to "further a personal agenda."

The *Navy Times*, civilian publication, put the MIR on the interactive computer network, America Online, and advised readers on how to access the document. The *Times* challenged Admiral Mobley's contention that publication of the MIR would destroy that valuable institution:

> We don't buy that. Isn't this the same Navy in which honor and integrity are core values? Do people tell the truth only when that truth isn't shared with the public? If that's the case, the Navy has deeper problems than the leak of a privileged report.[15]

Critics of the Navy's orchestration of the Kara Hultgreen tragedy pointed out that it is no reflection on the honor and respect given to the victims of aviation accidents to recognize that some kind of pilot error is usually the cause or a contributing factor. Thirty-one male pilots had been killed in F-14 accidents since 1981.

"Instead of standing on principle and insisting on candor in the Hultgreen mishap, the Navy opted for public relations gimmicks and equivocation," said Elaine Donnelly, president of the Center for Military Readiness.[16]

The Detroit News also took the Navy leadership to task:

> The Navy insisted that Congress allow women in combat squadrons. Now it has everything to lose if its social experiment fails. But open and honest analyses of crashes, so future errors can be avoided, is necessary for the safety of all pilots. Lieutenant Hultgreen wished only to be measured against her fellow pilots. By applying a double standard, the Navy has heaped dishonor upon her memory.[17]

Male pilots who served with Lieutenant Hultgreen knew that any mention of the Navy's handling of the affair would be a career terminator. Yet, at considerable risk, a group of junior officers sent an emotional plea to a publication asking that Navy leaders "free commanding officers from the requirements to institute social policy at any cost . . . and cease tacit approval of double standards which fail the American people."[18]

The letter writer added:

> The junior male officers that I serve with are all dedicated professionals who were shocked and saddened by the loss of one of our own [Kara Hultgreen]. But, because we are dedicated professionals, we refuse to allow a pervasive climate of absolute political correctness to deter us from initiating frank and open discussion of the factors which may have contributed to this horrible tragedy.
>
> We respected [Hultgreen] as an individual and held her in high regard as a Navy officer . . . If anyone were to question her loyalty to the nation, dedication to the Navy, or her unbridled bravery, we would certainly be among the first to come to her defense.
>
> In their haste to get women into combat billets as soon as possible, Navy leaders have declined unit commanders the tools that they need . . . Lieutenant Kara Hultgreen was an F-14 pilot with limited abilities who, had she been a male, would arguably never have graduated to the fleet.
>
> Such a politically driven policy serves no one . . . It is prejudicial to women because the [double standards] puts them into a highly hazardous profession without ensuring that they have the necessary skills to survive.[19]

While the Navy focus was upon the *Abraham Lincoln*, another carrier was returning to its home port on the east coast after six months at sea. That floating platform, too, would soon be engulfed in controversy.

30 ❖ A Sea Cruise Plays to Mixed Reviews

Thousands of well-wishers lined the docks in Norfolk to greet the return of the huge nuclear carrier *Dwight D. Eisenhower* from a six-month cruise first to Haiti, then to the Middle East and the Adriatic, where its jets patrolled the no-fly zone over strife-torn Bosnia-Herzegovena. Tradition had been shattered: for the first time, women had been integrated into the crew of a U.S. combat ship. It was April 1995.

Swarms of reporters, photographers, and television camera crews flocked to Norfolk to cover the homecoming. Later, *Time* ran a story with the headline:

A HISTORIC EXPERIMENT ON THE U.S.S.
EISENHOWER PROVES A ROUSING SUCCESS

That journalistic analysis varied with the view of many male junior officers aboard the carrier. Between the time the coed crew had come aboard in April 1994 and its return to Norfolk a year later, there had been thirty-eight pregnancies, fourteen of them after the ship had gone to sea, and other problems related to gender.

Commander Kevin Wensing, a Navy spokesman in the Norfolk head-quarters of the Atlantic Fleet, insisted that there was no indication that any of the pregnancies were the result of sex on board ship. The *Ike* had made several port visits during the cruise, he pointed out.[1]

The *Ike's* skipper, Captain Alan Gemmill, told reporters that women had improved the carrier's efficiency because of military skills. Another advantage of females being aboard, he added, was that foul language had been toned down. "I think we've become a little more civilized," he said.[2] It was not clear how more-refined language increased the ship's efficiency.

A bonus during the cruise, said another *Ike* senior officer, was that wives back in the United States noticed that they were receiving better gifts from their husbands. That was because, he explained, the husbands had women shipmates with them during port calls to advise them on shopping.[3]

Commander Jan Hamby, the *Ike's* female assistant operations officer, told the media about the relationship between men and women aboard ship.

"At first, women were intimidated," Hamby said. "But a comfort level was eventually established."[4]

Although the *Ike*'s skipper had strongly discouraged "dating," his stern admonition was largely ignored. "Fraternization" had been rampant, male junior officers disclosed privately. During the cruise, six couples had gone to Captain Gemmill and said they had fallen in love. Eventually, the couples would be split—half transferred to shore jobs of their choice, half remained on board.

During the voyage, Gemmill found himself saddled with yet another problem that had not been covered in his Naval Academy textbooks. A male seaman apprentice and a female recruit, both in their early twenties and married to other persons, videotaped themselves engaging in a sex act aboard ship. Later, the male sailor played the tape for fellow male workers at his station. The couple's activity became known to *Ike* officers when the tape was given to them by a crewman who had watched the film.

When the videotaped affair leaked to the media, Commander Wensing, the Atlantic Fleet's spokesman, declared, "The U.S. Navy has an unambiguous policy. Sexual conduct [aboard ships] will not be tolerated."[5]

Both of the participants in the filming pleaded guilty to "willfully disobeying orders" and to adultery. They were restricted for forty-five days and given another forty-five days of extra duty. Both forfeited one-half of two months' pay—about $850 each. A third crew member, a chief warrant officer with an unblemished record, was restricted for thirty days and given a punitive letter of reprimand. His offense was that he had viewed a portion of the video and failed to inform his superiors.

Crew members who were critical of the seagoing coed experiment could not speak out. "We have taken the focus away from being a potent fighting ship and made the *Ike* a showboat!" a male pilot complained privately. "We succeeded in this deployment, but will we succeed if we actually get into combat with a well-armed foe?"[6]

Shortly after the *Ike* sailed into Norfolk, it became known publicly that Deputy Secretary of Defense John Deutch (a Clinton appointee) on March 14, 1995, had signed a highly controversial directive that many in the armed forces feel politicizes military officers' promotions requiring approval of the President or secretary of defense or confirmation by the Senate.

Deutch's instructions permit alleged adverse information and unsubstantiated allegations of misconduct to be used against officers already selected for promotion. The directive replaced one issued in 1981, that was simple and straightforward. It called for consideration of the nominee's qualifications, such as tours of duty, current assignment, age, decorations, and leadership evaluation by superiors.

The 1995 Defense Department directive states:

> Normally the Department of Defense does not report alleged adverse information or other unsubstantiated allegations to the Senate. However, in extraordinary cases, such as where the allegations received significant media attention or when the Senate Armed Services Committee brings allegations to the attention of the Department of Defense, the Secretaries of the Military Departments shall include a discussion of the unsubstantiated allegations in the nomination package.

Syndicated columnist Richard Cohen called the new directive Post-Tailhook Traumatic Syndrome. "The prevailing theory is, 'Burn all the suspects to ensure the witches are punished,'" he noted.

Elaine Donnelly, president of the Center for Military Readiness, was highly critical of Deutch's directive. "Protection for the rights of the accused officers [selected for promotion] are conspicuously absent. A targeted officer may never know what one-sided 'summaries' of sensitive, incomplete, or false information are circulated from Pentagon bureaucrats or staffers to the secretary of defense, the White House, the Joint Chiefs, the Senate Armed Forces Committee—perhaps even to the *National Enquirer* [a scandal sheet]."

Potential for insider influence and abuse is enormous, Donnelly declared. She pointed out that there are no specific requirements that selectees for promotion be informed of and allowed to comment on adverse information, including unsubstantiated allegations, added to their files. "This creates inherent opportunities for cronyism and partiality," she added.

As an example of potential abuse, Donnelly referred to the case of the female Navy lieutenant who testified under oath that fellow male officers had gang-raped her at the Tailhook 91 convention, then later admitted that she had lied to cover up her own consensual sexual activity. "She was not punished for perjury or violation of Navy regulations forbidding false accusations, and she subsequently won her wings as a helicopter pilot," Donnelly said.

In May 1995, Lieutenant Commander Kenneth Carkhuff appeared before a Board of Inquiry at Mayport Naval Station in Florida. The tribunal of three Navy captains had been appointed to render judgment of his conduct for having privately expressed his belief that women should not be sent into situations of potential violence. Pentagon brass apparently had concluded that Carkhuff had not refused to carry out a legitimate order, or else he would have been court-martialed.

Carkhuff's three immediate commanders testified that even if he had made it clear that he would have led his helicopter detachment into battle if so ordered, his moral beliefs against women in combat were sufficient to render him unfit to command.

By this logic, Carkhuff's attorney, Stephen Gallagher, countered, most of the students at the Naval War College, where the service sends its brightest young officers destined for high command, would be disqualified for leadership roles and subject to dismissal from the Navy. He pointed out that an earlier poll taken by the Navy had disclosed the overwhelming majority of War College students was opposed to women being thrust into combat situations.

Carkhuff testified that he considered female pilots to be his equal, and emphasized that he had never refused to lead them and his detachment into battle. However, he explained, "The Bible clearly teaches that we should not subject women to violence. Combat is probably the most extreme violence that one can undergo."

Although the tribunal conducted the proceedings fairly, the Navy prosecutor ridiculed Carkhuff's religious beliefs by asserting that it made no difference whether he had gained them by reading the Bible or "the back of a Crackerjack box."[7]

Then the prosecutor fired a broadside at Carkhuff for his membership in Promise Keepers, a rapidly growing organization of tens of thousands of Christian men pledging faithfulness to their own families. Founder and leader of the fellowship was Bill McCartney, who had been coach of the national champion Colorado University football team in the early 1990s. The prosecutor tried to show that the Promise Keepers' family-oriented goals are subversive to the Navy.

At the conclusion of the day-long inquiry, the board voted unanimously to recommend the honorable discharge of Lieutenant Commander Carkhuff, only two years before he could have taken early retirement, on the grounds that he had "created a glaring and irreconcilable conflict with Navy policy."

Carkhuff's attorney, Stephen Gallagher, told reporters he was not surprised by the verdict. "The worst possible thing that could happen to a Navy officer [today] is to come down on the wrong side of the [Pentagon's] political correctness," he declared.[8]

After the inquiry verdict became known to the public, veterans groups, religious organizations, and individual citizens began bombarding the Pentagon suites of Navy Secretary Dalton and Admiral Boorda with letters of protest. Thirty-five senators and representatives urged the Navy to retain Carkhuff. One of them, Congresswoman Linda Smith, on behalf of sixteen legislators, wrote to Dalton:

> After reviewing the record, we are convinced that Lieutenant Commander Carkhuff did not disobey orders in this matter and that he has not been charged with any violation of the Uniform Code of Military Justice.
>
> In fact, the record clearly reflects that [he] has stated that he would lead women into combat if so ordered, despite his vocalized religious objections . . . Separation of such a fine officer sends the wrong message to those personnel on active duty who adhere to their religious convictions and still serve our nation honorably.[9]

As the result of what the Pentagon described as an exhaustive review, Secretary Dalton on August 18, 1995, approved the recommendation of Admiral Boorda to reject the inquiry verdict and allow Carkhuff to remain in the Navy. At the same time, Boorda sent a four-page memorandum to all Navy commanders citing Carkhuff's sterling record and the "unusual circumstances" of the case as causes for retaining him.

"The way in which [Carkhuff] treated people in his command, regardless of any factor (including gender), was without blemish," Boorda wrote. "His record of service and performance was impeccable."[10]

Dalton's action allowed Carkhuff to remain in the Navy, and, if he chooses to do so, take early retirement and draw full benefits. He was reassigned to Fleet Training Group, Mayport, Florida, as an antisubmarine officer, a job in which he would not be engaged in flight operations. Because he had been relieved of his duties, which is noted in his personnel record, Carkhuff's remaining years in the Navy probably will be brief.

At the same time in Natick, Massachusetts, the Army Research Institute of Environmental Medicine launched an experimental program designed to determine if women participants could become 75 percent as strong as men of equal size by means of ninety minutes of weight lifting and aerobics five times a week for twenty-four weeks. The project was funded by $140,000 inserted into the 1995 defense budget by Congresswoman Patricia Schroeder.

If successful, the program presumably would demolish the barrier that had kept females from being assigned to ground combat units—lack of sufficient strength and stamina. However, the Department of Defense had already collected voluminous evidence that, even with heavy physical conditioning, women on average have only about 50–60 percent of the upper body strength and about 73 percent aerobic capacity (essential for stamina) of men of the same size.

Retired Colonel David Hackworth, who had been awarded eight Purple Hearts, two Distinguished Services Crosses, nine Silver Stars, and nine Bronze Stars in the Korean and Vietnam wars, put the matter of strength into the perspective of the real-life battlefield:

> Not a single woman soldier of the hundreds I have interviewed [as a corre-spondent for *Newsweek*] has shown any enthusiasm for being put at risk doing jobs beyond their strength and endurance. Some artillery rounds weigh over one hundred pounds. In the Persian Gulf war, the average engineer's ruck-sack weighed eighty-two pounds. So far, scientists haven't figured out a way to put suitcase wheels on this heavy gear.[11]

Meanwhile, in Washington on July 1, 1995, General Charles C. Krulak succeeded the retiring General Carl Mundy as commandant of the Marine Corps. Almost within hours, Krulak climbed into a C-20 executive jet and lifted off on a whirlwind, one-day, five-stop tour of Marine recruiting stations in the South.

Krulak had completed his jaunt and was headed back to Andrews Air Force Base outside Washington, from Columbia, South Carolina, when the general went to the cockpit as the jet neared the Parris Island boot camp in North Carolina. He asked the pilot: "Can you land this airplane without them knowing it's the commandant?"

"No, sir," was the reply. "Telling the tower we're a C-20 would be a dead giveaway. We could say, though, that we're a transport."

"Good!" said the general. "Do it!"

The scheme worked. On landing, Krulak disguised his presence by tooling around the sprawling reservation in a beat-up old van.

"He likes to drop in on places," explained the commandant's spokeswoman, Major Betsy Arends. "That's when he can see what's really going on. It's not like he's trying to catch anybody. What it does, is that it motivates people."[12]

Krulak dashed from a messhall to a drill instructor school to a women recruits unit. Standing before the female newcomers, he asked: "Do you know who I am?" There was a long silence. Then one young woman leaped to her feet and hollered: "Sir, you are the commandant, sir!"

Krulak, who stands five feet six inches, has a dry wit. He joked if she had guessed correctly because he was short. No, the recruit responded, because of the four shiny stars on his uniform shirt collar. Grinning, Krulak said that he always knew that women Marines were bright.

At the time, females made up 4.7 percent of the Marine Corps, by far the smallest proportion of the uniformed services, although the share had grown in recent years. Lieutenant Sarah Deal, who earned her wings in April and then began training in a helicopter, was the only qualified woman pilot in the Marines.

Krulak, fifty-three years of age, is a decorated Vietnam veteran and the son of a retired lieutenant general, Victor Krulak, who had a distinguished combat record in World War II and Korea. One of Charles' first actions on taking the helm was moving the commandant's office from its traditional quarters in the Navy Annex into the nearby Pentagon. The announced object was to improve coordination with other services in the new era of "joint operations."

Along with the historic physical movement of his office, Krulak, a wiry man with a narrow face and close-cropped hair, told reporters right from the opening gun that "I am more on the side of women than most Marine generals." He said that he didn't doubt that women had the intelligence it takes to fight on the battlefield.[13]

However, Krulak came out firmly against assigning Marine women to combat units. "I'm a firm believer in women as a combat multiplier," the general declared, meaning using females in important support roles to free men to do the nasty fighting. "I am not a believer in women as walking 'point' for the second squad, second platoon, golf company. You're not going to see that."[14]

Krulak added: "It's just that it's damned tough being a grunt [ground combat Marine]. The physical challenge is simply too great. Humping a lot of heavy gear for a long distance and then putting steel on target [shooting rapidly and accurately] is too much to ask of women Marines."[15]

The new commandant also said he was toughening physical training for women—for their good and the good of male Marines. "What signal do we send to the Corps when at the end of a mile and a half [training jog] all the women drop off to the side and the men keep running?" he asked.

Krulak was aware that females had been dropping out of the Parris Island boot camp at a much higher rate than men. "I think there's a high attrition rate [among females] because Marine Corps recruit training is really tough," he said. "And I'm going to make it tougher."[16]

Infantry, armor, and artillery remain closed to women. However, most female Marines at Parris Island seemed to have no overpowering urge to engage an enemy directly in life-or-death, hand-to-hand fighting. "Males are meant to do the hey-diddle-diddle, right up the middle, so let them do it!" exclaimed Lieutenant Colonel Gloria Jane Harmon, commander of the female training battalion. "If the men get into trouble, we'll help them out!"[17]

Once through the gates at Parris Island, male and female recruits are basically subjected to the same dawn-to-dusk training rigors, with allowances made for the weaker strength and lesser endurance of women.

Physical fitness is not the only challenge the women recruits face at Parris Island. For most of them—and men, as well—the real test is the first encounter with the drill instructor. A choreographed mixture of physical, verbal, and psychological dominance, the confrontation leaves the recruits badgered, bewildered, and bawled out—and often bemoaning their decision to join the Brave and the Proud.

Sabrina Bonasera, for one, wondered whether she really belonged in boot camp. Her initial exposure to the drill sergeant was "terrifying."

"We didn't sleep for the first two or three nights," she recalled. "Most of the female recruits and I tried to motivate each other. They were in the same fix as I was. They wanted to stay, and they wanted to go home."[18]

Three months, countless challenges, and seemingly endless exercises later, those women who pass muster earn the right to wear the eagle, globe, and anchor emblem of the U.S. Marines.

31 ❖ Navigating Troubled Waters

Commander Robert F. Stumpf, leader of the world famous Blue Angels precision flying team, had been awarded the Distinguished Flying Cross and other decorations for leading his F-18 fighter squadron in twenty-two dangerous missions to destroy Iraqi Scud missiles during the Persian Gulf War. A 1993 fitness report by Rear Admiral W. R. McGowen described Stumpf as "our best" and saw in him "a gentleman" and "truly remarkable officer"—notable for his "exceptional, inspirational leadership."

Those who served with Bob Stumpf predicted that he would eventually reach four stars. In early 1994 he seemed to be on his way to that high plateau when the secretary of the Navy put him on a list for promotion to captain. His elevation was endorsed by the Senate Armed Services Committee and then confirmed by the full body on May 24, 1994.

Among those pushing for Stumpf's promotion were Navy Secretary John Dalton and Chief of Naval Operations Mike Boorda. When a year passed and Stumpf had not yet been officially promoted, Admiral J. L. Flemming, commander of the Strike-Fighter Wing, Atlantic Fleet, wrote:

> [Comander Stumpf] is unquestionably one of the finest officers I have ever known. A leader and a warrior with no equal, he will be a superb Airwing Commander. He is the kind of officer we need to lead naval aviation into the next century.

A high-profile officer because of his leadership of the elite Blue Angels, Stumpf had attended Tailhook 91 to accept an outstanding achievement award for his fighter squadron in the Persian Gulf conflict. He had spent a short time one night in one of the hospitality suites at the Las Vegas Hilton. Bawdy behavior had occurred in the suite, the ensuing investigation disclosed, but only after Stumpf had departed and retired for the night. However, he was caught in the post-Tailhook dragnet.

During formal weeklong proceedings before a three-member Court of Inquiry in 1993, Stumpf's superiors testified that the Blue Angels had performed flawlessly under his leadership, and they told of his involvement, on his own initiative, in helping young persons and in community volunteer activities. By a unanimous vote, he was found innocent of misconduct charges. After a private meeting with the forty-three-year-old Stumpf, Secretary Dalton recommended that he be returned to duty as commander of the Blue Angels.

Then trouble began for Stumpf from a source customarily ignored by responsible government leaders: A series of anonymous telephone calls to members of the Republican-controlled Senate Armed Services Committee, chaired by ninety-four-year-old Strom Thurmond. The calls came from individuals clearly bent on getting Stumpf's scalp.

Matters became complicated when the Navy informed the Senate Armed Services Committee that a clerical error had occurred. Stumpf's promotion package had not included a red flag indicating that he was on the "Tailhook list," even though he had been exonerated of any misconduct. Consequently, the committee put a "hold" on Stumpf's promotion.

Secretary Dalton wrote the committee a letter strongly reiterating his and Admiral Boorda's recommendation that Stumpf be promoted. He stated that his own exhaustive review of the case convinced him that the commander had engaged in no misconduct and deserved to be elevated in rank. He described a "record of distinguished and heroic service to his country."[1]

Dalton's plea cut no ice with Senators Thurmond and Sam Nunn, the ranking Democrat on the Armed Services Committee. On October 25, 1995, the panel met in a closed-door session without a quorum and voted 8 to 2 to withdraw endorsement of Commander Stumpf's already confirmed promotion. The two committee members supporting the highly decorated combat pilot reportedly were Senators Trent Lott and John McCain.

After the vote, one unidentified member of the committee informed the *Wall Street Journal* that there were reasons other than Tailhook for rejecting Commander Stumpf's promotion. What were the reasons? The senator refused to disclose them.

Stumpf and his attorney urged the committee to tell the world whatever derogatory information the senators thought they knew about him. The commander's legion of supporters claimed that it seemed unlikely that an officer harboring dark secrets would be publicly calling for a full disclosure.

Presumably by prior agreement, none of the members of the committee nor its staffers would reveal the source or the nature of the charges against the officer described by his superiors as "a leader and warrior with no equal." Nor had Stumpf been permitted to appear before the committee or to provide any written rebuttal to the "evidence" collected against him.[2]

Commander Stumpf was not only denied a promotion, but a pending assignment as deputy wing commander of his fighter unit, which was scheduled to deploy to Bosnia aboard the carrier *Enterprise*, was snatched away from him.

Under the new Defense Department directive, two more promising young officers became victims of "unsubstantiated allegations." Three years after he tried to assist a drunken woman who was later groped and molested by pilots at the Tailhook 91 convention, Lieutenant Aaron C. Flannery, a helicopter pilot and flight instructor, learned that his promotion to lieutenant commander had been dropped from the Navy's selection list.

Flannery had only been questioned by Navy investigators; he was not suspected of or charged with any wrongdoing. Yet his file was "flagged" with the all-purpose accusation "potentially implicated in Tailhook-related misconduct."[3]

Lieutenant John M. Cooney learned four years after Tailhook 91 that an unidentified "witness" had placed him near the scene of the lewd conduct that had taken place in the third floor corridor of the Las Vegas Hilton. However, on that Saturday night, Cooney was not even in Nevada. Credit card receipts and the testimony of others proved that he had flown back to San Diego earlier in the day.

Despite this solid-gold evidence, the Department of Defense inspector general's investigation reported that Cooney must have lied about his whereabouts on Saturday night. Consequently, the lieutenant's request for transfer from the Naval Reserve to the regular Navy was flagged and set aside.

Because he is proud of his third-generation Navy tradition, Cooney had to go to considerable expense to hire a civilian lawyer to clear his name. Then, in the wake of several media stories and television commentaries that scalded the Senate Armed Services Committee, that panel rescinded Cooney's status as a Tailhook suspect.[4]

In late October 1995, Navy Captain Everett Greene, leader of an elite SEAL commando unit, was the defendant in a court martial at the Washington Navy Yard in the nation's capital. He was the highest-ranking naval officer to face such legal proceedings since World War II.

Greene, who had an exemplary military record, was charged with "unduly familiar personal relationships" with two female Navy officers who had been his subordinates. Prior to the official complaints by the two women, the forty-seven-year-old Greene had been in line for promotion to rear admiral.

Neither of the women charged Greene with sexual contact. Nor was there even a hint that he had hindered the two women's careers. Rather, Lieutenant Mary E. Felix and former Lieutenant Pamela Castrucci stated that Greene made them feel perturbed by sending them cards and small gifts (such as chewing gum) and calling them on the telephone.

Before a jury of five admirals and three captains (including two females), Castrucci, age thirty, stated that Greene's alleged attentions made her feel "creepy." However, she admitted "there was nothing offensive about them."[5]

The twenty-eight-year-old Felix testified that "I didn't want to believe this was happening. He was a married man, my boss, and old enough to be my father."[6]

During a recess, Captain Greene told the media that the women had confused his interest in their well being for harassment. "You're dealing with perceptions," he said, "and I have no way of controlling how someone else might interpret an otherwise innocent event."[7]

For the accused, the stakes were enormous. Greene's promotion to rear admiral had been put on hold, and, if found guilty, he could be kicked out of the service, fined, or even imprisoned.

After a trial lasting several days, Captain Greene, who steadfastly maintained his innocence to the charges, was acquitted. However, his career had been stymied: There was little chance that his promotion would take place, Pentagon officials admitted privately.[8]

Seven thousand miles from the Washington Navy Yard in Baumholder, Germany, on a cold, gray Saturday morning in early December 1995, 20,000 soldiers of the U.S. 1st Armored Division stood at attention like long rows of corn as a twenty-one-gun salute heralded the arrival of the commander in chief, President Bill Clinton. Earlier, he had pledged these troops as part of a North American Treaty Organization (NATO) peacekeeping force in Bosnia-Herzegovina, where Muslims, Serbs, and Croats, who have been violently feuding for centuries, had been engaged in a bloody civil war for the past four years.

Clinton, who had flown from Washington to deliver a pep talk to the troops, spoke for twenty-two minutes. Soon after he took off, advance parties of Task Force Eagle (as the participating units were designated), departed for the tiny country in the Balkans. Other contingents then headed from Germany to Bosnia by road, rail, and air. Some of the big transport planes bringing in troops, supplies, and equipment, were flown by female pilots.

Most of the Task Force Eagle troops arrived in drab, snowy, cold Tuzla, headquarters for the American sector in northern Bosnia, where everything seemed broken, bent, smashed, or frozen. Included in the peacekeeping force were sizable numbers of women soldiers. For the first time since the Persian Gulf conflict, American servicewomen found themselves involved in potentially hazardous duty. Although not engaged in combat, they were susceptible to being blown up by one of the millions of mines that warring factions had planted during the civil war, or picked off by unseen snipers.

Back in the United States in early March 1996, yet another episode involving charges of sexual harassment surfaced within the Navy. Republican Senator John Warner, a member of the Armed Services Committee and a former secretary of the Navy, wrote a letter to Admiral Mike Boorda, the chief of naval operations, demanding to know why a Navy captain had been given a new command assignment after he had been accused of propositioning a subordinate female officer in return for a favorable performance report.

A convoluting series of events leading up to Warner's letter began on July 25, 1993, when Naval Reserve Lieutenant Commander Mary Murphy held a routine closed-door session in a room in the Pentagon to discuss her forthcoming fitness (or performance) report with the head of her logistics unit, Captain Charles Chadburn. Later, she would charge that he replied to a question, "The only performance I will rank you on is in bed."[9]

About two months after the meeting, Murphy somehow got hold of a draft of her performance report that had been created by Chadburn and members of his staff. It gave her B grades in three categories—which would no doubt deny her promotion. Then Murphy began telling other Navy personnel about her alleged harassment, and word of her remarks eventually sifted back to Chadburn.

Three weeks after the draft report, Murphy received the official document. It had a B in five categories. On November 1, 1993, she filed a complaint, charging Chadburn with sexual harassment and retaliation.

Navy Reserve Captain Marianne Drew was appointed to investigate Murphy's complaint. Drew, who had chaired a post-Tailhook committee to study means for providing more career opportunities for women in the Navy, promptly began an intensive search for evidence to corroborate the charges. She interviewed every woman in Chadburn's command.

"They unanimously refused to believe such an allegation [against Chadburn]," Drew stated. One woman officer described her boss as a "Mister Rogers," after the homespun, soft-spoken children's television program character.[10]

Chadburn called the Murphy charge "absurd." No one else was present, as is standard procedure when performance reports are being discussed, so it was her word against his. He swore that he and his staff had completed the final performance report before he learned of the sexual harassment complaint.

Drew's investigative report exonerated Captain Chadburn of any wrongdoing and stated that the fitness evaluation accurately reflected Murphy's performance. Drew found that the charges were unsubstantiated and recommended that they be dismissed.

That would customarily have concluded the affair. But when Vicki Golden, Murphy's lawyer, branded the investigation "character assassination" against her client, Captain Drew conducted another partial investigation and reached the identical conclusion as the first one.

Although Chadburn had now been thoroughly investigated, a third probe was ordered by the Navy hierarchy, this one by Naval Reserve Captain Alexander Williams III, a California judge. Williams's report questioned Chadburn's credibility and concluded that Murphy's poor fitness report seemed to have been the result of something other than her performance. However, Williams admitted that there was not enough evidence to support Murphy's complaint.

Then in September 1995, Bernard Rostker, assistant secretary of the Navy for manpower and reserve affairs, decided to ignore the findings of the three investigations and rule that "retaliation had occurred." Consequently, Murphy's weak performance report was permanently removed from her file. Chadburn was relieved from his command and assigned to head another reserve unit.

Murphy contacted Senator John Warner, allegedly to complain about Chadburn's being given another command. Warner's letter to Admiral Boorda, demanding an explanation, followed.

In his response to Warner, Boorda contradicted his boss, Bernard Rostker, and stated that there was no conclusive evidence of harassment or retaliation. But Chadburn had been "deficient in judgment" for submitting Murphy's performance report when he knew of her complaint against him. (Chadburn denied he had prior knowledge of her charges.) It was for that "error" that Chadburn was being relieved of his current command, Boorda explained.

Captain Chadburn was confused and bewildered. Being relieved of his command stained his sterling Navy record, he declared. He had not seen the third report that questioned his credibility in the eyes of Judge Alexander Williams, even though Chadburn had asked to see it. On the other hand, Murphy had either been given a copy by Navy officials or one had been leaked to her by a supporter in the Pentagon.

"I don't understand why the first investigation was not enough," said Chadburn, reflecting the view of most Navy professionals, including Naval Reserve Commander Elinor Bartlett. "It appears the Navy went shopping till it got an answer that supported his accuser [Murphy]," she said.[11]

More than thirty of Chadburn's colleagues, including many women, wrote to Navy officials and members of Congress in support of their relieved boss.

Captain Marianne Drew, who had conducted the first investigation, told Admiral Boorda in a letter that the handling of the Chadburn case by the Navy hierarchy could result in a severe blow to the aspirations and future career opportunities for women. She declared: "We will be further ostracized by male supervisors who are afraid of the havoc we can bring to their careers, without proof."[12]

In early 1996, there were signs that some members of the Senate Armed Services Committee were feeling the heat from their decision to deny a promotion to Commander Robert Stumpf, the former commander of the famed Blue Angels. On the evening of March 21, Senators Dan Coats, James Exon, Sam Nunn, and Robert C. Byrd one after another took to the Senate floor before a national television audience on C-SPAN to defend the committee's decision.

For nearly an hour, the senators reproached Stumpf, blasted his civilian attorney, and stridently expressed their extreme displeasure with news reports that had put the committee in an unfavorable light. Senator Byrd was especially bitter, charging that Navy leaders (Secretary John Dalton and Admiral Mike Boorda) had been guilty of a "cover up" by failing to flag Stumpf's file with the "possible Tailhook implication" cautionary.

Senator Exon castigated Stumpf's many supporters as an "old-boy network that took over for a top gun." Once he had vented his wrath and salved his ego, Exon concluded his remarks by saying: "In all likelihood, Commander Stumpf, if and when he is promoted—as I think he will be, eventually, to captain—he is very likely to become an admiral some day."

Commenting on what she described as an astonishing demonstration of personal pique, Kate O'Brierne, Washington editor of the *National Review*, stated:

> When [the senators took to the floor] to praise one another for their fair treatment of Commander Stumpf, not one of them saw fit to note that this Navy hero had been found innocent [of any wrongdoing] by a Board of Inquiry, that he did not engage in conduct unbecoming an officer.

Meanwhile, the groundwork had been laid over a period of years for a tragedy that would shock official Washington and reverberate throughout the Navy.

32 ❖ The Admiral Boorda Tragedy

In April 1996, just over two years since Admiral Mike Boorda had taken over as chief of naval operations, he was in Annapolis, Maryland, for a speech at the Naval Institute. Typically, the affable, pipe-smoking Boorda was brimming with good humor and self-confidence. Clearly, the soft-spoken admiral, who loved licorice and played Nerfball in his Pentagon office to relieve tension, was handling the enormous pressure of continuing Tailhook-related and other seemingly endless problems quite well.

In his upbeat remarks at the Naval Institute, Boorda urged his audience not to "fall into a trap and feel sorry for yourself because your problems are getting reported [in the media]. He also spoke forcefully about the duty of military leaders to be models and to be aware of both the misdeeds and the personal problems of individuals in the Navy.

"Can the sailor commit suicide and not have the leader know that he or she had been in distress?" Boorda asked. "The answer is no."[1]

About a month later, on May 16, just before lunchtime, Boorda was told that two *Newsweek* reporters had arranged an appointment that afternoon to question him about two small bronze V (for valor) pins he had once worn on a chestful of decorations and ribbons received during his nearly forty years of Navy service. A year earlier, when he had heard rumors that reporters were looking into whether he was authorized to wear the combat Vs for his Vietnam service, he took them off.

Instead of eating the lunch that had been delivered to his Pentagon office, Boorda told an aide that he was going home, but that he would be back in time for his 2:30 P.M. appointment with the *Newsweek* correspondents. Brushing aside his driver, the admiral drove himself to his quarters in the historic Navy Yard in southeast Washington. There he took a .38-caliber pistol, walked outside, and ended his life with a shot to the chest.

Boorda had quickly scribbled two suicide notes. One was to his wife Bettie, to whom he was deeply devoted, and the other was to "the sailors." In the latter message, he indicated that he was not taking his life in the belief that he had been "caught in a lie," but out of fear that the media would accuse him of one and blow up the incident into major proportions, thereby damaging the Navy as a whole.

The four-star admiral was buried in a private family service with appropriate military honors in Arlington National Cemetery across the Potomac from Washington. A few days later, on May 21, throngs of Pentagon and military personnel, leaders in Congress, veterans, and civilians crowded into the National Cathedral for a memorial service. One after the other, speakers eulogized the one-time apprentice seaman who had risen to the pinnacle of his chosen profession.

Among those struck hardest by the shock waves that rapidly rippled throughout the Navy was Rear Admiral Kendell Pease, the service's principal spokesman, who had been with Boorda when he left to go home at noon on the fatal day. Pease said that Boorda appeared "concerned" about the coming *Newsweek* interview but that he vowed to "merely tell the truth," that he might have worn the combat Vs by mistake.[2]

Appearing on ABC's *This Week with David Brinkley*, Navy Secretary John Dalton pointed out that retired Admiral Elmo R. Zumwalt, Jr., who had been a top officer in Vietnam and later was chief of naval operations, "had put out the word that those ships there were in the combat theater, [and] those people [like Boorda] were authorized to wear the combat V."[3] In a separate interview, Zumwalt said, "When I was chief of naval operations, I certainly would have told him to wear them."[4]

During the Vietnam conflict, Boorda had received two commendations, one of them while serving as weapons officer aboard the USS *John R. Craig* and the other while executive officer on the USS *Brooke* for fourteen months from 1971 to 1973. Neither citation specified that Boorda was qualified for the combat V. However, the *Washington Post* reported that a 1965 military awards manual appears to support Boorda's right to wear the devices.

Mike Boorda's wearing of the combat Vs on his chest amidst a maze of other undisputed decorations perhaps had resulted from his (or his aides') interpretation of the military awards manual and subconsciously influenced by the Pentagon's extravagant awarding of medals during the Vietnam conflict. Many decorations for bravery were justly earned there by soldiers, airmen and Marines in hostile actions. However, tens of thousands of GIs who had never heard a shot fired in anger and whose only exposure to danger was the possibility of falling off a bar stool in Saigon, returned home wearing "combat" ribbons.

"The weeks before I left Vietnam in 1969, my bosses rummaged around and came up with a Bronze Star for me, sort of a going-away present," recalled journalist Jeff Stein. "The citation said I had 'distinguished' myself in connection with military operations against a hostile force.

"The only 'hostile force' that I really had to worry about in Vietnam, was mosquitoes," Stein explained. "Like 85 percent of the 2 million soldiers, sailors, and Marines who served in or off the shores of Vietnam between 1962 and 1975, I spent most of my time guarding a desk."[5]

Most of the Washington-based media reported that Boorda had taken his own life because of the unfavorable publicity his former wearing of two combat Vs would bring to the Navy. Many fellow officers in the Pentagon, civilian acquaintances, and a few retired admirals found that explanation simplistic and unconvincing.

A retired three-star admiral, who had received every military decoration for valor during three wars and knew Mike Boorda well, had recognized that the Navy chief had been skewered on the horns of a dilemma. "As a uniformed officer, Mike tried to adhere as much as feasible to the 'politically correct' stance the Clinton administration and some members of Congress were trying to impose on our armed forces," he said. "Under this enormous pressure, he occasionally did dumb things on the altar of 'feminists' rights.'" At the same time, Mike was endeavoring to uphold Navy traditions and the basic principles of combat readiness.

"This no-win situation eventually crushed Mike's spirit and led to his fatal decision, in my opinion," the retired admiral declared.[6]

Elaine Donnelly, president of the Center for Military Readiness whose board consists of numerous prominent retired admirals and generals, held a similar view. She had often conferred with Boorda in the Pentagon and corresponded with him on a regular basis about her deep opposition to placing women in combat.

"The outwardly cheerful admiral was under enormous stress," Donnelly stated. "As the chief of naval operations it was his duty to carry out orders, even if he thought the consequences might be contrary to the best interests of the Navy.

"When the going got rough," Donnelly added, "he could always have said that the decisions had been made, as they say in the military, 'above my pay grade,' meaning, in his case, the [Clinton] civilian leaders. But he didn't. Admiral Boorda saluted smartly and did everything he was asked to do. The problem was: He was asked to do far too much."[7]

Prior to his taking charge of the Navy in the Pentagon two years earlier, Boorda had a reputation as a tough-minded military man. When serving as NATO commander in southern Europe, he often told visitors how he would finish the Bosnian war in weeks, if only the political bureaucrats in the White House and the Pentagon would employ the U.S. Army to "win," a word one is not supposed to use in today's armed forces.[8]

When Senator Joseph Biden visited his headquarters, Boorda told him that "President Clinton may have a lot of no-can-do generals in Washington, but he has a can-do admiral in Naples."[9]

On one occasion, Boorda was so enraged over the mass slaughter and burned villages perpetrated by the Serbs while inspecting the landscape from the air, that he ordered his pilot to buzz the Bosnian Serb capital of Pale from a few hundred feet. In Washington, the bureaucrats were horrified; those who still had principle thought it was great.

In the wake of Admiral Boorda's death, John F. Lehman, Jr., who had been secretary of the Navy during part of the Ronald Reagan years, fired heavy broadsides at elements of the national media and the Senate Armed Services Committee while a guest on the David Brinkley television program. Lehman also charged that President Bill Clinton and his White House aides had been guilty of "imposing policies of 'political correctness' on the armed forces."[10]

Lehman, who had been a Navy fighter pilot for more than two decades, compared Boorda's death to the 1949 suicide of Defense Secretary James V. Forrestal, who became depressed from a barrage of attacks against him from several sources on his policies and leaped from a hospital window two months after resigning his post.

"The Navy as an institution continues to be damaged terribly by the gutter reporting of some journalists out to find sandal in the [Navy] ranks." Lehman declared. He cited the ongoing accounts of the 1991 Tailhook episode as an example of how Navy officers were victims of "media character assassination."

"Following what should have been a minor story," he added, "fourteen admirals have been cashiered, [and] 300 naval aviators have been driven out of the Navy or their careers terminated."[11]

Lehman said that the Senate Armed Services Committee, led by such "friends of the military" as Strom Thurmond, "has stood by while the careers of more than 300 naval personnel were ruined, and now they are holding up the promotions of another 90 naval aviators allegedly tainted by Tailhook."

Lehman added: "Not one of the [Senate Armed Services] Committee members has stood up and said, 'Enough!'"[12]

Notes and Sources

CHAPTER 1. A NIGHTMARE IN VIETNAM

1. "History of the WAF Directorate," Maxwell Air Force Base, Alabama.
2. Ibid.
3. The Geneva Conventions provide for the humane treatment of prisoners and wounded men in wartime. Also set forth are the proper markings of hospitals and medical transports with red crosses. The first Geneva Convention, or Treaty, was signed by most countries in 1864, and new provisions were added in 1906, 1929, and 1949.
4. Eunice Splawn eventually retired from the Army as a full colonel.
5. *A War Remembered* by editors of Boston Publishing Company, Boston, 1986. p. 40.
6. Ibid.
7. Ibid., p. 42.
8. Other Hollywood celebrities who went to Vietnam to entertain the service-men and -women included: Lana Turner, Dale Evans, Julie Andrews, Jill St. John, Joey Heatherton, Nancy Sinatra, Anna Maria Alberghetti, Kay Stevens, Janis Paige, Ann Sydney, Ann-Margret, Ursula Andress, Fran Jeffries, Mary Martin, Carroll Baker, Anita Bryant, Racquel Welch.
9. Captain Harry H. Dinsmore was awarded the sea service's second highest medal for valor, the Navy Cross. The author was unable to find if the women nurses had also been decorated.
10. Truong Nhu Tang made his remarks after defecting and taking up residence in Paris.

CHAPTER 2. FEMALE TRAILBLAZERS

1. A yeoman in the U.S. Navy is one who largely performs clerical duties.
2. John Ellis, *Eye-Deep in Hell* (New York: Pantheon, 1976), p. 67.
3. After World War I, Paul von Hindenberg was elected the first president of the German Republic.
4. The League of Nations was dissolved on April 18, 1946, and replaced by the United Nations.
5. In 1949 Admiral Chester W. Nimitz, the U.S. commander in the Central Pacific in World War II, was quoted by a journalist as saying that Amelia Earhart and Fred Noonan had been picked up by the Japanese (and presumably executed as spies). Nimitz did not elaborate.

6. Some details of the Amelia Earhart account come from *The New York Times*, August 2–10, 1937; *Los Angeles Times*, August 2–22, 1937; *St. Louis Post-Dispatch*, August 8, 1937.

CHAPTER 3. "YOU HAVE A DEBT TO DEMOCRACY"

1. The Pearl Harbor sneak attack took place on December 8, 1941, Hawaiian time.

2. Douglas MacArthur had retired from the U.S. Army in 1935 and was appointed a field marshal of the army of the Philippines, to which Congress had voted commonwealth status.

3. Lieutenant Hattie Brantley was captured by the Japanese and was a prisoner for thirty-seven months.

4. Both Earleen and Garnet Francis survived three years of brutal Japanese captivity.

5. Lieutenant John D. Bulkeley was awarded the Medal of Honor for his actions in the Philippines during those early dark weeks of the war. Eventually he became America's most highly decorated warrior and retired as a vice admiral in 1989.

6. Eunice Young remained in the Army until 1949, when she transferred to the fledgling Air Force. She retired as a lieutenant colonel in 1961.

7. Louis Morton, *Fall of the Philippines* (Washington: U.S. Government Printing Office, 1959), p. 462.

8. Author interview with Jerry L. Coty, who had been a sergeant in the Army Air Corps on Mindanao and witnessed the episode.

9. The Angels of Corregidor were liberated when the U.S. Army captured Manila in February 1945.

10. Colonel Oveta Culp Hobby left the Army in July 1945, after Germany surrendered. In 1953 President Dwight D. Eisenhower appointed her to his cabinet as the first secretary of the new Department of Housing and Urban Development (HUD).

11. *This Fabulous Century* (New York: Time-Life Books, 1969), p. 176.

12. *The Register*, publication of Women in the Military Service for America Memorial Foundation, Fall 1995.

13. After leaving the service after World War II, Mildred H. McAfee became a member of a U.S. education mission to Japan.

14. U.S. Marine Corps pamphlet, "Marine Corps Women Reserve in World War II." Headquarters, USMC, Washington, 1968.

15. Sally V. Keil, *Those Wonderful Women in Their Flying Machines* (New York: Rawson, Wade, 1979), p. 237.

16. Ibid., pp. 237–38.

17. After World War II, Jacqueline Cochran became the first woman to be honored by the United States with the Distinguished Service Medal.

CHAPTER 4. SECRET MISSIONS

1. Dwight D. Eisenhower, *Crusade in Europe* (Garden City, N.Y.: Doubleday, 1946), p. 132.

2. Ibid., p. 133.

3. The Germans had nearly completed the long-range bomber to hit the United States when the war in Europe ended in May 1945.

4. R. Harris Smith, *OSS* (Berkeley: University of California Press, 1972), pp. 25–26.

5. *Air Force Times*, December 6, 1976.

6. Mattie E. Treadwell, *The Women's Army Corps* (Washington: Chief of Military History, 1954), p. 246.

7. Ibid., p. 250.

8. Aline, Countess of Romanones, *The Spy Wore Red* (New York: Random House, 1987), p. 17.

9. Ibid., p. 43.

CHAPTER 5. A CONSPIRACY TO MURDER HITLER

1. Joseph E. Persico, *Piercing the Reich* (New York: Viking, 1979), p. 48.

2. Ibid.

3. Hans Gisevius's book, *To the Bitter End*, translated by Mary Bancroft, was published in the United States in 1947.

4. Arguments over whether the Allied landing force was supposed to drive immediately for Rome or to dig in and await reinforcements continues into the 1990s.

5. Author interview with Charles H. Doyle, who had been a paratrooper and a patient at the Army tent hospital on Hell's Half-Acre.

6. Jeanne Holm, *Women in the Military* (Novato, Calif.: Presidio, 1982), p. 60.

7. Author interview with Major General John K. Singlaub (Ret.)

8. Douglas MacArthur, *Reminiscences* (New York: Norton, 1964), p. 157.

CHAPTER 6. LADY SPIES AND A BLONDE GUERRILLA

1. Author interview with Colonel Barney Oldfield (Ret.).

2. Ibid.

3. After World War II Kay Summersby lived in the United States and wrote a book about her relationship with Dwight Eisenhower.

4. Aline, Countess of Romanones, p. 269.

5. In 1947 Aline Griffith married a Spanish count whom she had met only hours after arriving in Madrid on December 31, 1943.

6. Mata Hari's widely ballyhooed espionage exploits have largely been debunked by most responsible historians.

7. Major General William J. "Wild Bill" Donovan, who founded the OSS in mid-1941, reportedly requested President Roosevelt to award Virginia Hall the Distinguished Service Cross, the nation's second highest award for valor.

8. Sarah Wilkins survived the war and returned to her native Brooklyn.

CHAPTER 7. A HAIR-RAISING ESCAPE

1. Mabel Jessop, *Front Line Surgeons* (San Diego: Frye and Smith, 1950), p. 106.

2. Ibid., p. 110.

3. After the war, Lieutenant Colonel Joachim Peiper was tried as a war criminal by the Allies as a result of the episode, which became popularly known as the Malmedy Massacre, although it took place in Baugnez. Even though Peiper had not been present nor had he issued an order to kill POWs, he was sentenced to

death. This verdict was reduced to life imprisonment, and after serving a few years, he was released.

4. Author interview with John Phalen.

5. *Yank* magazine, March 1945.

6. Mildred Bailey had planned to remain in the service only for the duration of World War II. She retired after twenty-seven years in the Army as a full colonel.

CHAPTER 8. TWO SPYMISTRESSES IN MANILA

1. Father John Lalor's espionage activities were discovered by the Japanese shortly before Manila was liberated in early 1945. He and several priests who had been helping him were executed.

2. Corporal John Boone "promoted" himself to major in keeping with his extra responsibility as leader of a large guerrilla force. After the war, General MacArthur permitted him and most other American guerrilla leaders, who also had elevated themselves, to keep their higher ranks.

3. Nearly all of the key members of Miss U's and High Pockets' underground were captured and executed by the Japanese.

4. After the war, Hollywood made a movie about Claire Phillips' adventures in the Philippines. Entitled *I Was an American Spy* the film starred a popular actress, Ann Dvorak.

5. Several years after World War II, a few American apologists for the Japanese claimed that Tokyo Rose had never existed. That revelation came as a surprise to hundreds of thousands of GIs in the Pacific who had heard her make countless broadcasts.

6. Sally Keil, p. 258.

7. *House Beautiful* magazine, October 1945.

8. *Harper's Bazaar* magazine, November 1945.

CHAPTER 9. CRACKING A MAN'S WORLD

1. The 38th Parallel roughly splits the Korean peninsula at the waist. It had been chosen as an arbitrary dividing line by the United States and the Soviets at the close of World War II.

2. Since World War II, Douglas MacArthur's title was Supreme Commander, Allied Powers (SCAP).

3. Forrest C. Pogue, *George C. Marshall: Statesman* (New York: Viking, 1987), p. 421.

4. Ibid., p. 435

5. Memorandum, George C. Marshall to Harry S. Truman, December 18, 1950. George C. Marshall Library, Lexington, Virginia.

6. Letter, J. Edgar Hoover to George C. Marshall, December 19, 1950. Marshall Library.

7. Letter, Margaret Chase Smith to George C. Marshall, December 11, 1950. Marshall Library.

8. Briefing by Colonel Mary Hallaren to DACOWITS, September 18, 1951. National Archives.

9. Jeanne Holm, p. 159.

10. Ibid., p. 183.

11. *Parade*, January 2, 1966.

12. *Air Force Times*, May 17, 1967.

CHAPTER 10. AN ORDEAL IN SOUTHEAST ASIA

1. *Readers Digest*, December 1967.
2. *Washington Post*, July 28, 1968.
3. *Dallas Times Herald*, January 25, 1981.
4. *Washington Post*, September 10, 1966.
5. Colonel Mary V. Strenlow, *A History of Women Marines* (Washington: History Division, USMC, 1982), p. 88.
6. Ibid., p. 92.
7. Jeanne Holm, p. 219.
8. Ibid., p. 220.
9. Ibid., p. 224.
10. Lynda Van Devanter, *Home Before Morning* (New York: Beaufort, 1983), p. 122.
11. Transcript, House Armed Services Committee hearings, September 28, 1966.
12. Ibid., September 25, 1966.
13. As a captain in the 82nd Airborne Division, J. Strom Thurmond landed in Normandy by glider before dawn on D-Day, June 6, 1944.
14. *Denver Post*, November 9, 1967.

CHAPTER 11. LADY GENERALS AND LADY BIRDS

1. *Chicago Tribune*, October 18, 1968.
2. *The New York Times*, January 4, 1970.
3. *Baltimore Sun*, June 12, 1970.
4. General William C. Westmoreland, *A Soldier Reports* (Garden City, N.Y.: Doubleday, 1976), p. 320.
5. *Congressional Quarterly*, 1973, p. 510.
6. *Norfolk Star-Ledger*, November 26, 1977.
7. Ibid.
8. Ibid.
9. Ibid.

CHAPTER 12. A PAINFUL HOMECOMING

1. *Washington Post*, August 25, 1970.
2. *The New York Times*, August 26, 1970.
3. In the early 1990s Ruth Bader Ginsburg was appointed to the Supreme Court by President Bill Clinton.
4. The Pentagon's legal basis for discharging military mothers was the result of an executive order signed by President Harry S. Truman in 1951.
5. *U.S. News & World Report*, May 28, 1973.
6. *Los Angeles Times*, July 12, 1970.
7. Stanley Karnow, *Vietnam* (New York: Viking, 1983), pp. 649–50.
8. *Baltimore News American*, January 26, 1982.
9. Ibid.
10. *Dallas Times Herald*, January 25, 1981.

11. Jacqueline Rhoads, *Nurses in Vietnam* (Austin: Texas Monthly Press, 1987), p. 22.

12. Lynda Van Devanter, p. 122.

13. Kathryn Marshall, *In the Combat Zone* (Boston: Little Brown, 1987), p. 91.

14. Martin Binkin and John D. Johnston, *All-Volunteer Armed Forces* (Washington: Government Printing Office, 1973), p. 3.

15. House Armed Services Committee, subcommittee on manpower needs in the All-Volunteer Force, transcript, April 22, 1972.

16. DACOWITS report, spring meeting, April 21–25, 1974.

17. *Redbook*, November 1973.

CHAPTER 13. CLASH OVER THE SERVICE ACADEMIES

1. Jeanne Holm, p. 305.

2. Ibid., p. 306.

3. Ibid.

4. *Washington Post*, May 12, 14, 17, 1974.

5. House Armed Services Committee hearings, transcript, p. 256.

6. Ibid., p. 263.

7. Ibid., p. 265.

8. Spiro Agnew pleaded guilty to taking kickbacks and received a suspended sentence.

9. DACOWITS report, fall meeting, November 14–18, 1976.

10. Ibid.

11. Ibid.

CHAPTER 14. FIRST CRISIS FOR THE COED ARMY

1. 1976 Annual Historical Report, pp. 12–17, National Archives.

2. C. A. DeLateur, *Murder at Panmunjom* (Washington: National Defense University, 1977), pp. 8–14.

3. Paul Bunyan was a mythical hero of the lumberjacks.

4. Author interview with Major General John K. Singlaub (Ret.)

5. Ibid.

6. Ibid.

7. *Airman*, October 1977.

8. Ibid.

9. A year later, Czar Nicholas II and his entire family were executed by the Communists.

10. *Congressional Record*, p. E-135, January 28, 1982.

11. *The New York Times*, January 8, 1982.

12. Lionel Tiger and Joseph Shepler, *Women in the Kibbutz* (New York: Harcourt Brace Jovanovich, 1975), pp. 189–90.

13. Lesley Hazelton, *Israeli Women: The Reality Behind the Myth* (New York: Simon and Schuster, 1977), p. 139.

14. *U.S. News & World Report*, May 22, 1995.

15. Ibid.

16. *Newsweek*, August 5, 1991.

CHAPTER 15. "YOUR MISSION IS TO WIN OUR WARS"

1. In 1955, the first class of 306 cadets trained at the Air Force Academy's temporary site at Lowry Air Force Base, near Denver, Colorado. The academy opened its permanent site in 1958.
2. Judith H. Stiehm, *Bring Me Men and Women* (Berkeley: University of California Press, 1981), p. 99.
3. Lois B. DeFleur, David Gillman, and William Marshak, "The Development of Military Professionalism Among Male and Female Air Force Academy Cadets," p. 168.
4. Judith H. Stiehm, p. 83.
5. Ibid., pp. 257–59.
6. "Committee on Integration of Women into the Cadet Wing" report, p. 1, July 1984.
7. Brian Mitchell, *Weak Link* (Washington: Regnery Gateway, 1981), p. 83.
8. *Life*, May 1980.
9. Brian Mitchell, p. 69.
10. Ibid.
11. *Washingtonian*, November 1979.
12. Ibid.
13. Ibid.
14. Ibid.
15. *Newsweek*, August 5, 1991.
16. Ibid.

CHAPTER 16. A NEW VIEW IN THE PENTAGON

1. Jimmy Carter, *Keeping Faith* (New York: Bantam, 1982), pp. 444–45.
2. *The New York Times*, January 22, 1977.
3. *Washington Post*, January 23, 1977.
4. Ibid., February 7, 1980.
5. Ibid., February 9, 1980.
6. *Baltimore Sun*, March 20, 1980.
7. After World War II, Audie Murphy, a handsome, wholesome young man still in his early twenties, became a Hollywood film actor and starred in several movies.
8. Report of the Manpower and Personnel Subcommittee of the Senate Armed Services Committee, April 17, 1980.
9. Ibid.
10. *St. Louis Post-Dispatch*, September 6, 1980.

CHAPTER 17. "GENERAL, YOU ARE A MALE CHAUVINIST!"

1. Braveshield report, Department of the Army, August 22, 1977.
2. *Washington Star*, January 10, 1980.
3. Braveshield report.
4. *The New York Times*, November 12, 1977.
5. *Washington Star*, January 10, 1980.
6. Ibid.
7. Congressional Record, p. E-136, January 28, 1982.

8. *Washington Star*, January 11, 1980.

9. *Congressional Record*, p. E-142, January 28, 1982.

10. *Army Times*, May 7, 1979.

11. Ibid.

12. *Newsweek*, February 5, 1980.

13. *The New York Times*, January 20, 1979.

14. Author interview with Major General John K. Singlaub (Ret.).

15. Ibid.

16. Ibid.

17. *The New York Times*, March 12, 1978.

18. *Norfolk Star-Ledger*, November 2, 1978.

19. Hearings before the Manpower and Personnel Subcommittee of the House Armed Services Committee, transcript, November 13–16, 1979.

20. Ibid.

21. *Minerva*. Quarterly report on Women in the Military, p. 95, Spring 1985.

22. Hearings before the Manpower and Personnel Subcommittee of the House Armed Services Committee, transcript, p. 238, November 12–18, 1979.

23. Ibid., pp. 332, 346.

24. Ibid., p. 372.

CHAPTER 18. A PLAN TO REGISTER WOMEN

1. Jimmy Carter, pp. 445–46.

2. Ibid., p. 188.

3. Release by White House Press Office, February 8, 1980.

4. Ibid.

5. *St. Louis Post-Dispatch*, February 12, 1980.

6. *Washington Post*, February 7, 1980.

7. Ibid., February 9, 1980.

8. Report of the Manpower and Personnel Subcommittee of the Senate Armed Services Committee, April 17, 1980.

9. Helen Rogan, *Mixed Company* (New York: Putnam, 1981), p. 287.

10. The remainder of the popular votes went to candidates of minor parties.

11. *Time*, February 23, 1981.

12. *Air Force Times*, January 19, 1981.

13. *The New York Times*, March 2, 1981.

14. *Washington Post*, March 5, 1981.

15. Supreme Court majority decision, June 25, 1981.

16. Supreme Court dissenting opinion, June 25, 1981.

17. *The New York Times*, June 26, 1981.

18. Ibid.

19. *St. Louis Post-Dispatch*, June 26, 1981.

20. *Washington Post*, June 26, 1981.

21. *Chicago Tribune*, June 26, 1981.

22. *St. Louis Post-Dispatch*, June 26, 1981.

CHAPTER 19. AN EPISODE IN PANAMA

1. As a four-star general in 1989, Maxwell Thurman was head of Southern Command, which was responsible for the Panama Canal zone and other regions at the time of Operation Just Cause.

2. H. Norman Schwarzkopf, *It Doesn't Take a Hero* (New York: Bantam, 1992), p. 235.

3. Brian Mitchell, pp. 134–35.

4. Ibid.

5. *Newsweek*, January 1, 1990.

6. *Denver Post*, December 23, 1989.

7. *Time*, January 8, 1990.

8. *The New York Times*, January 4, 1990.

9. Ibid., January 7, 1990.

10. *The New York Times*, January 10, 1990.

11. *Norfolk Star-Ledger*, January 7, 1990.

CHAPTER 20. SCUD MISSILES, CULTURE PROBLEMS, AND POWS

1. *Newsweek*, September 3, 1990.

2. Ibid.

3. H. Norman Schwarzkopf, p. 336.

4. Ibid., p. 337.

5. After their return from the Persian Gulf in 1991, several 82nd Airborne Division men (including a general) told the author that they spent part of their off-duty time during Desert Shield reading *Geronimo!* Published in 1989, the book was written by the author and told the story of U.S. paratroopers in World War II.

6. The five men killed in the Black Hawk crash were Sergeant Robert P. Brilinski, Sergeant First Class William T. Butts, Chief Warrant Officer Philip H. Garvey, Chief Warrant Officer Robert G. Godfrey, and Sergeant Patbouvier E. Ortiz.

7. *The New York Times*, March 7, 1991.

8. Major Marie T. Rossi was buried with full military honors in Arlington National Cemetery outside Washington, D.C.

9. Report by the Presidential Commission on the Assignment of Women in the Armed Forces, p. 89.

CHAPTER 21. "WE'RE TALKING ABOUT THE BATTLEFRONT"

1. *Air Force Times*, May 6, 1991.

2. *Washington Post*, April 30, 1991.

3. Ibid.

4. *Newsweek*, August 5, 1991.

5. *Military*, April 1994.

6. Ibid.

7. *Colorado Springs Gazette Telegraph*, October 28, 1990.

8. *Family Voice*, June 1991.

9. Ibid.

10. *Air Force Times*, May 6, 1991.

11. Ibid.

12. *Washington Times*, April 26, 1991.

13. Ibid.

14. *Air Force Times*, May 6, 1991.

15. *Washington Times*, April 25, 1991.

16. *Air Force Times*, May 13, 1991.

17. U.S. Air Force pilots, all lieutenants and captains, who signed the statement were: Paul R. Delmonte, William L. Sparrow, Joseph S. Matchette, Bryan K. Nordheim, Gary B. Guy, Brian M. Schaaf, Dean R. Ostovich, W. Gary Tew, Jon W. Walker, Reed L. Bowman, and J. R. Goodwin, Jr.

18. *Air Force Times*, June 17, 1991.

19. *The New York Times*, May 26, 1991.

20. Ibid.

CHAPTER 22. A SPIRITED DEBATE

1. Newhouse News Service, June 17, 1991.

2. Ibid.

3. *Washington Post*, June 19, 1991.

4. Letter in author's files, dated June 17, 1991.

5. *Newsweek*, August 5, 1991.

6. Report of Presidential Commission on the Assignment of Women in the Armed Forces, p. 115.

7. *The New York Times*, July 21, 1991.

8. Ibid., July 31, 1991.

9. Ibid.

10. Ibid., May 11, 1991.

11. Ibid.

12. Ibid, May 9, 1991.

13. *Washington Times* July 9, 1991.

14. Ibid.

15. Ibid.

16. Ibid., May 28, 1991.

CHAPTER 23. FALLOUT FROM A TAILHOOK CONVENTION

1. The 1991 Flag Panel consisted of Vice Admirals J. H. Fetterman, E. R. Kohn, A. A. Less, W. C. Bowes, Lieutenant General D. A. Wills, and Rear Admirals R. K. Chambers, W. R. McGowen, and J. L. Johnson.

2. CBS-TV *Evening News*, September 7, 1991.

3. Tailhook Association Report on the 1991 Convention, p. 5.

4. "Events of the 35th Annual Tailhook Symposium," Department of Defense, p. VII-1, 1992.

5. Ibid., p. VII-6.

6. Tailhook Association Report on 1991 Symposium, November 30, 1992.

7. "Events of the 35th Annual Tailhook Symposium," p. VI-1.

8. Ibid., p. VI-6.

9. "Events of the 35th Annual Tailhook Symposium, Part 2," Department of Defense, pp. F-51, F-52, February 1993.

10. Extracted from accounts in the *Washington Post, Washington Times*, and *The New York Times*.

11. Ibid.

12. *USA Today*, May 12, 1992.

13. *The New York Times*, June 27, 1992.

14. Ibid.

15. Ibid.
16. "Events of the 35th Annual Tailhook Symposium, Part 2," p. VI-1.
17. CNN newscast, June 26, 1992.
18. *The Backgrounder*, July 8, 1992.
19. *Washington Times*, August 28, 1992.

CHAPTER 24. "TODAY'S BATTLEFIELD IS MORE HORRIFIC"

1. Report of Presidential Commission on the Assignment of Women in the Armed Forces, p. 43.
2. Ibid.
3. Author interview with Elaine Donnelly.
4. Report of Presidential Commission on the Assignment of Women in the Armed Forces, p. 76.
5. Ibid., p. 77.
6. Ibid., p. 103.
7. Author interview with Elaine Donnelly.
8. Report of Presidential Commission on the Assignment of Women in the Armed Forces, p. 70.
9. Ibid.
10. *VFW* (Veterans of Foreign Wars), February 1995.
11. Report of Presidential Commission on the Assignment of Women in the Armed Forces, p. 64.
12. Ibid.
13. Ibid., p. 65.
14. TOW is abbreviation for a tube-launched, optically-tracked, wire command-link guided missile. Crewmen can steer it after launching.
15. *VFW*, February 1995.
16. Report of Presidential Commission on the Assignment of Women in the Armed Forces, p. 67.
17. Ibid., p. 68.
18. Ibid., p. 87.
19. Ibid.
20. *Chicago Tribune*, July 16, 1992.
21. Ibid.

CHAPTER 25. CHARGES AND COUNTERCHARGES

1. *Chicago Tribune*, July 17, 1992.
2. Ibid.
3. Ibid.
4. *Christian American*, January 1993.
5. Ibid.
6. Report of Presidential Commission on the Assignment of Women in the Armed Forces, p. 81.
7. *Washington Times*, August 2, 1992.
8. Transcript, hearings, House Armed Services Committee, July 30, 1992.
9. Ibid.
10. Ibid.
11. Ibid.

12. Ibid.
13. *The New York Times*, July 31, 1992.
14. *Washington Times*, August 8, 1992.
15. Report of Presidential Commission on the Assignment of Women in the Armed Forces, p. 117.
16. Ibid., p. 118.
17. Ibid., p. 115.
18. *Military*, February 1993.
19. Ibid.
20. Report of Presidential Commission on the Assignment of Women in the Armed Forces, p. 89.
21. *The New York Times*, November 4, 1992.
22. Ibid.
23. *Washington Post*, November 4, 1992.
24. Ibid.
25. *The New York Times*, November 4, 1992.
26. *Military*, February 1993.
27. Members of the Presidential Commission on the Assignment of Women in the Armed Forces were: General Robert T. Herres, chairman; Major General Mary E. Clarke (Ret.); Brigadier General Samuel G. Cockerham (Ret.); Elaine Donnelly; Brigadier General Thomas V. Draude; Captain Mary M. Finch; William D. Henderson; Admiral James R. Hogg (Ret.); Newton D. Minnow; Charles C. Moskos; Meredith A. Neizer; Kate W. O'Bierne; Ronald D. Ray; General Maxwell R. Thurman (Ret.); and Sarah F. White.

CHAPTER 26. TRIALS AND TRIBULATIONS

1. October 18 is the actual birthday of the U.S. Navy.
2. *Washington Times*, October 5, 1993.
3. Ibid.
4. *National Review*, March 7, 1994.
5. Ibid.
6. *Navy Times*, January 21, 1994.
7. Ibid.
8. Ibid.
9. Ibid.
10. *Washington Post*, February 9, 1994.
11. Author interview with Vice Admiral John D. Bulkeley (Ret.).
12. Memorandum from Defense Secretary Les Aspin to Congress, January 15, 1994.
13. *The New York Times*, January 14, 1994.
14. Press release, Department of Defense, February 10, 1994.
15. Ibid.
16 Memorandum from Deputy Inspector General Derek J. Vander Schaaf to Defense Secretary William J. Perry, February 11, 1994.
17. Ibid.

CHAPTER 27. TWO ADMIRALS WALK THE PLANK

1. H. Norman Schwarzkopf, pp. 424, 437.

2. J.G. is lieutenant, junior grade, the next highest Navy rank being lieutenant, senior grade.

3. In the fall of 1995, Senator David Durenberger, who retired a year earlier after being investigated or indicted for five years, pleaded guilty to misdemeanor charges after facing an October trial on a felony count of defrauding the government. Durenberger could have recieved a ten-year sentence on the felony count, but the misdemeanor brought him no jail time.

4. *Washington Post*, April 20, 1994.

5. Ibid.

6. Ibid.

7. *Congressional Record*, January 19, 1994.

8. Ibid.

9. Ibid.

10 Congress confirmed the appointment of Clarence Thomas to the Supreme Court.

11. *Congressional Record*, January 19, 1994.

12. Ibid.

13. Memorandum from the Secretary of the Army to the Secretary of Defense, June 1, 1994.

14. Ibid.

15. Transcript, testimony of Lieutenant General J. H. Binford Peay III, Senate Armed Services Committee, June 16, 1994.

16. *Military*, September 1994.

17. Ibid.

18. Ibid., October 1994.

19. Ibid.

20. *Washington Times*, June 7, 1994.

21. Department of Defense press release, November 10, 1994.

22. *VFW*, February 1995.

23. Ibid.

CHAPTER 28. THE *IKE* MAKES HISTORY

1. *Congressional Record*, October 30, 1994.

2. Ibid.

3. *The New York Times*, May 20, 1995.

4. Author interview with Elaine Donnelly.

5. *Washington Times*, May 18, 1995.

6. *Newsweek*, October 3, 1994.

7. Ibid.

8. *Time*, October 10, 1994.

9. *Washington Times*, October 16, 1994.

10. The Code of Military Justice was enacted by Congress in 1950. It established a system of military courts, known as courts-martial, to try a broad range of criminal charges. Many of the rights contained in the Constitution apply to the military, but their precise application varies from the civilian courts. Verdicts from the Court of Military Appeals, which has five civilian judges, may be appealed to the U.S. Supreme Court.

11. *San Diego Union-Tribune*, November 27, 1994.

12. Ibid.
13. *Washington Times*, July 11, 1994.
14. Ibid.
15. Ibid.
16. Transcript, testimony, *Paula A. Coughlin vs. Hilton Hotels*, May 19, 1994.
17. *AIM* report, November 1993.
18. Ibid.
19. *The New York Times*, October 5, 1994.
20. Transcript, testimony, *Paula A. Coughlin vs. Hilton Hotels*, May 19, 1995.
21. *The New York Times*, November 1, 1994.

CHAPTER 29. DISASTER ON AN AIRCRAFT CARRIER

1. "Mishap Investigation Report (MIR) of Lieutenant Kara Hultgreen's Fatal Accident," week of March 20, 1995.
2. Ibid.
3. *Nightline*, ABC-TV, February 28, 1995.
4. *Newsweek*, November 14, 1994.
5. Ibid.
6. *The New York Times*, October 30, 1994.
7. Naval Institute *Proceedings*, April 1995, Annapolis, Maryland.
8. America Online, March 20, 1995.
9. U.S. Navy press release, February 28, 1995.
10. Ibid.
11. *Detroit News*, April 9, 1995.
12. *Nightline*, ABC-TV, February 28, 1995.
13. *USA Today*, May 10, 1995.
14. *Newsweek*, March 27, 1995.
15. *Navy Times*, April 10, 1995.
16. Author interview with Elaine Donnelly.
17. *Detroit News*, April 9, 1995.
18. *V.I.P. Notes*, May 1995.
19. Ibid.

CHAPTER 30. A SEA CRUISE PLAYS TO MIXED REVIEWS

1. *Time*, April 12, 1995.
2. Ibid.
3. *Washington Post*, April 5, 1995.
4. *Chicago Tribune*, April 6, 1995.
5. *Time*, April 12, 1995.
6. Lieutenant's name and unit on file with author.
7. *The New York Times*, May 20, 1995.
8. Ibid.
9. Representative Linda Smith letter to Navy Secretary John H. Dalton, June 30, 1995.
10. *St. Louis Post-Dispatch*, August 20, 1995.
11. *Military*, April 1994.
12. *Philadelphia Inquirer*, August 12, 1995.
13. Associated Press, August 14, 1995.

14. *Washington Post*, August 14, 1995.
15. Ibid.
16. Associated Press, August 14, 1995.
17. *Baltimore Sun*, July 6, 1995.
18. Ibid.

CHAPTER 31. NAVIGATING TROUBLED WATERS

1. *Wall Street Journal*, March 12, 1996.
2. Ibid.
3. *San Diego Union-Tribune*, February 4, 1996.
4. Ibid., February 18, 1996.
5. *Time*, October 23, 1995.
6. Ibid.
7. Ibid.
8. Ibid.
9. *U.S. News & World Report*, April 1, 1996.
10. Ibid.
11. Ibid.
12. Ibid.

CHAPTER 32. THE ADMIRAL BOORDA TRAGEDY

1. *Baltimore Sun*, April 18, 1996.
2. *Time*, May 27, 1996.
3. ABC-TV, May 19, 1996.
4. *Time*, May 27, 1996.
5. *Baltimore Sun*, May 26, 1996.
6. Author interview with retired admiral who asked not to be identified.
7. Author correspondence with Elaine Donnelly.
8. Article based on reporter Ed Vulliamy's 1994 interview with Admiral Jeremy Boorda, *The Guardian* (London), May 23, 1996.
9. Ibid.
10. ABC-TV, May 26, 1996.
11. Ibid.
12. Ibid.

Index

About the Author

WILLIAM B. BREUER is a decorated combat veteran of World War II who landed with assault waves in Normandy. He is one of today's most popular military historians and the author of twenty-five books since 1982. Ten were selections of the Military Book Club, six translated into foreign languages. "A first class author who writes with an emphasis on human drama," says *The Wall Street Journal.*